Distant Parents

Distant Parents

JACOB CLIMO

RUTGERS UNIVERSITY PRESS
New Brunswick, New Jersey

Library of Congress Cataloging-in-Publication Data

Climo, Jacob, 1945–
   Distant parents / Jacob Climo.
     p. cm.
   Includes bibliographical references and index.
   ISBN 0-8135-1796-6 (cloth)—ISBN 0-8135-1797-4 (pbk.)
   1. Parent and adult child—United States.   2. Aging parents—
United States—Family relationships.   3. Autonomy (Psychology) in
old age—United States.   I. Title.
HQ755.86.C55 1992   91-32605
306.874—dc20   CIP

British Cataloging-in-Publication information available

To My Distant Parents,
Leonard Salem Climo and Adeline Seltzer Climo

CONTENTS

I first became aware of the importance of distant relationships between adult children and their elderly parents when I read Herbert
Gold's autobiographical novel, *Family*. In this deeply moving work,
Gold, now a successful author living in California, telephones his
aging father in Cleveland to tell of his plans to visit:

> My father grew old. He sat and waited in Cleveland. He slept
> and ate and sometimes trudged in the hall, past my brother's room,
> past my mother's room, past the laundry room, and then back to
> his room, or he could walk around the block if someone took him.
> He used to be entertained by his troubles. Now they gave him no
> pleasure.
> "Dad." I yelled across the long distance connection. "How are
> you?"
> "What? What? Are you here?"
> I was trying to poke through the shriveled nerves of his ears.
> "No, no, Dad, I'm in California, but I'm coming to see you soon."
> And so I flew back to visit him and he touched me, he reached
> for my hand, he was nearly blind, he touched my face, he asked,
> "Are you here, son?"
> "Of course I'm here, Dad."
> "No son, you're far away. I'm far away."

That passage struck me in an intensely personal way and brought
some of the frustration and pain of my own distant relationships
into sharp focus. Since then I've never been able to think of my
distant relationships, or to communicate with my distant parents,
in quite the same way. I felt a profound need to explore the rela-

tionships and communications that adult children and elderly parents maintain over long distances. This book is the result of what I discovered from my exploration.

Much of my life, both past and present, has prepared me for the task of writing about this subject. Both my professional training as an anthropologist and my personal background give the study special meaning and facilitate deeper levels of comprehension that I might otherwise not have.

Before I became a professor and father of small children I experienced the stresses and strains of living away from home first as a college student, then as a graduate student, then as an anthropologist conducting field research for a year in a remote rural village in Yucatan, Mexico. As a newly married man I again lived away from my natal family for several years, in Ethiopia. Through each stage I tried to maintain feelings of family solidarity and to communicate with my distant family as well as I could. When I finally settled down into my current work as a professor some fifteen years ago, it was at a distance of 250 miles from my parents and sister.

Yet for most of those fifteen years my relationship with my parents was plagued by our mutual inability to accept the reality that I could live a satisfying and productive life away from them, and that our relationship could be close in spite of the distance that separated us. As long as we agreed on these principles our relationship was destined to be troubled; neither generation could acknowledge that my new environment could be authentic and satisfying with respect to work, friends, or family. For many years I suffered from a painful sense of loss coupled with a strong desire to move home and reunite with my family. I began writing this book in part out of my inability to accept the loss of my familial relationships. Now I realize that prolonged separation in the context of distant living inevitably means loss. Confronting that loss is painful indeed. But it is also necessary.

In the book I paint a picture of the conscious and unconscious efforts distant adult children and parents make to conserve the essential qualities of their relationship so that they can retain a sense of family, security, and permanence in a rapidly changing social world. I document the difficulties, complications, and limitations distant conflict places on their relationships, and I examine the contacts they use to overcome such problems and reinforce their bonds. I also suggest ways to improve distant relationships and communications that enable both children and parents to emphasize the positive aspects of their bonds and derive greater satisfaction and emotional stability from one another.

ACKNOWLEDGMENTS

I wish to acknowledge many colleagues and friends who helped me during the time this book was conceptualized and written: Eunice Boyer, Joe Chartkoff, Bertram Cohler, Claire Collins, Ken Corey, Kent Creswell, Shlomo Deshen, Bradley Fisher, Doris Francis, Christine Fry, Bernard Gallin, Rita Gallin, David Gutmann, Gunhilde Hagestaad, Iwao Ishino, Eva Kahana, Boas Kahana, Sharon Kaufman, Jennie Keith, Jack Knott, Eugene Litwak, Harvey Livix, Miriam Moss, Corinne Nydeggar, Robert Rubinstein, Marjorie Schweitzer, Dena Shenk, Jay Sokolovsky, Rene Somera, Rachael Stark, Art Vener, Maria Vesperi, and Otto Von Mering.

Many of my students listened as I tested my ideas out loud. In the spirit of intellectual inquiry they added their thoughts and experiences to mine. There are too many to mention, but Heide Stidt and Jennifer Klann were particularly helpful in transcribing taped interviews.

Writing a book often engenders a special kind of ordeal for one's family. I am grateful to my wife, Martha, and to my sons, Avi and Simi, for showing tolerance while enduring hardships for many years while I conceived and gave birth to these ideas. I am especially grateful to Martha because, as a fellow traveler and writer, she conveyed to me her own high standards of honest self-evaluation and inquiry.

Distant Parents

CHAPTER 1

The Challenge of Distant Living in the Aging Revolution

In a world where many social relationships are transient, ephemeral, and bounded by current instrumental goals, the parent-child bond remains distinctive because of its capacity to thrive and endure throughout the lives of both generations. But no one can say for sure how it will respond to the newest challenges of modern civilization. Together, distant living arrangements that result from frequent moves and the aging revolution that has dramatically increased the human life span present major new challenges to the adult child–elderly parent relationship. In this book we will explore the impact of distant living and prolonged separation on that relationship in contemporary America.

The parent-child bond, the most fundamental of all human relationships, finds its roots deep in the history of human social life. In his influential study of the origins and nature of the mother-child relationship, psychologist John Bowlby (see Weiss 1983) proposes that under the dangerous conditions of early human existence, nature bonded mothers and small children together for protection, for no less important a purpose than survival. Affectionate bonding and its correlate behaviors "attachment" and "proximity-promoting mechanisms" or the tendency for bonded partners to remain in proximity to each other, "caretaking behavior" or the behavior shown by the parent to the young, and "separation anxiety" or the emotional experience of loss whenever we wish to be close to our mother figure but cannot find her are all normal, healthy elements of human nature experienced from the cradle to the grave.

Throughout our lives we remain children to the parents who love us. For many of us, our parents' opinions are almost as important in adulthood and even old age as they were when we were youngsters. For example, in 1984 the Detroit Tigers won the World Series. Immediately following the final game, Tiger coach Sparky Anderson was interviewed by television reporters as he made his way through a mass of people from the playing field to the locker room. One reporter asked how he felt at this moment, the peak of his career, when he had just accomplished what every coach spends his life dreaming about. Anderson paused. His large square face and shocking white hair seemed slightly out of character for an instant: his victorious smile vanished, revealing a serious man deeply moved by emotion. He answered, "I only wish my father was alive so he could see me today."

The role model of parents for children persists throughout the duration of their relationship and beyond (Hagestad 1979). When Lillian Troll (1982) asked individuals at different life stages to describe any individual who came to mind, people more often described parents than any other person (see also Cummings and Henry 1961). Parents also depend on their children throughout their lives. Vern Bengston calls one critical theme in the relationship the "developmental stake" that parents have in their offspring. Many elderly parents identify strongly and vicariously with their children's accomplishments (Frank 1980; Krause 1978; Gelfand 1982), often regarding their children on a deeper emotional level as a link to their own immortality. Rafael (see Moss et al. 1985) claims that a child is many things: a part of the self, and the loved partner; a representative of the generation past; the genes of the forebears; the hope of the future; a source of love, pleasure, even narcissistic delight; a tie or a burden; and sometimes a symbol of the worst parts of the self and others.

But human social life has changed radically over the millennia. During the long course of human cultural evolution, a wide variety of family types and elaborate institutional forms have emerged. In modern societies wherever social and environmental conditions encourage the endurance of family solidarity throughout the life course, these institutional forms can assist even the most basic relationships in their caretaking tasks. The adult child–elderly parent relationship is not perpetuated automatically in every society under any circumstance, however. Cross-cultural studies reveal instances in which the adult child–elderly parent relationship is sacrificed for other cultural priorities, especially when resources are limited or unstable, and when the elderly lose control over important skills, knowledge, information, ritual functions, and personal autonomy (Rubinstein and Johnsen 1982; Glascock 1990).

No doubt affection bonding begins today the same way it did thousands of years ago, appearing first in early infancy and continuing throughout the life cycles of the partners. But unlike the earliest conditions of human social life, contemporary civilization seems to transform even the most basic human relationships.

THE CHALLENGES OF THE AGING REVOLUTION

Recent technological advances in medicine have lengthened the human life span, thrusting us into the "aging revolution," a period characterized by vast numbers of people living into their seventies, eighties, and nineties. By significantly increasing the human life span, the aging revolution has temporally lengthened the parent-child relationship, thus presenting a challenge of major proportions, especially toward the end of the family cycle. For the first time in human history, not only a handful of people but a large proportion now live up to twenty or thirty years beyond sixty. This "new frontier," as Ethel Shanas (1979) once called it, requires that we adopt a new way of thinking about old people and old age in general, and about parent-child relationships in particular. For the adult child–elderly parent relationship to endure over the expanding life course, it must be stable enough to retain its essential affectional and emotional qualities of parental stake and child involvement, while at the same time remain dynamic and flexible enough to adapt to the newest pressures and challenges of our world.

Gerontologists must revise the traditional explanations of parent-child relationships in the late-life family now that such bonds commonly last twenty or thirty years longer than ever before. How do middle-aged children and elderly parents adapt their behaviors and attitudes toward each other? What aspects or qualities remain stable throughout the life course, and how do the generations deal with change in order to adapt successfully to the new era? We not only need to understand how aging individuals adapt to the final, extended segment in their life course, but also how their relationships with adult children must change if they are to endure to the end of the family cycle. Thus, the aging revolution demands that we focus attention on the adult child–elderly parent relationship itself—its stability and continuity, on the one hand, and its changes and differences between generations, on the other.

On the positive side, more elderly parents will be alive for their children's transitions into middle age, and even retirement and widowhood. Elderly parents can potentially provide role models for such transitions (Clark 1967; Francis 1984).

Yet recent evidence suggests the development of a negative side too. For many parents and children emotional attachments late in the family cycle are characterized by great intensity and ambivalence. People often assume that emotional closeness is synonymous with loving and that alienation indicates consistent negative feelings— that we love those relatives we feel close to and hate those we feel distant from. Evidence suggests we cannot separate positive from negative feelings in this way. Where feelings run high they are rarely only positive or only negative. Where love is found so is hate.

Furthermore, there is probably an ebb and flow in most family feelings. People may feel warm and loving in the morning and neutral or hostile when tired or disgruntled in the evening. Adult children may feel very close to their elderly parents when things are going well but may feel overburdened and even hostile during times of illness or economic difficulty (Johnson and Bursk 1977). Parents of adult children are proud of them when they are successful but worry when they need help or fail in their endeavors. Such intense feelings, uncertainty, and flux continue to swing back and forth regardless of where grown children live (Rosow 1967).

An even greater concern arising from the lengthening of the life span has been a growing awareness of widespread conflicts and problems in the adult child–elderly parent relationship. The basic dilemma for more and more families is that by extending the life cycle the aging revolution has increased the need for adult children to provide assistance, especially health care and domestic services, for their elderly parents as they approach the end of life.

This increasing need is transforming the adult child–elderly parent relationship more than any other single factor. Today in America more adult children provide more care to elderly parents for longer periods of time and for a wider range of needs than ever before in our history (Brody 1988). It is estimated that adult children provide 70 to 80 percent of all services to noninstitutionalized elderly parents. Furthermore, the responsibilities of adult children are increasing rather than stabilizing or declining. In the 1990s, most adult Americans will have some major responsibility caring for an elderly parent, since the eighty-five-plus age group is the fastest-growing population segment.

The demands on adult children seem to mount with few social supports from the larger society and without any limits on obligations. The relations of many adult children and parents have become more difficult, stressful, painful, guilt-ridden, and complicated than they ever imagined, in some ways threatening to undermine the emotional foundations of the bond itself.

The lengthening of the life span also poses serious and unprecedented moral, ethical, and legal problems for the family. What constitutes a catastrophic illness? How should society deal with an adult son or daughter who pulls the plug on a comatose elderly parent, or provides poison, or shoots and kills a mother or father who suffers from excruciating pain and begs the child to end it all? At what point should the family choose extraordinary life-saving technology for a terminally ill elderly parent? What legal steps can an aging parent take in preparation for a prolonged period of illness and dependency without surrendering complete control of his or her estate? The list of unprecedented dilemmas expands with no end in sight while acceptable, clear, ethical solutions continue to evade us.

Despite widespread stress we have neither recognized nor acknowledged that the aging revolution has changed our most intimate relationships. The most remarkable conceptual difficulty to emerge from this study of distant relationships is the concept of the "adult child" itself. Since our society is experiencing rapid demographic changes in which unprecedented numbers of people now live well into old age, many more adults remain "children" to their parents far longer than expected. The concept of "adult child" amused many of the people I interviewed. No one disapproved of the term, yet many adult children felt that the term is inherently contradictory—"adult" versus "child"—or that it is confusing. And the reasons for their comments soon became clear.

At this moment we are disoriented, bewildered, and even overwhelmed by rapid demographic changes that are rocking the foundations of our most basic relationships. The fact that our language has not yet invented a new word to acknowledge the change and thereby assist us in coping with this new social reality complicates matters. It also indicates that our mental images have lagged behind our new social reality, so most of us remain in a mild state of confusion. But our linguistic lag also reflects our ambivalence about the dramatic changes in the life-cycle events of family members. Many adult children are bewildered with their new role for good reasons. The responsibilities of this new social role are overwhelming us because they are unprecedented. Only recently have middle-aged adult children found themselves responsible as "children" for their dependent, elderly parents. And there are no answers for us yet.

THE CHALLENGES OF DISTANT LIVING

Contemporary civilization is characterized by prolonged separations of family members and distant living. This fact of life is difficult for many of us to accept. Yet separations affect most of us directly in one way or another. The theme of distant relationships appears again and again in articles and television specials that try to teach us how to cope with the loneliness resulting from constant travel obligations in corporate occupations, from commuter marriages where young married couples try to remain happy while they work in different locations, and from teenagers leaving home and parents prematurely, by modern standards, to seek their fortunes in distant places. Even the most basic human relationships, those between parents and children, must adjust to the effects of distant living.

The distant adult child–elderly parent relationship is a social bond involving at least one elderly parent and one adult child who live too far away to permit regular, frequent, face-to-face contacts. Though not a statistical majority, distant relationships are abundant in America wherever rural to urban or interregional migrations take place or political and economic circumstances necessitate long-distance separations of family members for prolonged periods.

Americans' extraordinary geographic mobility plays a crucial role in the establishment of distant households and relationships. Large numbers of Americans move from the places they were born and raised, often several times in their lives. Whether they are employed by the military, large corporations, universities, or are students or retired persons, they will uproot themselves and move to a new locale.

What makes such moves different from international and other migrations which Americans experienced historically is its nonfamilistic quality. Walter Zenner (1981) distinguishes the more traditional familistic migration involving "some form of chain migration whereby an individual goes to work in X city and calls for his former countrymen, especially relatives" from "individualistic migration," in which a single individual or a married couple moves to a community and is not followed by any other relative. There is no chain, just an isolated household. Such individualistic migrations arise for the purpose of work or self-fulfillment (Gmelch and Zenner 1980:142).

According to census data more than 46 percent of the population has moved within the last five years. Either adult children or parents may leave the "home" location permanently over a period of years, thus initiating a distant relationship. The distant family household, however, is primarily a middle-class phenomenon, since low-income groups have generally not migrated in search of occupational mobility. Poorer adult children have few options in caring for their elderly relatives, who often live nearby or with them (Litwak 1982).

The distant household is initiated most often when the young adult or late adolescent child decides to leave home to marry or seek educational or career opportunities. Middle-aged parents and young adult children together set the family's highest priority on the child's pressing developmental transition—the quest for independence and educational, occupational, and economic advancement. With few exceptions, young adults leave their parental homes to begin their adult lives in a separate household, sometimes at great distances from their parents. From the perspective of both children and parents, the major transition lies in the developing independence of the adult child as expressed in leaving the parental home and establishing a separate household, rather than in the distance created in the parent-child relationship.

Yet the high geographic mobility involved in this transition is startling. According to a national survey of 58,000 households in 1982 (Kennedy 1986), the peak age of American movers were young adults in their twenties, of whom more than one third changed residence in the last year. Young adults in their early twenties were more than twice as likely to move than those in their late teens, and although some settle down in their mid-twenties, about 20 percent are still changing residences frequently into their early thirties.

An increasingly common occurrence during a later stage in the family cycle is the migration of elderly parents. Such elderly migrations are facilitated by independent income (Longino et al. 1984; Schorr 1980) and lend support to the notion that frequent migration in America is itself a middle-class phenomenon. Those who can afford it migrate to retirement regions (Gober and Zonn 1983) and to communities in Arizona, California, and Florida. During the 1970s there was a 54 percent increase in the number of Americans of retirement age who migrated from state to state (Longino 1979). Although only 4 percent of those over age sixty changed the state of their residence between 1965 and 1970 (Bigger et al. 1980), recent studies indicate that migrations by the elderly have been increasing and that the trend has not peaked (A.S. Lee 1974). Greater residential separation between middle-aged (sixty-five to seventy) or older parents (seventy-five plus) and their children also indicates that the elderly of the future may have more distant children (Treas and Bengston 1982).

In a small but growing number of cases elderly parents initiate distant living by moving away after adult children have established separate households near them, or by migrating for all or part of the year to a distant location. A *New York Times* article reported a middle-aged daughter's anger and grief when her elderly parents "shook our roots loose" by selling their home in the suburbs and moving to Florida. The author writes: "They taught me the value of family, urged me to settle in town, nurtured the love of my children and then left" (Collins 1983). Needless to say, not all adult children respond with such anger when their elderly parents move.

Yet at least one study shows that postretirement migration did not lead to greater family isolation for the aged. The parents see their children infrequently but not any less often than if they had not moved (Bultena and Wood 1969). Litwak and Longino (1987) have documented the return migration of the elderly from Sunbelt retirement communities when they become infirm and need care. When they retire and grow old, some parents migrate to be near one of their children (Bultena and Wood 1969).

Some evidence suggests that distant children may assume increasing importance in the lives of their aging parents. In the first place, adult children in particular become relatively more important in the social networks of aging parents (Brody 1988; Rosow 1970). Social contacts for many elderly Americans tend to decrease over time. Important relationships often become altered or are ended through death, so regardless of distance many elderly parents desire and need to perpetuate meaningful contacts with their children.

The loss of consistent, satisfying relationships can have harmful effects. One study of older people found that low social interaction is strongly related to depression, and that the majority of those who lost a confidant were depressed. The study underscores the importance of stability in relationships and the desire of older people for harmonious familial and personal bonds (Lowenthal and Haven 1968).

Finally, elderly Americans today have fewer children than in the past, and the elderly of the near future may have yet fewer. The number of elderly with only one child has increased in the last decades (Shanas and Sussman 1981), so that the need for contact with children regardless of distance will remain significant in the coming years and may even become greater.

In fact, distant relationships are very significant to our way of life. As Hagestad (1979) has pointed out, as long as we continue to study households, the physical structures in which families reside, we will never begin to understand the dynamics of family life in America. Since we know familial relationships reach far beyond the household, we must study the impact of distance to identify the true sentiments and activities that prevail in American family life.

For a significant minority of American children and parents, distant contacts represent the most important ways for them to maintain their familial bonds. An insightful analysis (Moss et al. 1985) of the Schooler (1979) data base revealed that almost half of today's elderly parents had at least one child living over 150 miles away, and one third (32 percent) had at least one child living over 500 miles away (Federal Council on Aging 1982). Conversely, 26 percent of the children had an elderly parent who lived more than 150 miles away and 17 percent had a parent over 500 miles away. A random sample of American men reporting distance from their fathers yielded figures of 30 percent over 150 miles and 22 percent over 300 miles. And another recent study of deceased people aged sixty-five and older revealed that 25 percent had no surviving children or siblings residing near enough to provide regular direct assistance (Hays 1984).

From these investigations it appears some 25 percent of all elderly Americans have no adult child living closer than 100 to 200 miles. Estimating conservatively, about 25 percent or seven million elderly American parents have only distant children as potential filial supports, and an additional 50 percent, or fourteen million elderly parents, have at least one distant living adult child. In other words, there are roughly twenty million distant elderly parents plus at least twenty million distant children, or a total of approximately forty million adult children and distant parents in America today.

As long as our civilization promotes and rewards high geographic mobility it is likely that a sizable minority of young adult children will continue to leave their parents' households to pursue opportunities far away. Some who leave will eventually return, since some people return in middle age to the geographic areas where they grew up (A.S. Lee 1974; Litwak and Silverstein 1987). But a substantial and virtually neglected minority, a group of people numbering in the millions, will remain apart indefinitely, many for the remainder of their lives.

Despite the significance of distant relationships, surprisingly little is known about the feelings of distant adult children and elderly parents and their efforts to keep their family bonds intact. For a variety of reasons, mostly unspoken, there exists a fairly strong trend on the part of gerontologists and the lay public to deny and neglect the importance of distant relationships.

Instead, current gerontological research has emphasized that most elderly Americans live near at least one of their children. Ethel Shanas (1979) found that three out of four elderly parents live either within a half hour of a child or with a child. Other studies show that both children and parents are most satisfied when they live in separate households but near each other. American parents move in with adult children only when they don't have enough money to live alone, their health is so poor that self-care is impossible, or their spouses have died. It is the least popular solution, mainly done out of necessity. A private household not only symbolizes independence for the elderly but also provides a setting for them to lead their lives as they choose.

Because distant living is not the dominant pattern of American family life, most studies imply that we should concentrate our efforts in trying to understand how the majority rather than the minority lives. Though the phenomenon of distant living has been widespread for some time, neither scholars nor practitioners have ascribed any special importance to it. The dominant perception that distant relationships do not need to be investigated as a separate type of relationship remains unchallenged.

Moreover, it is supported by four misleading or mistaken assumptions about parent-child relationships and distance that are generally accepted without question in our current thinking. If we are ever going to improve our distant parent-child relationships, we must first identify the limitations of these assumptions, then move beyond them.

1. Near and Distant Emotional Attachments Are the Same

The first assumption contends that the nature and quality of relationships between near-living and distant-living adult children and elderly parents are fundamentally the same; that both the stable as well as the changing qualities of relationships between generations occur independent of distance. Research supporting this view is abundant and impressive. The available evidence confirms that distant relationships are identical to near relationships in emotional attachments, love and affection, obligations, and endurance over time. Moreover, the parent-child bond can maintain cohesion under conditions of limited face-to-face contact and is very resistant to the effects of geographical separations, socioeconomic mobility, and even developmental changes (Moss et al. 1985; Adams 1968; Lee and Ellithorpe 1982; Dono et al. 1979:406; Bowlby 1983; Troll and Smith 1976:158). Other studies of independent and relatively healthy elderly suggest that family composition tends to remain stable in spite of distance (Moss et al. 1985:135).

The overriding conclusion is that although distance certainly diminishes the frequency of contacts, the quality of affection and feelings of parents and children remain the same regardless of distance (Litwak 1960, 1965, 1981, 1985; Moss et al. 1985; Adams 1968; Lee and Ellithorpe 1982). This evidence confirms the traditional belief that early social bonding will continue to provide the necessary social glue to perpetuate our most fundamental human bonds. But the explanation seems simplistic or reductionist in the absence of concrete descriptions and qualifications. It tends to overlook the tremendous pressures of modern life—economic, social, cultural, psychological—that pull people in separate directions. In fact, most of the evidence is based on survey questionnaires alone; there is no ethnographic study of the distinctive features involved in maintaining long-distance relationships. Until we explore distant relationships from the perspective of those who experience them, we should not accept the assumption of sameness as more than a recognition that the emotional quality of child-parent relationships endures.

2. Geographic Distance Reflects Emotional Distance

This assumption calls special attention to those who live far away and emphasizes a perceived distinction in filial devotion: that those who are physically close are also emotionally close, and more importantly, that those who are physically distant are emotionally distant as well. At a glance, this assumption seems to contradict the assumption that near and distant affectional attachments are fundamentally the same; for instead of denying important emotional differences between near and distant family members, it asserts them.

The notion that distant-living adult children are emotionally alienated from their elderly parents and do not want to provide supports for them was popular in the 1960s when several prominent gerontologists and scholarly writers suggested that many distant-living adult children had abandoned their aging parents, and that distant living itself symbolized emotional and social distance between the generations. According to Shanas (1979), the strongest evidence to support this "myth of alienation" was distant living itself; the fact that many old people lived apart from their children, "the assumption that old persons who live alone or apart from their children are neglected by their children and relatives is implicit in the alienation myth."

The problem with this assumption is that it underestimates the complexity of distant parent-child relationships. By suggesting that emotional attachments and assistance cannot survive prolonged geographical separations, it generalizes on the motives for separation. Certainly, some young adult children leave their natal families because of emotional conflict. Others experience emotional conflicts after they leave. Many experience relatively little emotional conflict; they live far apart because they took advantage of economic opportunities. Some children never return to the place where their parents live yet maintain strong familial bonds throughout the years.

These issues are complicated and require further investigation. Even now, however, it seems clear that many distant children maintain strong emotional attachments to their parents. There is no good evidence to assume that distant children feel any greater emotional alienation than near-living children.

3. Only Near-Living Children Provide Face-to-Face Services and Health Care

For a long time gerontologists have assumed that the distant child cannot contribute directly or routinely to the immediate health and social support needs of elderly parents (Seelback 1978) and that the number of kin geographically available to the elderly limits the amount of help they receive in practical everyday living. Hence, a practical explanation for the exclusive focus on near-living relationships is that elderly parents confronting declining health require increasing face-to-face services. Everyone acknowledges the obvious limitations distance places on the frequency of contacts; as distance increases, the frequency of communications diminishes. Litwak, Kulis, and Worth (1982) have demonstrated that the kinds of services children provide to elderly parents decreases as distance increases. At a distance of about ten city blocks, for example, telephone calls begin to replace visits from distant relatives who, in that study, are defined as those living within a half hour's drive. Since near-living adult children can provide regular face-to-face services but distant living adult children cannot, the practical response is to focus attention on near-living adult child–elderly parent relationships (Climo 1988).

Indeed, certain kinds of routine help such as personal care, health care, housework, and transportation do require proximity (Moss et al. 1985; Gelfand 1982) and can be provided only by kin living near enough for face-to-face interactions, causing many people to ignore distant-living relationships or the assistance children provide for their distant parents. Litwak and Silverstein (1987) found that kin, spouses, and friends provide different types of face-to-face services. As independent older retirement community residents experience transitions to widowhood and chronic illness, they increasingly require face-to-face, routine, household services. Friends among their age peers are too frail, neighbors lack the desire for long-term commitments, and paid help is too hard for distant children to supervise. Only children have both the long-term commitment and the necessary resources. So frail, older, ill, and single people leave retirement regions to be closer to a child; those disabled and ill in 1978 were more likely to have moved closer to their helpers by 1986 (Litwak and Longino 1987). Thus, distant living limits assistance but distant children are clearly assisting their parents in various ways.

4. Little Can Be Done to Improve Distant Relationships

This final assumption represents the logical outcome of the others: a passive acceptance that distant relationships must remain as they are and there is no way to improve them. Of all the erroneous assumptions this is the most damaging, for it not only denies and negates the problem but leaves us in despair.

In fact, a growing number of adult children are beginning to recognize the negative impact and limitations of distance on their relationships with loved ones. Some children seek assistance from formal agencies to provide support for a distant parent only to discover that organized social service agencies are not yet ready to help them. Many federal agencies take the position that once the family has taken over, it's their business (see Shanas in *Newsweek* 1985). The few private agencies with national networks are limited and costly. An increasing number of distant children would like to assist their elderly parents but don't know how, leaving all concerned extremely frustrated and stressed.

Furthermore, American core cultural values require acquiescence and placid acceptance of the distant relationship. An adult child is usually in no position to complain about distant living. The situation was usually created by the children themselves as they made their own life choices—a situation basic to the construction of their careers or marriages and fundamental to the organization of modern civilization. An individual who finds distant living distasteful may seem to challenge some of our most cherished values: generational independence, normal individual development, separation from the natal family, ego identity, individualism, achievement, success, upward mobility—in short, the pillars of the American dream itself.

Many adult children speak with their spouses or friends about their problems and conflicts with distant living but do not recognize that distance is more than a personal problem. It is a social problem shared by literally millions of people and has the potential of being resolved, yet it remains an isolated, private, individual, or family dilemma. Its true dimensions are not identified. It is misread, unclear, unapproached, and unapproachable.

If we accept these four assumptions as unimpeachable truths they will prevent us from inquiring further into the problem. Each assumption carries some elements of truth, but when they are generalized they become false, incomplete, inadequate, and misleading. Although they attempt to explain our life-style, they do not address the unique impact of distant living on our relationships.

By endorsing these assumptions we have not yet acknowledged that high mobility, distant living arrangements, and prolonged separations not only aggravate normal generational conflicts but also create new ones. It also explains why we have been unable to develop an understanding of the unique features of relationships with distant parents, including intergenerational communications and contacts, patterns of assistance and care, and expressions of feelings.

Finally, it is important to study distant parent-child relationships because in order to improve them we must first understand them. The limitations of distant relationships must be redefined as temporary challenges rather than permanent obstacles.

PROFESSORS AS DISTANT ADULT CHILDREN

I began to investigate the distant adult child–elderly parent relationship informally by asking people at parties about their parents who lived far away. I listened carefully as friends and acquaintances spoke about their distant parents. My decision to study university professors as distant adult children grew naturally out of these experiences.

I use an ethnographic method which examines the meaning of distant relationships from the inside, from the point of view of those actively sustaining such relationships, in this case by interviewing a small group of people whose members were easily accessible. The advantage of such a group is that it approximates the face-to-face anthropological method of participant-observation and, over a period of time, allowed me to come to know the participants as people. Such ethnographic analysis indirectly sheds light on our larger, complex social reality by illuminating a microcosm in a universe of cultural diversity.

Although I use the ethnographic approach I am aware that the participants do not constitute a community in the traditional anthropological sense. Professors as distant-living adult children do not have a consciousness of themselves as a naturally existing group whose members share a common identity. Nor do they distinguish their relationships from those of other children and parents who live near each other. In fact, a few individuals who are deeply engaged in personal problems in their relationships with distant parents are only dimly aware of distance as an aspect of their relationship. I focus on their attempts to maintain familial bonds through distant contacts, in spite of many obstacles.

SELECTING PARTICIPANTS AND THE FIELD RESEARCH

For my original pilot study in 1985–1986 I developed an open-ended questionnaire which I used to interview forty adult children—twenty men and twenty women—who lived 200 or more miles away from their parents. I deliberately chose adult children who wanted to talk about their distant parents. A few of them are friends and colleagues whom I have known for years. In some cases, when I remarked offhandedly that I was studying distant relationships between adult children and parents, they volunteered to be interviewed before I could ask them. In other cases I called on the phone to set up an interview. My original pilot sample was biased toward adult children willing to discuss their problems with distant parents openly and wishing to get some insights to improve them.

Our informal discussions usually lasted about an hour and focused on their distant communications. I gathered information especially on the frequency and content of visits and telephone conversations with the distant children's biological parents and the subjective meaning of such communication to the child. In a few instances the father's health influenced the discussion, but most information from the discussions revealed the importance of emotional relationships and communication with distant mothers.

My questions also addressed children's attitudes and feelings during visits and telephone calls, their thoughts about the future, especially their anticipated response to their parents' declining health and loss of independence, and the role of their past relationships, especially past adolescent conflicts that may have carried over into their present adult relationships. I also asked them to express important life-style and generational differences between themselves and their parents and to speculate on their ability to maintain distant relationships and communication.

In these pilot interviews a large number of married people referred me to their spouses, resulting in thirty-two interviews with sixteen married couples. I interviewed wives and husbands separately about their own parents rather than relationships with parents-in-law because I wanted to understand the way each individual experiences his or her own distant family relationships. Later I realized I had not interviewed any divorced or never-married people, or anyone who was married but childless. It was clear that in the next phase of the research I would need to interview such individuals to develop a broader picture of the distant adult child–elderly parent relationship.

After analyzing the pilot responses descriptively, I revised the questionnaire. My second, more formal closed questionnaire integrated the range of responses and answers supplied by the pilot group. The revised questionnaire also elaborated some areas where more information was needed, especially regarding intergenerational financial assistance, adult children's recollections of the process of making decisions in early adulthood to leave their parents' home to form a distant household, current emotional conflicts and technical difficulties associated with distant telephone communications, and reports concerning intergenerational affection and assistance in their families.

I interviewed a second group of forty faculty and their spouses in 1988 using this revised questionnaire. The sample was selected formally using a snowball effect. I chose distant adult children through networks of friendship and collegiality. I called each person and asked if he or she would participate in my study. When they agreed, I asked them to fill out the revised questionnaire, which I sent through the mail. After reviewing their returned answers I interviewed them for one or two more hours, asking them to elaborate selected answers that I felt were unclear or held special interest to the study. I encouraged them to discuss any questions they found particularly challenging. A second group of questions in that interview concerned their current use of the telephone and their memories of leaving home in late adolescence.

I conducted most of the formal interviews in their offices. A few preferred to come to my office, and several spouses invited me to their homes. I always allowed the participants to choose the place and I always told them they should choose an environment in which they would feel comfortable talking about their distant parents. Only two people refused to be interviewed. One couldn't make the time commitment; another explained she did not want to mix her personal life into our professional relationship. Some initial reluctance or a delay in an interview often cued me about difficulties in the distant relationship. Once a distant daughter did not show up for a scheduled interview in her home. When we eventually met she described a long, strained relationship with her mother.

A few individuals were uncomfortable talking about family relationships. It was simply too personal. One son asked me if I ran into much resistance. He said he has worked with a colleague for five years and they have talked openly about politics, religion, sex—virtually everything except family. Obviously such people are not well represented in this study. Moreover, I found that when people are in the middle of a family crisis they usually do not like to be interviewed. Either their emotions are too strong or they feel they cannot discuss such personal problems with a stranger.

I tape-recorded most of the interviews except on two occasions. On the first I realized I had forgotten to bring a tape, but after the interview the adult daughter said that she would not have spoken as freely on tape. On the other occasion a son was very defensive about the entire study. He did not want me to record the interview. He also asked me to sign a document promising not to reveal his or his parents' names. I signed, anticipating some exciting information, but as it turned out his relationships proved disappointing.

Eventually my participants came to know me as a kindred spirit—a distant adult child like them whose parents live far away and visit only occasionally. I believe this commonality helped me establish rapport. Later on it helped some sons and daughters reveal and explore more fundamental problems in their relationships rather than keeping the discussion at the superficial level. In one remarkable interview I entered a colleague's office, whereupon he told me: "I don't ordinarily spend a lot of time filling out questionnaires that come through the post. A lot of them from the various units on campus definitely are neither very well hatched nor very worthy for one reason or another. This one is a different story. The questions you're interested in here seem to be the right questions. I've really given a lot of thought to that myself."

After each interview I asked the participants to recommend one or two people they knew who would be appropriate and willing to be interviewed. In order to limit the bias of such referrals so that not all individuals are connected to each other in some way I took only one referral from each person. I consciously guided the sample selection only to make sure that there was an equal number of men and women and that it included distant children who were never-married, divorced, and married without children.

People had a tendency to refer me to others in their own academic departments, resulting in a stronger representation of certain disciplines. Nevertheless, the adult children represent a wide variety of professions within the university, including administration, business, the social, biological, and physical sciences, literature and languages, arts and letters, classical studies, and the health sciences including nursing and medicine. In my presentation I shift disciplines to protect the identities of the participants. In some cases, for the same reason, I also change the location of their parents' residence, though I keep the distance and region precise.

As I delved more deeply into the meaning of distant relationships two things became clear. First, my inquiries initiated an amazing degree of concern and involvement in the participants. Second, after my initial interviews I began to realize that the whole field of distant parent-child relationships was emerging in my thoughts as an important yet neglected social problem. I had to address a number of key questions concerning distant relationships and communications that had no precedence in gerontological research.

As an academic anthropologist and gerontologist I had a sense from the beginning that many distant-living adult children and elderly parents could derive some concrete benefits from the information I planned to gather. I reasoned that the subject of distant familial communications and relationships is of concern to many people, but I never suspected my interviews would engender such a strong and immediate response. Some participants began to call me to find out more about their own relationships in the hope of improving them. At first a few, then several of the adult children asked to see the professional papers I wrote as a result of this investigation. Some continued to call me periodically and others contacted me regularly to update me on current happenings in their own relationships. Much of this information focused on key transitions in their family developmental cycle such as the institutionalization of a distant parent or the special difficulties of an adult child whose widowed mother in Florida had recently become disoriented and was losing her memory.

The distant children were tied only loosely to the university community and the study only very marginally related to university life. In other words, I could not participate or observe a community in the traditional sense of a group of people bounded somehow by space. In spite of this limitation, as an anthropologist I could not resist any opportunity to participate in distant parent-child relationships, communications, and family events as they arose. Over a four-year period I was invited on several occasions to the homes of adult children to meet and speak informally with their visiting elderly parents during vacations and holidays. I also attended memorial services in town, usually held several days after distant (natal-home) funeral services.

On one occasion a man's mother called him on the phone in the middle of our second interview in his home. It gave me the rare opportunity actually to witness a distant telephone communication firsthand. But he began talking to his mother about the interview and laughing about their relationship: "What a coincidence, I was just talking about you with Jacob Climo. Only saying good things, of course . . . ," and I felt my very presence had altered any "natural" parent-child interactions I might have witnessed.

Over the last three years I held several follow-up conversations with sons and daughters to keep abreast of important changes in their relationships. These changes included major transitions such as the local community response to the sudden death of a distant parent, the relocation of a distant child or parent causing them to be closer or farther from each other, the birth of a child, a parent's retirement, or a major family reunion. I listened carefully to the attitudes adult children expressed about proximity to aging parents in planning relocations, changes in the health status of a parent or child, the response to various disabilities parents experienced, the death of a father and the mother's transition to widowhood, and the death of a mother and the surviving father's remarriage. I documented changes in attitudes and behavior corresponding to other major transitions such as the failing health and death of a terminally ill distant parent.

What began as a study of adult child relationships to distant elderly parents in a Midwestern university community spread gradually yet naturally to include many people beyond the study's original boundaries. Some sons and daughters referred me to their friends who are currently experiencing conflicts with distant elderly parents, encouraging them to tell me their points of view and to seek information about my study, which they could then use as informal advice. To round out my perspective I spoke to geriatric physicians from nursing homes; to social workers, lawyers, clergy; and to nursing home administrators, especially about their experiences with distant adult children who had sought advice or communicated with them about distant elderly parents. I also presented some of the more obvious findings to my classes at the university, and a number of students came after class to speak informally with me. To my surprise, most of them were on the verge of leaving home permanently and establishing distant households for the first time. I wanted to know how they and their parents felt about this initial stage in the formation of distant households.

In broadening my perspective I realized that in some minor ways university professors as distant adult children are distinctive; certain events are unique to their life circumstances. For example, they and their parents visit each other longer and more often in the summer than in other seasons. Because of the teaching calendar, professors have more freedom in the summer than people in other occupations. In addition, they usually have the economic resources to make long-distance travel more possible.

Still, the meaning of distant relationships is fundamentally the same for them as it is for others. Along with other Americans, professors are entering the aging revolution. Like other adult children, sometime in the 1990s most of them will take on major responsibilities in caring for an aging parent in need, and, with others, they share in the development of routine patterns such as telephone communications and visits. Their feelings and stories can apply to distant children throughout the country. Their personal difficulties, satisfactions, conflicts, and solutions to problems typically reflect what I have come to regard as the natural limitations of distant communications and the shape of distant relationships, no matter what one's occupation is.

CHAPTER 2

Understanding Relationships with Distant Parents

The central thesis of this book is that the distant adult child–elderly parent relationship is unique, that we must begin to see ourselves and our significant others differently when we are separated by space and time. This is especially true of our parents, whose actions and opinions influence our daily lives and our ongoing social definitions of ourselves. Three cultural concepts provide the key to understanding relationships with distant parents: (1) the individualized self; (2) independence and separation; and (3) ambivalence toward love and distance.

THE INDIVIDUALIZED SELF

I am especially concerned with the concept of self within the distant parent-child relationship. Without losing their traditional cross-cultural perspective, anthropologists concerned with the concept of the self are beginning to open a dialogue with existential philosophers on one hand and with psychologists on the other. Even at this early stage of intellectual exchange we know the results will challenge many of our current assumptions, especially those dealing with the relationship of the individual and the self in society.

In open-ended discussions, the distant adult sons and daughters in the study often moved back and forth between several distinct self concepts (See LeVine 1982:296). I began to classify their presentations of self into three types. First, they used an autobiographical self when they wanted to distinguish the present meaning of relationships from the past or when referring to attributes that are continuous and integrated through their life course, as in the comment, "Mother always complained about my weight." Second, in presenting their public self, distant children stressed social conventions, forms, and acceptable codes of conduct in their parent-child relationships, as in the statement, "Of course I keep in contact with my mother." Finally, in presenting their interpersonal self, distant adult children focused on relationships with parents as fluid and ongoing through time and space, a self that is dependent on feedback in continuous intimate relationships with significant others, as in the comment, "Talking with Mom over coffee and listening to her praise Ann, my child, is the most satisfying part of my visit."

Distant relationships seem to weaken the interpersonal self, the self we have come to consider necessary for a complete sense of emotional attachment to our social worlds. The interpersonal self is fluid and changing throughout our lives. As we choose options for our actions and develop attitudes that support our actions, we depend on interpersonal contact and dialogue with significant others to reinforce our self image. Thus, in the absence of our parents we are confronted by our individualized self, isolated and incomplete.

A main obstacle to understanding the self in distant relationships is the predominant cultural assertion that the individualized self rather than the interpersonal self should be the focus of our concern, that distance has little impact on our feelings toward one another, and that our most intimate relationships are unaffected by distance. Such cultural interpretations of the meaning of distance rely on the powerful cultural image of the individualized self, independent and autonomous.

At a deeper level of meaning, however, we must question the adequacy of this cultural interpretation of distance vis-à-vis subjective experience. Since we believe distance does not have a major impact on our relationships, we have not developed an articulate conception of what is missing when aging parents are absent from our lives. Yet the meaning of distance in an individual's experience always draws on the interpersonal self. The Western cultural concept of the individualized self encourages us to deny our feelings of loss and emptiness in distant relationships or interpret them as something different.

INDEPENDENCE AND SEPARATION

The extremes of this view of the individualized self can be found everywhere in our behaviors and attitudes. But they are nowhere more apparent than in our popular conceptions of independence and separation, the accepted relationships between parents and children. We isolate infants and babies, putting them to sleep in cribs in separate rooms away from their mothers. Such "privacy," we believe, builds independence and autonomy despite the fact that it flies in the face of everything we know about the human infant's developmental need for physical closeness.

In another area of parent-child relationships, therapy continues to recommend that we must consciously separate ourselves emotionally from our parents in order to live independent, satisfying, normal emotional lives. In each case normal development is viewed as the responsibility of the individual, a responsibility which demands that individuals somehow separate themselves emotionally from ongoing interactions with parents.

Our view of the need to separate ourselves emotionally from our parents derives from important developments in postindustrial civilization. In many traditional agrarian societies, economic interdependence of families shapes the boundaries of relationships between generations. Parents and children are tied to each other economically wherever geographic mobility is limited. In contrast, our postindustrial civilization is characterized by diminishing economic interdependence of families and greater mobility and economic independence of individuals. In the postindustrial world both economic supports and intimate bonds may be found outside the influence of the natal family.

In this atmosphere of increasing individual freedom, parents and children can decide for themselves how close or far they want to live, how much contact they want and need from each other, and what the quality of their relationships should be. Most adult children do want to maintain a continuing, fluid relationship with their distant aging parents. Perhaps because of the universal difficulties of finding and keeping intimate relationships anywhere, most adult children cling tenaciously to their distant parents, sometimes at great emotional cost. As a result of distant living and prolonged separations, the parent-child relationship is often characterized by a strenuous, even monumental effort on the part of both generations to make it work.

AMBIVALENCE TOWARD LOVE AND DISTANCE

Yet because many actions and expectations are often misdirected, misunderstood, and filled with emotional conflicts from the past and distortions caused by distance in the present, ambivalence often dominates the feelings of both adult children and distant parents. Ambivalence underscores the intense, unresolved nature of distant relationships. Distant children in the postindustrial world find themselves stationed somewhere in between the interdependence of traditional societies and the individual choice of postindustrial civilization. For unknown reasons, distant living arrangements put stress on the interpersonal interactions necessary to perpetuate definitions and redefinitions of the self in adult life.

One important source of ambivalence may be traced to ambivalent attitudes toward distant love relationships found in Western culture. Embedded within these attitudes are the mental maps that reveal the meaning of love in our relationships with distant parents.

On the surface, traditional Western culture seems to have developed an ambivalent approach to distant love relationships. In the idiom of modern American English, two apparently contradictory positions have been passed along to us. The first contends that distance is the enemy of love, that love withers and dies when people are separated from one another. At its roots is the belief that human relationships are founded, nurtured, and flourish when people live in close physical proximity.

The clearest, idiomatic expression of this position is found in Homer's *Odyssey:* "Out of sight, out of mind." Paradoxically, the odyssey resolves the dilemma by accepting an alternative position, for in the end when Ulysses finally returns from his adventures, his love is unaltered for his faithful wife, Penelope. Thus an apparently contradictory position remains important in Western civilization, contending that love prevails over distance, that "absence makes the heart grow fonder." At first glance the two principles seem contradictory. We cannot have it both ways: either "out of sight, out of mind" or "absence makes the heart grow fonder," but not both. However, when we look at these positions at a deeper level, they remain problematical but not contradictory.

In Western culture the difference between the heart and the mind is clear: the heart is the center of emotion, the mind of reason. Thus the two views are not complete opposites. Perhaps our common parlance has retained both sayings because both are accurate. "Out of sight, out of mind" means that everyday pragmatic and rational necessities and events must proceed without the distant loved one. Reason must prevail in the daily practical decisions and activities of life. Though needed and longed for, distant loved ones cannot help. Yet absence also makes the heart grow fonder. Love can grow and persist despite distance. When people truly love one another they become part of each other's lives forever. Even long separations do not diminish love. In some ways distance even enhances our desire to be together again.

These key cultural concepts have profound implications for distant parent-child relationships. Many adult children in the study are faced with the realization that satisfying relationships between them and their parents are extraordinarily difficult to attain. The themes of the individualized self, generational independence and separation, and ambivalence characterize their distant relationships.

The distant sons and daughters in my study noted three areas in which generational differences cause stress in their relationships with distant parents: occupation and financial position, education, and ideology and religion.

In income and occupation both parents and children in the study are upper-middle class. Ninety percent of the distant children and many spouses are university professors or administrators. The remaining spouses hold jobs in professions outside the university such as a high school principal, school social worker, science writer, teacher, and civil servant.

Eighty-five percent of the parents are retired from middle-class occupations. Prior to retirement many fathers had worked in the professions (48 percent) and in small business and trades (27 percent). Professional fathers included a dentist, lawyers, college professors, schoolteachers and administrators, an editor, and two ministers. Several fathers worked for corporate businesses as engineering consultants and biologists. Other fathers owned small businesses or worked as salesmen; others included a sea captain, a barber, a carpenter, and a mechanic.

Seventy percent of the mothers had been housewives, though many worked irregularly over the years. Some mothers had worked as college professors, librarians, schoolteachers, nurses, or secretaries, and one owned a real estate business. For the vast majority of children, their academic careers are very different from their parents' occupations.

Half the adult children claimed their parents, though retired, are better off than they are. A quarter said they are better off, and another quarter said they and their parents are the same financially. More than 85 percent owned their own home. About half said their parents helped them materially or financially in the last five years. Another third said neither generation helped the other financially, and 15 percent claimed they helped their parents financially.

Children claiming better-off parents report many instances of parental gifts and loans, including "an interest-free loan for my computer," "paying for us to fly there because she knows two plane tickets would probably be more than we saved for," loans for a down-payment on a house, and tuition payments for grandchildren because "on my salary it would have been quite a financial burden." Only a few children help support their parents. In most of those instances sons or daughters provide money or an apartment for their widowed mothers.

A third say that neither they nor their parents are financially dependent on each other. These children describe their distant parents' circumstances as adequate for their needs, as a son reports:

> Help goes in neither direction. They have enough money, although they're by no means rich or even well off. They live very simply, and they own this property that they have been selling off a little bit so they can travel, which is fairly expensive. But they haven't needed any money really. And I haven't either.

Most of the distant sons and daughter are more educated than their parents. More than 80 percent have a graduate degree, while only a quarter of their parents hold graduate degrees and another quarter Bachelor's degrees. About half only graduated from high school. Fathers were clearly better educated than mothers; about half the fathers hold graduate degrees compared to only 15 percent of the mothers.

Children with well-educated parents view their own achievements as a generational continuity. Several recall that in their childhood homes academic achievement was expected, as one daughter points out:

> There was a strong message of achievement. My mother's father was a chemist for Goodyear and my father's father was a banker. So there were white-collar expectations three generations deep. It was just of course you go to college, of course you do the best you can. So high achievement was built into the family.

Most highly educated parents and children regard geographic mobility as part of the package of achievement, yet not all children are pleased with the resulting separation of generations, as a daughter explains:

> My mother wanted me to go to school in New York. But I didn't want to go there and live at home. I wanted to be away at school. I went to college near Boston, at Radcliffe. Then I got a job and moved back to be closer and lived in New York. I wish I could move Michigan back there. Not only to my parents but also to New York City. I'd like to be close to my parents and friends.

Sons and daughters who come from less well-educated homes often trace their achievement motivation to individualistic and internal sources or to external sources beyond the family. One son from a working-class family says that his drive was influenced by his university professors. A daughter recalls that

> I don't think they stressed achievement for me as much as I did for myself. First, Linda was going to get married and have children. Then, if I went to school I would be a teacher or a nurse. Those were practical things. But I knew I wanted more than that.

Another son recalls that his family's demand for academic achievement did not prove to be a raving success in his youth:

> My father had made the jump from working class to professional. The message I heard as a kid was that I had great potential in academia and that I had to achieve. I also got the message that I never quite lived up to that potential. I almost flunked out of high school. I think it was an unconscious way of lowering everybody's expectations; that was a kind of adolescent rebellion.

Sons and daughters from working-class families often claim that their educational achievements opened a major gap between the generations; their poorly educated parents failed to understand their career choices. One son recalls:

> They didn't know what was going on. Neither of them had been to college. Their level of knowledge of what to expect was what they learned from *Newsweek* and *Time*. I remember my father saying to me once as he was reading *Newsweek*, "You ought to be a nuclear physicist." It sounded good to him, sounded like big bucks and lots of prestige so that's what he thought I should do. It kind of struck me that that's not advice. It's a joke. Worse.

A daughter from a Midwestern rural farming family remembers how difficult it was to convince her parents to support her plans for higher education:

> My parents didn't support my going to college. I can remember real battles. They said, "Why go to college when you're only going

to get married. You're never going to use that. Why don't you go to an airline school and you can learn to be a ticket reservationist?" And they made me take business courses and typing and shorthand in high school. Then they wanted me to go to teachers' college, which was less tuition.

A number of parents were supportive of their children's initial undergraduate education but couldn't understand why they chose to continue in higher education. A son from an urban working-class family explains how complicated it was to convince his parents to accept his plans to go to graduate school away from home:

> I commuted from home as an undergraduate. Then I went to the University of Pennsylvania for graduate school. They were both upset about it. One reason was they couldn't understand why I was still going to school. Neither of my brothers did this. I was the first one to leave. Actually, they didn't mind so much that I was a full-time college student. But then when I wanted to go to graduate school they didn't understand. Especially in political science. Who does that? They could understand if I were going to be a lawyer or a doctor or an accountant. But what does a political scientist do? They said, "How are we going to pay for it?" I promised them they wouldn't have to pay for it.
>
> I got a tuition waiver, guaranteed student loans, and I was working every summer. It didn't cost them anything. So they were upset about my just going on and not getting a job, and about the potential expense they would have. And they were upset because I was leaving home and going to Philadelphia.

The education gap created social distance between most children and their parents, as a daughter explains:

> I'm afraid the course of my adult life has put me at more of a distance from them. My mother would have preferred that I stop my education and become a high school teacher. I always wanted to be a teacher and that's the way my family talked about it. Going on in higher education was something she didn't understand. It would be so much easier if she could talk about her daughter, the high school teacher.

A son claims his father only really acknowledged the value of his decision after he became economically independent. Though respected by parents, the academic life-style is unfamiliar to most of them and makes visiting uncomfortable. A daughter explains this with reference to her mother's clumsy relationship to her husband:

> It took them a while to adjust to Arnold. He was different from anyone they had ever known. And my mother always respected him but was not always entirely comfortable with him. My parents don't have a college education and I am a Ph.D. and my husband is a professor. It's a different world from where my parents come from. My husband and she maintain a good relationship, but the problem is to relax her enough so she doesn't feel totally like a guest. She tends to be very passive when Arnold is around. When we do things alone I can get her into better conversations about the family and what we have in common. I have a better time with her by myself too. We'll go shopping or I'll take her to a concert.

Ideological and religious differences between generations are startling. Sixty percent of the adult children were born Protestant, 30 percent Catholic, and 10 percent Jewish. Two thirds described their parents' religious practices as moderate to traditional, and a third claimed their parents were nonpracticing or practice religion minimally. In sharp contrast, 75 percent describe their own religious practices as nonpracticing or minimal and only 25 percent said they were moderate or traditional. Furthermore, many adult children said their parents are prejudiced or racist and that this is a continuing source of conflict between them. A son in his fifties explains what happens when his parents make racist statements: "It's uncomfortable. They'll make some racial slur and I always correct them, and it always cools off the conversation. It's hard for me to let it ride. They would actually disagree that they have racial feelings, but I think it's there." A daughter believes such prejudices are generational. Another tells how she has tried to break away from the prejudice she learned from her parents. She is convinced she cannot change them:

> I really don't like the way they talk about other people. I'm convinced that it comes from their feelings of inadequacy. I find that

deeply offensive. I worked like a dog to rid myself of it. So did my sister. So when I see it expressed in one way or another in them it's like a red light comes on, "Oh no, here we go again." But I know it's something I can't do anything about.

For some children questions of prejudice and social justice are closely linked to religion. They have rejected their parents' religiosity because of its prejudicial overtones. About 75 percent are nonpracticing, 5 percent minimally practicing. Sons and daughters often explain changes in their religious affiliation as an adjustment to marriage or as an attempt to find an ideological environment compatible with the way they want to educate their children, as this daughter claims:

> I avoid the church thing. I've made a change and she knows about it. But I don't ever elaborate the reasons for doing so beyond the very superficial reason that the minister whom we liked, who married us, left and we didn't like the new minister. We left and we began looking for another church experience that would allow us to feel more comfortable and also give us a place to take our children.

Some parents are not happy that their children do not practice religion. Other parents used to complain but have abated in later years. An unmarried son says he visits more now that his parents stopped complaining. A daughter reports:

> My parents' relationship to the church is very significant. And my mother is concerned that the rest of us don't have that and are not active church members. It's a recurring theme with her. Recently, she has backed off from all the remarks that we weren't going or participating.

A couple of children recall that social drinking, a basic part of the academic scene, was a major life-style change for them and raised conflicts with their parents' religious beliefs. One daughter relates her internal struggle:

> My mother was very much a teetotaler and was critical of drinking because her father had been an alcoholic. We were pretty

straight in college and didn't have much experience, so as a young married couple we wanted to have a bit more of a social life. We went out to a bar at that time and I felt like a real hypocrite. I could not balance having something to drink and going to church. It took a long time before I felt you could be a good Christian *and* drink.

The focus on ideological differences does not imply that generations have nothing in common. A few children claim they hold the same religious values as their parents, but their formal commitments have changed. Even when they disagree, parents and children continue to see each other. Many distant children mention areas of generational continuity with their parents, especially in terms of values. A daughter shares her parents' deep commitment to finding satisfying work. A son enjoys a strong bond with his father in sharing a common interest in science and literature:

My father is a biologist and one of my specialties is science and literature. He loves and really understands the things I write about academically in journal articles. And I always feel it's a very nice gift to him when I do something in that area because it says something about the connection between us and the importance that he's had in my life.

In their interviews, adult children identify a number of characteristic features of their familial relationships with distant elderly parents. The distant, isolated, nuclear family represents the clearest behavioral expression of postindustrial America's cultural value that encourages generational independence. In distant relationships both adult children and elderly parents are free to develop attitudes and life-styles independently from each other, and make life choices with as much or as little involvement of the other generation as they desire. Nevertheless, many distant children remain unprepared to deal with all the emotional requirements of this new lifestyle. Frequently neither adult child nor elderly parent is satisfied with so much independence. For along with nuclear-family freedom, distance brings a subtle yet gnawing sense of the demise of certain key emotional and affective as well as supportive elements of extended family protection and security.

35

The geographically isolated nuclear family and the independent households of elderly Americans are both frail and vulnerable social units. Marital relationships and child rearing, for example, fall entirely on the backs of young husbands and wives, many of whom lack preparation for the ominous responsibilities required. One study of migrating families found that marital problems could be attributed to the separation of a wife from her relatives (Gray and Smith 1960). Some recent surveys suggest that executives are not as eager to move as they used to be (Weiss 1983). A significant number of distant-living elderly parents also experience emotions and anxieties associated with separation, such as anger and longing (Parkes 1981). Loneliness can make distance intolerable for some widowed elderly parents (Lopata 1981).

Family size and composition can be a support system as well as a source of strain in relationships with distant parents. The most obvious factor is whether an aging parent lives alone or as part of a couple. Other factors such as the number of adult siblings, the location and birth order of children, the presence of other extended family members in the vicinity, and the marital status of adult children all influence the nature of distant communications and the availability of adult children and other relatives to help when elderly parents need it.

The more children an elderly person has the greater the potential for contact, assistance, and affection as he or she grows old. Family planning represents a major twentieth-century revolution in human reproduction. New techniques of preventing pregnancies have significantly reduced the average family size of those who practice birth control. The first generation to have made use of artificial birth control methods during the post-World War I period and the depression is now entering old age.

Does the fact of fewer adult children in these families also mean there is less assistance available to aging parents? Certainly childless married couples or individuals will have no children to help them out in old age, which may account for the higher numbers of childless elderly residing in nursing homes. The answer is more complicated, however. Often even one adult child is sufficient as a caretaker, since one child rather than a committee of children usually takes the major responsibility of caring for an aging parent.

However, for the aging couple with only one child—a distant-living child—problems of communication and assistance are compounded significantly. A distant only child's ability to assist an aging parent is severely curtailed even though his or her sense of filial obligation remains strong.

Slightly more than half the distant children in this study had one or more siblings living near their parents, while only 20 percent of the parents live near their own brothers and sisters. Several daughters and sons report that their entire family is spread out around the country. One daughter from a large family explains:

> We're pretty scattered. One in California, one in Houston. I'm here and two others are in Chicago. One of the stepbrothers is at home. He could have taken a job elsewhere. And two or three others are two or three hours from home. One of the youngest sisters is living in an apartment in town. Another sister has an easy drive to where my parents live.

At a certain level, distant sons and daughters with siblings near their parents feel less stress because they appreciate their siblings' help. Yet sibling relationships often become strained during transitions as a result of different expectations toward each other and toward parents.

Distant children from families with many siblings often report less concern about face-to-face care or material assistance for aging parents since even a small amount of money collected from many brothers and sisters is adequate, and siblings living near their parents usually help them with services. At the same time, distant children from large families claim their parents initiate fewer calls and visits since parents have so many children to communicate with. Holiday visits are often described as fun but chaotic and without much chance for quiet conversation. Telephone calls are more personalized one-on-one because there is less chance to withdraw or disengage from the conversation and the interaction is focused.

The proximity of extended family members, especially aunts and uncles, nieces and nephews, cousins, and even grandchildren also influences distant relationships. Distant sons and daughters with extended families near their parents visit and telephone their parents more often than those without such extended families. A large number of extended family members increases communications, though not necessarily the quality of relationships. In some cases differences between generations arise from a distant child's lack of emotional closeness to extended family. A son remarks:

> I'm more nuclear-family focused. My parents are much closer to their brothers and the extended family. Both sets of my grandparents were immigrant children from southern Italy. This instilled in my parents a strong set of family values. Then there's a breakaway that comes with the first and second generation kids of immigrants. I think it came in my generation. I would have broken away from my uncles and my brother and sister more than my father would from his brothers and sisters. When we go home we have to visit our cousins and aunts and they put pressure on us to do that.

Unmarried children often express stronger feelings toward their parents since their filial devotion has no formal competition in a spouse. For the same reasons, however, the likelihood is greater that an unmarried child will perpetuate conflicts from adolescence into the distant adult relationship.

Sons and daughters commonly call attention to differences in family obligations between themselves and their distant parents. A few daughters without children of their own consider this a significant life-style difference between them and their mothers. One unmarried daughter from a very large family elaborated the implications of this generational difference for her relationship with her distant mother:

> I don't expect to have kids and they did. My mother was pregnant fourteen times. There's a lot of communication that comes with shared experience. In many ways my mother has more in common with my sisters who have kids than with me. That's an area of shared experience that I won't have with my mother. The grandparents being present is something I won't have.
>
> If I had children my mother would be more likely to move in with me and I'd be more comfortable with that. Having children is something that just doesn't interest me. I suspect that teaching gives me a sense of passing on to the next generation in the sense of parenting.

In the same vein, a married daughter without children realizes how much more important her friends are to her compared to her mother, who centered her life around her family:

> I feel more independent. I have my own life to lead. I am sensitive to my mother's needs but my life centers around friends much more than it does on family. I have not been able to make close contact with cousins and aunts and uncles. I never see them and it doesn't bother me. In that way I'm different from my mother. I think my mother also thinks it's unfortunate that I've grown away from the family.

Several married daughters with children commented on their mothers' greater dedication to family and domestic tasks compared to their own commitments, which include a career:

> She had been an elementary school teacher. But she only worked for one year after she was married; it was really frowned on then for married women to work. Now I understand why she had no interest in going back to work. She was much more committed to her children. She was a very meticulous housekeeper. I guess it's taken me a while to realize I'm not. I'm never going to be and it doesn't fit with my life. But now I understand better why. With two jobs it's incredibly difficult with kids. If my child is out of school it's a tremendous problem in scheduling because my husband teaches too. When a kid is sick it's very hard to keep things going.

Adult children with their own children often impose the grandchildren into their relationships with distant parents. This has a negative effect on their own distant relationship when their parents do not satisfy their expectations as grandparents. Couples whose parents live in the same town visit more often and split their visits between their respective distant parents.

All the mothers and fathers in my study were living independently, with the exception of one institutionalized mother. Most distant children perceive their parents as very self-sufficient. Only a quarter said one parent has a few dependencies or their parent is dependent for a number of important things. About half said one of their parents has a chronic medical condition and 40 percent said that a health condition limits their parents' activities in some way. Older daughters and sons (in their fifties) with parents in poor health complained more of serious stress and frustration in their relationships than younger children with healthy, active parents. These older children were trying to help their very frail or ill parents, but their efforts yielded few satisfactions and much guilt.

Our culture promotes sexual differences in expectations between parents and children. Both sons and daughters provide assistance for their distant aging parents, but differences in parental expectations of sons and daughters influence communications and assistance. The predominance of American women as caretakers and communicators with elderly family members represents a perpetuation of the traditional role of women in our society. One result is that elderly mothers often expect far more services and assistance from daughters than from sons regardless of where they live. Aging mothers express unhappiness and disappointment when distant daughters cannot comply. Yet these same elderly mothers commonly expect far less from their sons and express extreme gratitude for any small favors.

The elderly mother–adult daughter bond is often described as the strongest (Troll 1972). Mothers with sons comes next, followed by fathers with daughters. Father-son relationships are often problematical in terms of communications, affection, and assistance, possibly because of the narrow expectations involved in the male role. Some adult daughters report difficulties communicating with their distant fathers, though most communicate well.

In general, daughters are socialized to express their emotions openly and provide more nurturance and care giving than sons. Sons, on the other hand, are expected to repress their emotions or at least not express them freely. The implications of such socialization practices for telephone communications are clear: daughters, in general, do it better and derive more satisfaction from it. Yet distant daughters do not call or write significantly more often than distant sons.

On the other hand, distant daughters report having visited more recently, and significantly more often, than sons: 95 percent of the daughters compared to only 65 percent of the sons visited more than two times in the last year. Consistent with this, 35 percent of the sons, compared to only 5 percent of the daughters, visited only once or not at all in the last year. In addition, daughters also complain more of feeling lonely for their parents. Neither they nor their parents are satisfied with the frequency of visits. Several married daughters feel sad and disappointed because their distant parents cannot take a more active role in their children's socialization. Finally, daughters express more frustration and guilt that their parents are not present to give and to receive help and nurturance.

In recent years an important family problem has emerged because more women are entering the work force. Since working women do not have sufficient time to care for both children and aging parents, many women must make a choice (Brody 1981). Their dilemma implies further limitations of the family as a support system for distant elderly parents in the near future.

A common complaint among daughters was their distant mother's lack of interest or insensitivity to their jobs. This generation gap reflects an important social change since few of their mothers had careers. In a few cases daughters-in-law assume the responsibility of communicating with their husbands' distant parents.

All of the sons and daughters in this study migrated from other parts of the country, leaving their parents and extended families behind in the Midwest (30 percent), in the East (30 percent), in the South (20 percent), and in the West (15 percent). One child's parents live in England and one retired father lives in Puerto Rico.

Many live quite far from their parents: 40 percent live more than 800 miles away, 35 percent more than 400 miles, and 25 percent more than 200 miles. Thirty percent must travel more than five hours by plane. Forty percent drive between four and twelve hours to visit, and another 40 percent drive more than thirteen hours.

The average distant child has lived in his or her current residence for eight years. Half have lived in their current residences for five years or less, and 20 percent have lived there more than sixteen years. Asked to consider a hypothetical move to their parents' location, only 15 percent said living close to their parents would be an important consideration in such a move; 95 percent said they would never move to their parents' location.

In general, distant parents have a highly stable residential history. Half have lived in their current residence for more than twenty years; 25 percent more than thirty years. A son remarks:

> My mother is seventy-two years old and has lived in the same place for sixty years. She was not born in that house, she moved there as a child. After they were married they just moved into the same house. She bought it and the estate from her parents. Currently, she's widowed and living alone.

Only 25 percent of the parents have lived in their current residence less than five years, and many of them made retirement moves within the last few years but previously lived for many years in the same residence. Only 20 percent of the parents moved frequently over the years. Most children expect their distant parents to continue living where they are. Only 20 percent thought their parents would consider moving near them. About 60 percent expected their parents to make housing changes in old age, but not nearer to them; 25 percent believed their parents would eventually be institutionalized.

The length of time parents and children have lived apart also has an important influence on their relationship. Adult children who moved away only recently claim more often that their distant parents sustain the hope that they will relocate to live near them; their parents also express greater dissatisfaction and lack of acceptance of distant living. Children who have lived in their current residence for less than six years also express more dissatisfaction with the frequency of visits. On the other hand, children who have been separated longer adapt better and report more stable patterns of contact. In time, most people learn to accept distant living as a permanent aspect of their relationship.

To understand the development of the distant relationship over time, I interviewed children and parents from several age groups, representing distinct stages of the distant family cycle. The average distant child was forty-four years old; the youngest was thirty-one, the oldest fifty-six. Half were between forty and fifty years old, a quarter were between thirty and forty, and another quarter over fifty. Distant children answered questions about sixty-two parents, including thirty-seven mothers and twenty-five fathers. The average parent was seventy-four years old; the youngest was sixty-two and the oldest eighty-eight.

The developmental cycle of the distant family is based on the ages and age differences of adult children and their parents. Expectations, communications, and emotional attachments between children and distant parents change over time as a result of the normal family-development cycle. For example, as the age gap between generations increases, the frequency of visits in both directions decreases. Parental visits decrease in frequency because of increasing disability and frailty; however, visits may last longer when they do occur. Younger sons and daughters visit their parents more than older children, and those with mothers younger than seventy express a stronger desire to call and visit more often. When a parent becomes sick or frail, however, telephone communications increase in importance both for emotional support and assistance. Because of a strong correlation between aging and declining health, communications of children over fifty focus more on the need for assistance, whereas communications of younger children focus more on mutual exchanges and affection.

Such developmental changes help explain the ambivalence adult children commonly express about distance. At one stage they may feel pleased and satisfied with great distances between them and their parents, whereas at another stage in the cycle the same distance may seem like an insurmountable obstacle.

The first stage of the distant relationship begins sometime during the young adulthood of the child. The stage is initiated through independent living. The most common way distant living begins is when the young adult child migrates to seek educational, occupational, or marital goals in a distant location. Both parents and children cooperate in this early adult transition, calling on a series of cultural values emphasizing the independence of generations and justifying the process of generational separation. During this period the primary issue in the expectations of both generations is the child's normal adult development, including marriage, educational and occupational achievement, financial and emotional independence from the parents, and separating emotionally from childhood bonds of dependency. Once a child has established a distant household, the characteristic parent-child conflict is in the memory of past dependency, which reasserts itself in the present relationship.

During the second stage in the distant family cycle, children and parents maintain and reinforce bonds of affection and family solidarity within a framework of mutual nondependence. This stage may begin as a continuation of distant-living arrangements formed earlier by migrations of young adult children, or by new migrations of middle-aged children or elderly parents in retirement. In general, adult children have now accomplished their educational, marital, and occupational objectives, or at least settled into a life-style in which such goals do not dominate over their relationships to distant parents. Parents are decreasing their occupational roles, ending their child-rearing tasks, and beginning to face transitions of middle age and early old age. Some measure of familial assistance may be part of this stage. Help is usually provided by the generation best able to do so. But assistance, though important, does not dominate the relationship.

Communications and contacts maintain and reinforce bonds of affection and family solidarity. Patterned telephone conversations and routine visits may characterize this stage in the family cycle for many years. The generation gap is the chief source of ambivalence and conflict at this stage because emerging life-style differences are difficult for each generation to understand or accept in the other.

The final stage of the distant-family developmental cycle is dominated by the elderly parents' declining health, increasing frailty, and social-status changes such as widowhood or retirement. The key issue for adult children and distant parents is the need to adapt their relationship to the life-cycle transitions of the aging parent.

When distant elderly parents begin to require face-to-face assistance and care, it becomes extremely difficult for both generations and much strain is placed on the relationship. Such transitions often generate feelings of ambivalence and anxiety both in the elderly parent who wishes to remain independent, and in the distant adult child who experiences intense emotions because of the parents' increasing dependence on them. On the one hand, the adult child feels responsible for providing assistance, including face-to-face care and services when needed; on the other hand, because distance creates obstacles and complications in providing assistance, the adult child often experiences guilt, role stress, divided loyalty, conflict, frustration, and, of course, ambivalence.

I have come to regard emotional attachments to distant parents as an ambivalent connection, a persistent feeling of uncertainty about distant communications and relationships. I believe these ambivalent attitudes arise out of the emotional insecurity children experience trying to maintain close relationships with parents over distances in spite of many obstacles. At the same time, ambivalent feelings strain distant relationships and contribute to feelings of alienation, frustration, powerlessness, anger, and loss.

Although distant adult children express a diverse range of attitudes toward their parents, ambivalence is expressed at some time by almost everyone; 90 percent of the distant children expressed uncertainty, mixed messages, loneliness, loss, and guilt about distant living and their relationships with distant parents. A son in his forties typically wonders if his ambivalent feelings toward his widowed father are normal:

> Now there's one feeling that I've not come to grips with yet. There's something very curious about my relationship with my father. This distance is not normal in the sense that I always imagined that sons need to have closer relations and stronger feelings with their fathers. And I don't feel that need. I love him dearly. But I'm not crazy about him.
>
> As I was reading through the questions I was thinking, "God, I must sound like a very cold fish in my relationship with my father because I don't have those strong feelings of warmth that one normally has." I don't think it would be different if we lived closer. I think that my distance from my father has its origins in the fact that I was raised for the first three years without him because he went off to the war. The major figures in my life were women—my mother and my grandmother.
>
> Then, when I was a kid my father was never a man who expressed his emotions. So he didn't pat me on the back. We didn't do things together very often. The school had father-son trips and he always did it. But one had a feeling he was doing his fatherly duty. He may very well have enjoyed these things. But our relationship was such that he wasn't expressing that, and I wasn't sure.
>
> I would have more in common with him had my mother remained alive. She was clearly the center of the family. It's interesting

45

because I probably felt much closer to my father when my mother was alive. She sort of moderated the relationship.

A daughter's relationship to her parents is typical in its combination of leftovers from the past and worries and guilt in the present. Her feelings arise from distortions in communications along with a sense of deterioration in the relationship resulting from distance and prolonged separation:

> In lots of ways they are still trying to treat me as they did when I was a teenager in terms of offering advice that has a little more status than just advice. I think also they're still coming to terms with the fact that I may be able to cope on my own. For a long time they were in a state of shock. But since it's gone over twenty years now I think perhaps they're ready to accept it.
>
> It's very difficult for me in part because it comes in sort of quantum leaps. If you don't see someone for six months or even twelve months the difference is much greater. More than the physical it's the emotional deterioration. It's difficult because I know I can't do very much in the three weeks I'm visiting there, nothing that's lasting.
>
> I think the feeling of separateness is much more acute for me with my mother than with my father. My sense of distance between my mother and me has been troubling me for a couple of years now. I feel she and I are farther apart, have more difficulty really talking closely than my father and I do. That's where my guilt comes in. I fear that she thinks I've abandoned her, that she'd like me to be at home and more accessible to take care of her. And she'd never say that. I think about that issue, that my relation with her would be better if I returned. I assume I would see her more. And my fantasy certainly is to be in a situation where I could pop in on her for a cup of tea once a week or so. Well, it's not satisfying.

Such ambivalent attitudes range from the response of some sons and daughters who are glad to live apart from their parents because of unresolved past conflicts, to others who wish to reunite with parents through migrations and cannot reconcile long periods between face-to-face visits. A few distant children even express diverse attitudes within a single interview. One minute they feel distance is to blame, the next minute they say their conflicting feelings reside in the relationship itself. Later still they feel the conflict is resolved. Typically, such sons and daughters twist and turn from positive to negative, from intense attachments to aloofness, from rational expressions to deep feelings, from jokes to tears. As circumstances fluctuate, so do emotions. A son who explains that he lost contact with his mother for ten years as a result of conflict says in the next breath that she can move in with him if she needs help; she is welcome. A daughter at first expresses how happy she is that her mother lives far away and cannot intrude on her life. Later in the interview she claims her relationship would improve if her mother and she lived in the same city.

Clearly, the distant relationship is emotionally powerful and in flux. Many distant children do not understand the situation themselves. Although they struggle to understand their emotional attachments to distant parents, no single pattern emerges of distant emotional attachments, only expressions of ambivalence.

CHAPTER 3

Distant Emotional Attachments in Three Voices

In the early stages of my investigation I was struck by the diversity of responses of the participants. Everyone seemed to stress something different, some special quality that distinguished his or her feelings and distant relationships from everyone else's: one man was abandoned by his father in early childhood, a woman's mother developed Alzheimer's disease, a distant father was dying of a terminal illness, someone's mother was domineering and set unrealistic expectations, a widowed mother had become very dependent emotionally. Slowly, diversity gave way and themes began to emerge: loss and grief, anger and frustration, unresolved conflict from adolescence, emotional repression in the natal home, religious and ideological differences between children and their parents, parents' health transitions, and anxiety about the future.

But the most universal and dramatic theme to emerge was the expression of ambivalent feelings toward distant parents. Regardless of the specific life events or incidences daughters and sons used to describe their distant relationships, three distinct voices consistently characterized their emotional attachments to distant parents. Of forty distant adult children, eight (20 percent) presented a displaced voice, twenty (50 percent) a well-adapted voice, and twelve (30 percent) an alienated voice. The displaced voice is not satisfied with distant living and expresses a desire to reunite with parents. The well-adapted voice accepts distant living as a normal result of occupational and educational mobility, maintaining close contact and strong affection without desiring to change the situation. The alienated voice is glad to live away from parents because relationships are unsatisfying, filled with unresolved conflicts from the past.

A distant child can have different voices or change from one voice to another as the stresses of divided loyalties increase or decrease, corresponding to life transitions and different stages in the distant-family cycle. In this chapter I will describe the general characteristics of each voice, then present narrated case histories from a few participants selected because they best illustrate the ideals of each type.

THE DISPLACED: WHEN THE HEART GROWS FONDER

For displaced sons and daughters absence makes the heart grow fonder. They express negative feelings about distant living along with a positive relationship to their parents. They will not be satisfied until one or the other generation relocates to be closer. Their emotional attachment to distant parents is a source of comfort and support rather than stress or conflict. They often complain about economic and social forces that require continued separation. They accept the reality of distant living and prolonged separations in their daily lives but complain that it has destructive effects on their ability to maintain bonds of affection. They perceive any conflict with parents the result of living far apart—a by-product of distant living.

Displaced sons and daughters interpret the basic cultural value of generational independence to mean separate households, but living nearby. They believe living·closer would be mutually beneficial. They feel a continuing sense of urgency resulting from feelings of separation and loss. They reject the notion that distant living is permanent. They and their parents strive for reunification, either by returning to their parents' location or having their parents move closer to them. Displaced children acknowledge that reunification would require adjustments in their life-styles and attitudes and would be difficult for their spouses and children. Nevertheless, they believe the advantages of relocating outweigh the difficulties.

Displaced children express a desire for more contact with their parents. Current contacts are inadequate for sharing their lives and for personal growth. Relative to other distant children they report very frequent calls and visits. They are always making plans to travel back and forth and visit. But the calls and visits are too short and unsatisfying: they end too soon. Displaced children say, "We barely begin talking and the visit is over, we must separate and go home." They want stronger bonds but distance interferes. After a visit they feel incomplete, a sense of loss.

Displaced children idealize memories of the past and describe their early adult separations from parents as free of conflict. They did not leave to escape from an oppressive emotional relationship but for external reasons, for economic mobility through education and career or for social mobility through marriage. Many express regret that life's circumstances have prevented their return. They left strong ties to parents and friends behind them.

Displaced sons and daughters are unhappy with their current life-styles. In varying degrees they are critical of their own careers, friends, families, and cities. They stress generational continuities, family histories and traditions, ethnic backgrounds, close ties to their grandparents and extended families, and they feel stronger attachments to their native regions. They see few advantages to the isolated nuclear family and complain that their extended families cannot help because of distance. They emphasize the material and emotional supports extended families provide and nuclear families lack: grandchildren cannot get to know grandparents; relationships with siblings suffer; and, after so many years they have lost touch with the stream of their parents' lives.

Displaced sons and daughters feel they need to live closer so they and their parents can help each other in times of need. They experience anxiety in anticipation of parental dependency because of illness or disability. They often become frustrated when their parents show signs of increasing need because of their inability to help directly. Life-cycle transitions, particularly parents' declining health and growing dependencies, generate intense feelings of guilt and reinforce negative attitudes toward distance. Though they try to overcome such feelings through frequent visits and phone calls, the financial and emotional costs are high.

A Displaced Son

The first case is a forty-two-year-old biology professor whose perspective is best summarized by his comment, "If only I could live closer to my parents."

I'm a very family-oriented person who's achieved upward mobility and suffered a lot from distance. Everyone is normal in the sense of functional in my situation. It isn't that I want to go back to Cleveland to help some poor, helpless, senile old parent. I mean, given the opportunity I'd like to go back because there is an awful lot there.

I never had adolescent conflicts. I left when I was twenty-two to go to graduate school at Berkeley. Mom didn't like it at all and she felt that I could have chosen a place that wasn't so far away. But they came out to visit regularly. They did send me money for a plane ticket to visit them and gave me some financial support. She appreciated that I was doing this because it was exciting to work with the people I really wanted to work with. She just didn't want to see me go.

It's almost identical the way they treated their parents and the way I treat them. They were closer in miles but they were there all the time just the way we are. I never rejected any opportunity to live closer. Even when I was in California I was very homesick for my family.

Marlene's parents are so much more helpful to us financially than my parents. They do things that Marlene and I can't possibly do for our kids. It isn't even that their income is so great, it's just that they don't spend it. So every time we turn around they've got another gift of $5,000. So when we wanted to move to a bigger house they said here's some money. And there is absolutely no sense of our having to pay them back; no strings attached.

Marlene's parents live about six blocks away from my parents. And they play bridge regularly. Both sets of parents have encouraged us to move to Cleveland. Neither set of parents has been happy with us living here. My father thinks this town is a hopeless waste of real estate. Regularly Mom in particular wistfully asks if we're going to move home. Marlene's parents, on the other hand, have campaigned eagerly to get us to Cleveland. And we haven't discouraged them either.

Marlene's parents called this weekend to say that the university is looking for "fact-finding" people, whatever that is, and immediately that jogged our memory about other things that we've talked about in the past. The location has a number of small colleges. So there are academic jobs. One of the problems we face in thinking of moving back to Cleveland is that it is not one of the places in the country with the best job market. Nevertheless, it's of serious enough importance to me that I think of leaving this altogether and getting something else, even outside of academia.

I'm not saying I'm unhappy being an academic. What I am unhappy about is being an academic here. If we're already in this part of the country, both of us would like to be within fifty blocks of our parents or a little bit more. Part of the reason is that my mother's almost sixty-nine and Dad's seventy-three and my younger daughter is two and my older daughter is six. The younger daughter says now on a fairly regular basis, "Go home to Grandma and Grandpa," which is the way we describe it, as going home. And so it's this grandchild-grandparent relationship. I had a lot of it. Marlene had even more.

My grandparents lived about two hours away from Cleveland. We were there about twice a month. My grandparents were truly important to us. Marlene's grandparents were even more important to them and they lived down the street. It's that continuity, that relationship which our kids aren't getting that is one of the central issues.

Another issue is that I feel dislocated from where my sense of self is. I identify myself in many ways with where my parents are, where my brother is, where many of my high school friends are with whom I'm in constant contact. My parents are one part of a complex of things which says a lot about what I am. And so to be in Cleveland would mean not just my parents but all the things they stand for which is home. So there's clearly an emotional aspect to this.

I think my connection with my parents in many ways is tighter than my brother's connection. My brother lives within a few blocks of them but they sometimes say I see them more than he does. I think Tom feels much more secure knowing my parents are nearby even though he doesn't see them often. I think about Tom a lot when I look at my kids who are also four years apart. Tom was my older brother and my best friend probably until I was twelve. We spent almost every weekend with each other until I was almost in high school, when Tom went to college.

So when I go home to Cleveland now, basically it's a very cool relationship. He's in public relations. That's why I would have that job opportunity there. The problem for me is that since I don't see him very often, when I do see him he will unload everything that's wrong with everyone in the world all at once, which I'm not at all pleased to hear. So basically, I just sort of get a glaze over my eyes and stare off into space. But I really think that if I saw Tom twice a week I'd enjoy him a lot more. I feel intensely close to all these people.

I was brought up in an ethnically diverse neighborhood. I spent a lot of time at the Y and there was a lot of neighborhood activity. Cleveland has a fairly rich culture. There's a great tavern which has wonderful duck dinners for five dollars and so on.

Well, Lansing is a white bread, Midwest, dull as dishwater place. I find that disappointing because it's not what I expected. At Berkeley I lived in the Bay Area. In Cleveland there is diversity but the city is dirty and grimy and the people don't have enough money. But California has the vitality and it's beautiful and everybody seems to be rich or they're trying to look like they're rich.

Gradually we have moved inward in Lansing so that what we do as a family matters an awful lot. It's just like what my parents did too. We had our first daughter after we were here for four years. We've been spending most of our time dealing with the family. Also as assistant professors we've both spent a lot of time writing lectures, creating courses, and doing research, all those work obligations. The fact that all the vitality I'm used to isn't here has probably made it in some funny way easier because we're not distracted. Michigan outside Detroit is a place you go when you don't want to be bothered by anything.

So some of the things that I missed here are bothering me now only because the girls are becoming a little older. We like to take the girls on the weekends to see things. After a half dozen things you've sort of run out of things to do, so we're going farther and farther afield, to Toledo for example. In Berkeley, there's just so much that one could do with kids. So all that's missing.

Another thing that's missing is the kind of intensity of relationships that I've always been used to. Not in the California sense that everybody is talking about their feelings, because I haven't really been involved in that in my life. But they're very intense because my friends and I are committed to each other.

I don't have friends like that here. Some of me says that it's because I never was an academic before so how can I compare being a college professor to being a student when I had such relationships. But I know that some people in other universities have had these kinds of strong collegial contacts. I find that this university is cooler. I don't know why. Maybe I haven't tried all that hard to become good friends to people my age. But I do miss that kind of companionship.

I'd like to talk with my parents on the phone more often because I like my parents, and if I could talk to them daily that would be more helpful to me; it's a natural part of our lives and we problem-solve that way. We call each other about equally by formal arrangement. Every Tuesday night somebody calls. My parents are like everybody's parents who grew up in the Depression. The telephone is for exchange of information and when someone is sick, not for conversation. They get scared when the phone bill comes.

They are good listeners. My folks don't always give appropriate responses. Sometimes they'll say things that are off the wall, but there's some relationship to what's been said and they are paying attention. My parents are the opposite of holding anything back. On the other hand, a little more discretion could go a long way. We have a history in my family, not exactly of destroyed dinners, but of dinners in which the digestive systems weren't working all that well because everyone is saying what they sincerely feel.

We go home for every vacation. For Christmas we'll sometimes go home for three weeks. During the summer we go home for a month. Everything is very satisfying when we're there visiting. We were there two weeks ago and we'll be going again in a week, then we'll be there again four weeks later. My parents and Marlene's have been here this fall.

It doesn't seem likely that my parents would ever move to Lansing. I would really prefer to move to Cleveland to be closer to them and I'd prefer to do it soon. Next year I have a sabbatical. We've talked about doing a sabbatical in California. But more and more I'm thinking that if the granting agency will come through and Marlene can find something to do in Cleveland, that's what we'd really like to do. It's kind of a probationary period. We would go to Cleveland for a year, and if that works we would stay.

I know that as my parents get older I'm going to be spending a lot more time in Cleveland on emergency business. It hasn't happened yet. Both of them come from very long-lived roots. I spent a lot of time driving back and forth to take care of my grandfather when he was in his high eighties. I saw my parents doing the same thing so that in all sorts of ways it would be better to be where they are.

THE WELL ADAPTED:
CULTURE AND THE INDIVIDUAL IN HARMONY

Well-adapted sons and daughters express harmony between the values of culture on the one hand and the needs of the individual on the other. The characteristic feature of the well-adapted voice is its abiding tone of security in relationships with parents. Well-adapted children are satisfied with distant living arrangements and have no desire to change. Moreover, they express consistently positive emotional attachments to their parents. Distance has no special impact; their relationships are good and would remain so, near or far. Both generations share expectations and a common perception of the meaning of distance.

Well-adapted sons and daughters recall leaving their parents and natal homes as part of a normal process in attaining adult status. Their desire for higher education, career opportunities, and marriage led them toward greater self-reliance, autonomy, achievement, and success in the adult world. They are grateful to their parents for supporting them financially and emotionally in their quest.

They often recall adolescent conflict with parents during their adolescence and early adult separations. But they interpret such conflict as a normal part of growing up. The conflict is confined to the past, with no spillover into their current adult relationships with parents. Several well-adapted children recall one key conflict they had to resolve. Many point to a period in adulthood, usually their late thirties, when they resolved their adolescent conflict with their parents.

Well-adapted sons and daughters continue to support the cultural values that originally encouraged them to establish a distant household: the desire for career mobility, individual achievement and fulfillment, independent living in an autonomous nuclear family, and the separation of generations. They view their careers as a logical outcome of professional training and hard work. They are proud of their achievements and their parents are proud of them.

Well-adapted children hold positive attitudes toward their current life-styles. They are pleased with friends, neighbors, work associates, leisure-time activities, their locations, children's schools, and optimistic about future opportunities. They praise the autonomy of the nuclear family while acknowledging its limitations, such as raising small children without any relatives nearby. Their middle-class incomes, however, allow compensations such as baby-sitters and housekeepers.

Well-adapted sons and daughters grant the same autonomy to their parents, claiming they are happy in retirement, enjoying their leisure, independence, friends, and local communities. Life-style differences between the generations do not detract significantly from their relationships. Conflicts are temporary and resolved quickly through the good will of both generations. Awareness of generational continuities provides an important source of family solidarity.

Well-adapted children regard routine telephone calls and visits as realistic ways of maintaining emotional bonds to their parents. In general, they are satisfied with the content and frequency of contacts, though objectively the frequency varies greatly. Invariably they say, "We call enough. If I wanted to call more I would and the same for my parents." They are also satisfied with the content of communications. Telephone calls are rarely problematical. Rather, they are mundane and ordinary, lacking drama. Typically they say, "We generally talk about what we've been doing, how we feel, and the children. It's good to know my parents are in good health."

Visits are equally satisfying. Planning reunions is a pleasant experience. Well-adapted children say they enjoy being with their parents; there is much to talk about and experience together. They could schedule more visits if they wanted to but do not need to. Most well-adapted children believe their parents share this view:

"If my mother wants to see me more," they say, "she knows she would be welcome here. I could go more often if I wanted to, but really we visit enough to maintain our feelings for each other."

Well-adapted sons and daughters see themselves and their parents as mutually independent or providing mutual assistance, depending on their stage in the family cycle. They stand ready to help when they can and express confidence that their parents would do the same for them. Should their parents decide to move closer they would try to make them welcome.

They are satisfied with the help they contribute to their parents' physical and emotional health, though most parents are healthy and independent so children rarely contribute much beyond emotional support. Some well-adapted children whose parents need assistance regret they cannot do more but cope well. Most express doubts about assuming primary responsibility for a dependent parent and relief when their parents are in professional hands. Because they believe distant living has imposed legitimate limits on their filial obligations, they express little guilt when their parents need professional care.

Finally, several well-adapted sons and daughters have developed conscious strategies and attitudes to help them with potential emotional conflicts. They express confidence that they and their parents can solve problems with mutual respect for each other as adults. They avoid sensitive topics from the past and do not hold unrealistic expectations of their parents. They are pleased when their parents solve their own problems and they try to avoid dumping their problems on their parents. The key rests on asking for assistance when needed and avoiding unnecessary emotional dependence.

A Well-Adapted Daughter

"I'm satisfied living far away from my parents."

Carmen Flory is a fifty-four-year-old university professor. She misses her parents but is not longing to relocate or wishing they would relocate. She focuses attention on her parents' health problems rather than on her own relationship with them.

> In a large family the middle kids like me don't have many problems. My older brother and sister had many many more conflicts

with my parents over dating and early marriages, a pregnancy, all the life problems. My brother and I really didn't have major conflicts with our parents. We just went to school and did our stuff. I think we came out pretty unscathed.

My parents started treating me like an adult around the time I was coming out of school. After that I wanted to see the world, literally. I became a stewardess with the airlines. I would have been independent of my folks even if I had been there. My sister lived sixteen miles away when she was first married and she was independent. They never expected us to stay near. I never regretted leaving town, only that I'm convinced it's really a good small town. But the work I wanted to do was never there. My family instilled in us a strong need for achievement and success. It was just what they said and their values. Anything I've ever done has been OK with them. They always gave me moral support.

My mother is seventy-seven and isn't in good health, but Dad is. It would be easier if they would live closer because we would see them more. When they had their fiftieth wedding anniversary ten years ago I was really surprised because all of these young people, I mean people my age, were there. They will never move because they have all their friends there.

My husband and I are from the same small town. After his father died in 1971 his mother moved to town, just around the corner from my folks. When we visited we stayed at either place, depending on what was going on with my folks—if the younger kids were home or not. Now my mother-in-law's got more room. Or, if we wear them out we can leave and go to the other one. Now, half our meals are with both my parents and Hank's mother. Our mothers are neighbors now, and friends. They use the same hairdresser and go to the same church.

My sister is on the other side of the state close to Minnesota. And I have three brothers in California. There's nobody there. Dealing with siblings is ragtag. One tells me I don't know how to do anything, and I'm never available. It ranges from that all the way up to making real practical steps and being involved. We had this family business meeting over how to fund my dad's autobiography. Actually, I have one brother who's really rich; he just came up with the money up front. Then when we had a family reunion the next year we just divided up who owed who to help fund it.

Recently, Mother was in the hospital for a perforated bowel.

While she was there she had peritonitis and underlying it all she has a heart condition. She barely lived. They decided they would go to the city sixty miles away to do some more surgery. Then she came back and had a temporary colostomy for about four months. She's like many frail elderly. She's got multiple systems that are going down simultaneously, not quickly. But she's got an absolutely fantastic medical backup there in that small town. My dad is there too.

My mom especially has changed. When we were little kids she worked very hard and was very controlling. When we all left she was really lost for a while and suffered. Then she got into other activities. But this critical illness was a big, big thing. She's really mellowed out. None of us kids could believe what a great patient she was. The nurses who took care of her sent her a birthday card. She's totally different from the person she was when she was younger.

We went to China in 1986 and never called, so we had our kids call periodically and make sure my parents and Hank's mother were OK. The grandparents had someone to talk to. In phone calls we exchange real information. Sometimes I need to stay on a while to get the information. I am satisfied with the call. They've changed too. They used to never phone. Now they use it. For example, I should call when I come back from traveling, but if I don't my father calls me. If I called them more often they would think I was really worried. A normal amount of calling has the right feel.

Mother is really much more explicit about what's going on with her. Dad doesn't talk as much. But he certainly called us in the middle of the night from the hospital when Mother was critically ill. He was very straightforward. We just stood by the phone because there was nothing we could do.

The only thing I ever got any static on is if they haven't gone to see the doctor and I rag them a bit about that. But they're still really in control. They're good listeners. I was telling her about my canary having a problem. There is still enough mutual territory and enough gossip about relatives to fill up time too. We always talk about health and Mother always asks me how my kids are.

We definitely withhold information about health. We've had some crises here that we have not passed on. I had some polyps that were being tested. There's no way I would have shared that with my mom and dad. There's no reason, if they can't do anything about it, to burden them because they'd just really worry about it a lot.

We would use them to help make some decisions. Like when we decided whether we were going to China we talked to them. They tend to do what they want to do. All of us kids can give them ideas but they decide. We don't argue in any way. We tried to influence them two years ago to see us in London. But they were just moving from the family home to a little home they built, and they thought the house was more important. It's typical. They decide what they want to do.

I feel relaxed and happy they are doing so well. But the distance is too great and we are too busy. I'd enjoy more visits and I think they would too. The most satisfying thing is that both my parents are alert and interesting people. They are the people I like to see and who like to see me. The most satisfying part of a visit is to see how well they look after each other. The most unsatisfying part is to look at Mom's swollen ankles, knowing what they mean.

I helped Dad make a lot of decisions during Mom's crisis. Dad and I were talking twice a day on the phone, so I'd catch him in the daytime at the hospital and after he got home at night. One time I was talking to Dad and one of the partners in the medical practice came into the room. Dad said, "Oh here's the doctor now." He got on the phone and said that I shouldn't come home to take care of everything, then leave, because that wouldn't help them learn to cope. He wanted them to use the extended-care facility, learn to cope with the colostomy, and then go home. He said if I was to come home it should be for emotional support but not to help set up the home care. They were getting good advice.

They both want to remain independent. They only ask help when they really need it. Still, I would like to be available at a few minutes' notice in emergencies. This is the result of having a critically ill parent. I've been most helpful in explaining medical terms and supporting their own independence in handling medical situations. Mom told me that one of the pamphlets I sent from a hospital here was helpful in terms of the equipment they ended up getting.

The house is small enough so one person can manage it. If my father died, my mother would need much more help but now she can manage. It is unlikely that they would move here, but since our children are grown and not at home it would be good. I think we would do well with any of them, including my mother-in-law. But they would be lonesome for their hometown friends. Also they have good housing and excellent doctors there.

THE ALIENATED: OUT OF SIGHT, OUT OF MIND

"I'm glad to have distance between us."

Alienated children maintain positive feelings about distant living and negative emotional attachments to their parents. They often express a strong lack of emotional closeness and often choose to live as far away as possible.

Some alienated children experienced strained and unsatisfactory relationships when they first established distant households. Since then their relationships with parents have gotten worse. Others believe prolonged separation itself eroded their relationships. Most alienated children express open hostility and anger because of past conflicts that persist. Sometimes they feel indifference.

Looking back on their original decisions in young adulthood to live far from home, alienated children recall distant living as an important component in their search for identity and their struggle for separation and autonomy from their parents. They did not leave primarily because of economic or social advancement like displaced and well-adapted children, though these may have been their surface motives. Instead, they left because they did not want to care for dependent parents or because they felt they could not develop normally if they remained close. In any case, the emotional costs were high. They sustain deep internal wounds.

Many alienated children established distance to achieve emotional freedom and independence they could not achieve nearby. Leaving home was part of a rebellion against oppressive or difficult family relationships. Alternatively, as young adult children they experienced an unconscious need to flee from a family breakdown— parents divorcing, separating, or fighting. In yet another scenario, the original decision to leave was a result of conforming to parental or peer-group aspirations for them, which they passively accepted at the time. In every case, their relationships to parents became more distant emotionally over time. For some, negative attitudes toward distant parents emerged as a mechanism for coping with the reality of distant living.

Alienated children believe generational life-style conflicts would dominate and become intolerable if they lived close to their parents.

Typically they say, "The responsibility of living near them would be overwhelming. I'm glad they're in good health because I couldn't do much for them even if they needed it." Visits and telephone calls are tolerable only because they are infrequent, involving no permanent need for them to adjust to extended face-to-face interactions with the parental generation.

In addition, their spouses, and even their children, do not get along well with their parents. And such feelings are mutual. Parents become irritable and unable to deal with their nuclear-family problems. Alienated children say, "Our parents don't really want to help us or they can't help us. They have too many of their own problems. They don't want us to live near them anymore than we want to."

Neither generation is happy about such conflicts. Alienated children often express remorse and a sense of loss. But neither children nor parents do anything to change the relationship; both generations seem resigned to accept it. Like other distant children, families come together periodically for holidays or life-course transitions. But for them, such rituals are hollow; they go through the motions of renewing family bonds out of a sense of obligation but they derive no personal satisfaction.

Most alienated children feel they have too much contact with their parents. Visits and calls are filled with problems and regrets. Visits are too long. In some cases poor communications and misunderstandings are partly responsible. But past conflicts also perpetuate unsatisfying relationships. Infrequent contacts are adequate to maintain their bonds of family solidarity. Frequent communications are problematical; frequent calling means that their parents are making unreasonable demands. For the same reason, alienated children prefer having their parents visit because they have more control over events. Face-to-face contacts always call to memory negative feelings and unresolved conflicts from the past.

In forging separate family units with negative feelings about their parents, alienated children pay the full price of isolation in upward social and economic mobility. They often rationalize their alienation by claiming that our culture neither requires nor encourages children to maintain strong familial bonds across geographic separations. Nevertheless, many grieve the loss of past closeness.

Most alienated children remain emotionally attached to their parents; alienation rarely includes a lack of desire to help during life-cycle transitions. Only a few alienated children do not try to assist their parents in time of need, and no one severs the bonds completely. Yet their contribution to parents' mental and physical health needs are minimal. Most feel strongly that they cannot help their parents now or in the future because of the painful legacy of past conflicts in their relationships. Some call attention to life-style differences and generation gaps. Typically they say, "I really provide no emotional supports to them and they provide nothing to me. I can't help them in physical health care either because of continuing conflict in our interactions. Our contacts are not satisfying to me or to them."

An Alienated Daughter: Was There Incest in My Family?

Jennie walks into my office and sits down. She begins to clear her throat, then coughs and coughs as if she's choking. While I'm waiting for her to regain her composure I remember that I met her earlier when I interviewed her office mate. Margaret chose to be interviewed in her own office. During my interview with Margaret, Jennie came into the office and after Margaret introduced us Jennie made a disparaging remark about our forthcoming interview. I should have realized she was afraid.

She began with a criticism, then answered a number of questions sharply:

> I'm not sure what that question could mean. Could I afford to call more often? Of course I could afford to call more often if I wanted to. Most of the time I don't even think about it. I tried to call last Sunday because my dad had been sick. But there wasn't any answer so I called to talk to my sister. But I haven't tried to call them since then.
>
> My father is seventy-six, and my mother is sixty-eight. I am concerned with siblings because I have a lot of them. I'm forty-seven, the oldest of sixteen children. I have four brothers and ten living sisters. Four sisters and one brother live near them.
>
> My parents consider Lansing close by comparison to California, where I used to live. It's only recently that I've moved closer. My parents are very self-sufficient. When I lived in California I made it a practice of calling once a month. Now that I'm here I see them

more but I don't call as much. In a way there's more distance now. I don't miss them a great deal. They call, on my birthday once a year, that's all.

I generally stay with my sister when I go there. I stopped staying with my parents. Well, our relationship has become more and more distant, and then there's this additional business going on in my family—that one of my sisters has come to believe that she was sexually abused by my father as a child. She's in the middle of the family, the ninth child. She's married and she has children of her own. It's too bad.

She talked about it for a year and last spring she wrote a letter to him. And you know I didn't really get in touch. I didn't know what I was going to say. It turned out that hardly anyone got in touch with my parents. That's really made strain all over because, I mean, I find it hard to believe . . . but I also am unwilling to say that it didn't happen.

My mother's response was, well, she just couldn't believe it when everyone didn't call and say, "Well, I know you couldn't have done this." But it makes everything tense. Our family wasn't close anyway.

Except for one brother who said, "Oh, this just couldn't be," it has brought up everybody's issues. I couldn't tell my parents what they wanted to hear when they came to visit for a day shortly after that. They were kind of in a mood . . . let's just not talk about this at all. They were going to kind of chat and they wanted to avoid it. Well, I wouldn't have minded avoiding it myself. But I didn't figure that was possible. I just couldn't say that I know this didn't happen. It was difficult for me to not say that, after a lifetime of trying to say things that please them. The night before they came I even called my sister, "What am I going to say?" I felt trapped.

I don't even know what the outcome of the letter is at this point. But my father wrote a letter to the family saying basically that this didn't happen. Then he did a strange thing. He added another line at the bottom saying that we shouldn't talk about it at all, and that we should destroy all these letters for the sake of the family name.

Amy claims this happened when she was about two years old. A couple of my other sisters about the same age have some waking-dream kind of memories that seem to point in the same direction. I wasn't around then, with that middle group of kids. I haven't talked to Amy for a while. I guess I find it hard to discount entirely.

I think what it's done to us is to make it more difficult to sort of pretend that various kinds of problems weren't there. I find it very difficult to have any conversation with them about anything. And I feel that's been the problem for many years even before this; there are all these unresolved issues between me and my parents. And I can't even tell them what they are, but a lot of times my feelings are those of indifference. It's involved in all sorts of things about me.

I guess I don't argue with them; well, sometimes politics turns out to be the safest. I guess I also notice some of the sexist ways he treats my mother, the expectations and demands of what she'll do for him. I suspect this was there but I didn't recognize it; a sort of low-level brooding about women, that they ought to stay home and take care of the children.

Our feelings about sex, well, there are a lot of associations of guilt. My parents sort of divided up who was going to talk to whom. My father apparently took care of the boys and my mother took care of the girls. I think her own reticence intervened. More damaging ultimately than this issue of sexuality is my mother's accepting of the traditional religion, the old business that women are responsible for seeing that men don't get out of control. It's more damaging that there was no effort to build up my self-esteem. But it was always important not to ruffle people's feathers. And having feelings were bad. I still find that I have great trouble knowing what I feel because it was always very important in my family not to express our feelings. But the feelings were there. Disagreement was not OK. So it seems to me that not being in touch with my feelings was ultimately more damaging than whatever they had to say about sex.

It's better to come in touch with one's anger, if one can express it. If one can't express it, it becomes repressed, and it doesn't go away. One becomes emotionally needy too when one can't understand how one feels. I married an alcoholic. Several of my sisters married variations on the theme of alcoholism and emotional dependencies—for example, drugs, or emotional distance, a person who's there but not there, he's never really home.

I think this has more to do with family dynamics and family disorders. Then there was this emotional upheaval of dealing with all my feelings about that letter. Before the letter, I felt that I had a handle on some of the problems with my parents. There was one time when I did try to talk with them about these things. It was just frustrating. Well, my mother just totally misunderstood. She can't hear or understand. I have to say the same thing seventeen times. Then if I whisper and I don't want her to hear, she will. My father was avoiding or denying or explaining away. Neither of them will respond to feelings. Their whole attitude is that problems shouldn't exist. And if they do, you're somehow doing something wrong. He says, "Sometimes even the truth shouldn't be spoken." I never again tried to talk about it.

I found that coming to Lansing was incredibly stressful on every level. I was kind of overwhelmed and just didn't try to deal anymore with the family issues that I had begun to deal with in therapy. I put most of it on hold just to cope.

After my husband and I split I realized that we had consciously avoided living near his parents for many years, but that I had no particular desire to live near my parents either. When I came to see them after I got this job, I found that I would just withdraw. I had no desire to be near them even when I was only thirty miles away. I did turn down a job nearer to them but it wasn't as good as this job. It was the job, not the question of distance. The fact that it was near them was no drawing card for me.

I'm not dissatisfied on the phone because we don't attempt a great deal. I have a very low expectation. It's mostly obligation and does not reinforce my feelings of affection for them. We have no disagreements because I don't voice disagreement. This is part of the problem. I think it's both a lifetime habit as well as a sense of the uselessness of being in conflict with them and trying to talk to them about my issues because they have all the solutions. I don't try. I don't trust them to respond the way I want them to respond.

I'm withholding a lot. I'm sure they must. But I don't have a sense they're not saying how they feel. This issue is hanging over my head. I simply haven't called them since August when my brother was married. I called last week because I thought it was really odd they didn't answer. Clearly my father feels very threatened by this issue. It was impossible for me to go there Eastertime. It was immediately after the letter came, and I was enormously relieved because I had made plans to go to Detroit. One of my sisters there called to tell me Father had told everyone who planned to come that he thinks we should have our family gathering as planned. But he said, "I don't want us to have any discussion of Amy's letter."

Of course, Amy wasn't there. Another sister couldn't do it, couldn't handle the pretending. Nobody came from out of town but it's never been a tradition for everyone to get together then. I go in for Christmas. I heard about what happened from one of the sisters who went. Finally, after dinner my mother said, "I can't stand it that

66

no one called." And my sister who couldn't discuss it left the table, and the rest of them who were left proceeded to discuss it. Father didn't get his way because my mother was so upset.

One of my sisters refuses to talk about the letter. Another sister is on the outs of the family anyway. She's semiexpelled. The problem is who she's not married to there. She hadn't known about the letter. When she found out she contacted them right away to say she couldn't believe it. She behaved the way they would have liked. The other two sisters actually tried to talk to my parents. One of them wouldn't talk to him about it except in the presence of a therapist; it was just too emotional for her. I think it is the issue of finding a safe place. It's the sort of safety where you will be protected from his reaction. And so she and my other sister went to the session with my parents and this counselor. I guess Gail said some of the things she needed to say, but she would only do it again with a person she chose herself.

I know that everyone has been reading a whole lot of books about incest. One brother is apparently in therapy himself. It seems to me that within the family it has had the effect of getting people to deal with things they haven't been dealing with. That's really what's been happening to me.

One of my sisters, who's also divorced, is near Amy's age. She has some recollection of the time Amy is talking about, that she can't put into words and feels that it might be true. The sisters and I are concerned about the footnote my father put at the bottom of the letter, asking to destroy the letters and not discuss it because it's part of that whole issue of denial of problems and covering things up and making the surface nice. One sister said she found it annoying because it seemed like he was more concerned about that than about Amy. He had really no expression of concern about her in the letter. It said, "Dear family, these things didn't happen." Maybe there was another sentence. But certainly no concern for her. It's not in character for him to be unconcerned.

I had talked to Amy prior to the letter. I think I was supportive. I guess I've been unwilling to push her to prove anything. I really haven't been skeptical. I'm in the middle of a family crisis at this point. I don't think there is a resolution. Nothing like this has ever happened. The only way it could be resolved is if he said, "Yes, it happened." Then everybody would know the truth. Otherwise the question is always there. I guess what I remember is what I remember.

An Abandoned Son: A Different Kind of Mother

I am married and have four children. It's unlikely but possible that I would move to where my mother lives. My parents divorced when I was two. My mother's been divorced and remarried again three times since she divorced my father.

My father is retired. He remarried and lives with his current spouse. He has two other sons with his present wife. I have good relations with them. We see each other when I'm at my father's. One of my half-brothers is thirty-years old and lives at home. The other lives close by.

I was the only child when my mother divorced my father. After the divorce my father wasn't available to me. But my mother was even less available because she is extremely selfish and self-absorbed. She doesn't do anything now and she never really did anything other than masquerade as a housewife. After my mother remarried I lived with her, my stepfather, and two younger half-brothers. One is dead. He was killed in Vietnam. The second one is lost. He is out there. No one knows where he is. He moved to California from New York.

We were raised together until I was fourteen, when my stepfather left my mother. He reappeared one morning and took my two half-siblings away to Pennsylvania. They were his children. He would have taken me, of course, if I had been his child. So I was left with my mother, abandoned and unstable and no supports, a boy of fourteen.

Before that I was required to raise the boys. I was responsible for their behavior, for maintaining the kitchen and cleaning up, for the outside grounds. It was really quite a dismal experience. I had such an atypical relationship with my parents that the normal adolescent conflicts, staying out late with the car and so on, weren't even possible. In my adolescent rebellion I dropped out of high school; I quit. I got involved with drugs and I spent time in jail.

I didn't have any contact with my mother for about eight years. I lost touch with her but there are common relatives, so somehow I knew she was somewhere in California. She didn't know where I was either although we both knew how to get in touch with each other if we were determined.

I was married once before and my first wife died from cancer of the abdominal tract. I can't say I recall discussing my wife's death with my mother. It was certainly not an issue that I dwelled on with her. I had a son from that marriage and I went to New York because my mother had promised to help out. But then she decided she wasn't capable. She was too preoccupied with something else. Then she moved to California.

The main cause of conflict was her inability to help with my son. But it antedates that. That's just something that comes to mind immediately as an example of my mother in some way abandoning me when I most needed help. She had actually said she would be available, then wasn't, which I think is very typical of her. But that isn't the only time it's happened.

She has a sense of duty to the children that is centered in social values: mothers should take care of their children, mothers should dress their children well, mothers should provide for their children's education and cultural experiences, piano. But, in fact, it was just a formulaic way she had of dealing with us. I don't have bonds to my mother that really go beyond a biological accident.

We don't have any miscommunications on the phone. No emotional exchange, only polite. I call one time a month or less. My mother and my father both call me more often than I call them. I wouldn't call more often if I could. They call every two or three weeks, not when they haven't heard from me. In fact, their calling is quite erratic. There can be a number of calls that will come in succession, maybe two or four times a month. Then several months where there's nothing.

I don't know why he calls more often than I do. I suppose now that he's retired he has more time to think about his children. He may also feel guilty about not being available as a parent. And in his own Scandinavian way he is trying to make up for that. When I say in his own Scandinavian way I mean it's not direct. I think his efforts began in earnest after my grandmother died; he came to my Ph.D. graduation that summer.

Well, I'm open to the idea. I have no problems with him working out his own psychological difficulties. I feel quite enraged at both my parents. They didn't give any of us guidance; there was more left unsaid than should have been. And there was a kind of hands-off approach to child-rearing that masqueraded as enlightenment. But in fact it had its roots in indifference and in an inability, a problem making serious contacts and emotional commitments.

I was seeking models of conduct of behavior for career goals, some direction on how to conduct myself, how to focus on what's meaningful. I think that the values formed in those early years are particularly meaningful later if the source of the values can be tied to your parents. In my case, my wife's, and several of my friends, our parents did not give us direction. They just weren't available. They felt that by keeping their hands off us we would find our way. I found my career after stumbling into an overseas studies program in Sweden. After the program I went to the Soviet Union, where I decided I liked Slavic culture better than Nordic.

My mother calls several times a year. I tend to let her talk. If I don't the conversations are interminable. She just called Sunday to say she was going somewhere and would be away. She was telling me that they're playing golf. And she suddenly said, " Are you feeling well? Are you tired?" And I said, "No." She said, "Well, you're not saying anything." That's when I realized that I needed to strike a balance. So I asked a few questions about golfing. I remember thinking about saying more but I caught myself thinking: don't say more because then you'll be on the phone for another half hour. All I have to do is feed into the conversation just a little too much and there's no end. I suspect she withholds information out of a perverse sense of suffering as a virtue. I hardly ever discuss any important issues on the phone.

I see my father at least once a year. It's difficult for me to visit either of them because of the distance. They've both made more effort in recent years to reach out to me. I'm doing better now with my father. My father is extremely stable. His visits are fine. He's extremely congenial and at ease with people. He can talk to the children and us. He makes eye contact. We don't have to entertain him.

My mother came to visit us twice in Michigan, both disasters. The first visit my wife had never met my mother; I was married for twelve years before they met. They never spoke on the telephone either. Then she called up one day out of the blue. She came and stayed for eight days. My wife was put out and very angry that my mother had suddenly some back into my life, acting as if nothing had ever happened. I felt inconvenienced. And eight days is a long time; even with the most wonderful parents it can be quite trying. But this was tense because my mother was unaware how my wife felt regarding her intrusion, that she had come out of the blue when I and my wife were going to work every day. And she and her husband expected us to entertain them. They were interested in the children but only inasmuch as they enjoyed having them close by but they didn't interact with them. That's when I really began to see how my mother had been with me: concerned on the surface but underneath it all quite distracted and preoccupied with herself. She's a different kind of mother.

I anticipate such visits with some dread. Following a visit I feel anger, of course, but I make every effort to forget as quickly as possible. If I could change anything in visits it would be to include more friends and have more open discussions of the past; and a more forthright discussion of emotions. It was repressed in my childhood.

I don't think it would be necessary for me to express anger. That might be at another time. I think right now I'd be more interested in learning more about my parents' relationship. Why did they marry in the first place? My mother is only sentimental, not approachable. And it is cast in formulas. "Oh yes, we were young. We wanted to get away from home." That kind of thing, lost innocence. It was during the war. They were looking for ways to find meaning.

The most satisfying event of a visit is when my mother tells her departure date. It is unsatisfying adhering to formal parent-child relationships. She's actually quite clever about imposing that structure on relationships. I'm not happy with that. I wish to be far away. It's important to be independent. The main source of stress is the parents' health. I'm still worrying about that.

I would have negative feelings if she decided to move to Lansing. My wife would have them if they were unable to manage. That responsibility I feel is the legacy of formalism. You've said this attitude of responsibility doesn't seem to fit well with the rest of the alienation and anger I've expressed. But it does. It fits precisely because of what we've been saying concerning my mother's way of structuring the world. One way of looking at it is to say emotionally neglected children are looking for more interaction with their parents. The other way is the pattern, this formalized way of relating to people through teacher-student, or parent-child relationships; this is something my mother is masterful at.

I believe morally and abstractly that children have a responsibility to take care of their parents. I think that belief is reinforced powerfully in me by this pattern of formalism my mother has shown me all through her life. It's the right thing to do. It's expected. Therefore the responsibility has to be taken.

Yes, it's emotionally difficult for me. But then I become a Scandinavian because the emotional issue is secondary. Maybe if she really were here I wouldn't be able to shove my emotions under the rug. But I think I would. I'm sure my wife would do the same because her view of her parents is very similar. One doesn't bring in emotions to family obligations. I wouldn't be looking for any resolution either.

As far as they are concerned, I would also hide my own rage. I would think about it myself. It is something I'm aware of. And my wife feels the same way. So we talk about things like this and we're anxious to work them out. But we realize that we never are going to be able to work this out directly with our parents. But we can try to work them out through discussion, reflection, and analysis.

A few alienated sons and daughters do not express anger but indifference, claiming distant living has had no impact on their emotional attachment and that their distant relationships are the same as they were before they left home. Either they have denied their true feelings about being distant or refused to consider them. But indifference is always temporary, a holding pattern. Sooner or later their emotional limbo must give way to a more direct confrontation with intense emotions.

Indifference within an unchanging family system suggests that alienated children retain the same feelings for their parents that they held years before, as if both generations by mutual agreement had frozen their attachments in time and space. The family system of the past consists of memories of expectations that dominate current interactions. Like other alienated children, most of their memories are of conflict during their adolescent quest for independence. Parents are just as intrusive now as they were then.

For indifferent children the chief purpose of contacts is to maintain the rituals of family solidarity. The medium is the message. There is little discussion of affection. Telephone communications and visits are unpleasant because parents are demanding and intrusive. There is a lack of trust in the family. Indifferent children typically say, "Even if I lived close to my parents our conflicts would not change. I would not see more of them; I would like to see them even less."

Indifferent alienated children rarely make an active contribution to their parents' needs. As long as parents are not dependent they can perpetuate their rituals of family solidarity through infrequent calls and visits without ever confronting the meaning or the dynamics of the relationship itself. Ultimately, however, some emotional price has to be paid for this denial of intense emotional attachments. By denying the limitations distant living places on their relationships, they have burdened themselves unnecessarily with added responsibilities. Their relationship becomes more difficult to balance as they and their parents move to the next stage in the family-development cycle.

In the end, they may hold themselves responsible for more than is humanly possible because they cannot distinguish between factors within and beyond their control. Such an orientation dooms them to disappointment and further unhappiness. Crises often find indifferent children off balance and with few skills to adjust or prepare for change. Less helpful than they would like to be during transitions, they often experience a rude awakening when they are forced to confront their emotions.

An Indifferent Son

It would be the same if I lived closer.

In high school and maybe even earlier, I spent most evenings at friends' houses. I didn't like the family sitting around discussing. My brother was four years younger and my sister was nine years younger. My parents wanted everyone to just sort of be together and have a nice conversation, but it didn't work out very well because the children were so far apart. I've never gotten to know my sister. When I moved out to go to college she was about nine years old.

I went to college against my father's expectations. I guess I really cut loose totally then. I consciously chose a liberal arts college they didn't want me to go to. My father and his brother and his parents were all Cornell people and that was where they wanted me to go. After I went away to college I didn't consider that I was living at home. And it felt very uncomfortable going home for vacations. I thought I made a decision at the time because it was the college I preferred. It may not have been a rebellion. Maybe I made up the rebellion side of it. They were upset about the choice.

Our parents were good friends. They had wanted Christine and me to get married for a long time. But we didn't have anything to do with each other until we were both living in New York for graduate school. My father didn't want me to go into higher education. He wanted me to do something that would make money. And his brother was a very successful lawyer at a large foundation. In fact, his brother came to visit me and Christine in New York when I was in graduate school. He offered to pay my full way if I'd go to law school and drop out of graduate school. I didn't do it. My father wasn't happy about that.

They always wanted us to live there. I never could figure out why. And I rejected several opportunities too, at the University of Pittsburgh. Being close to them was the reason why I didn't go there. I consciously chose not to be there. I'm the only one who doesn't live close; my brother and sister live within thirty miles.

Also my father worked at the university. We're independent-minded and we wanted to make our own way. I didn't want to be judged at all for anything until after I had become a professional and done my own work. At Pitt there would always be this problem: are people treating me this way because, well . . . I'd just much prefer to be totally on my own. My father and mother both wanted us there. They put a lot of pressure on us over the years. They kept informing us of all the opportunities. I was nominated by somebody else for a position in administration there and I just didn't want to be a candidate. I wrote a letter explaining quite honestly that I didn't want to be in the same institution with my father.

We have retained a strong dislike of Pittsburgh as a city. Every time we visit we talk about how yuppieish the place seems. Where I grew up it was a family town just north of the city. Most kids going to high school rode school buses. Now the whole thing is just malls, concrete and yuppieish.

I go to Pittsburgh to see her one or two times a year and that's enough for me. My mother says she isn't satisfied. It's a conscious choice in that we never find it easy or convenient to go to Pittsburgh. There's no other reason to go to Pittsburgh other than seeing them. And we don't make time. My mother expresses anger toward me for lots of things. That we don't come to visit. How could we turn down such a wonderful job opportunity. Actually there hasn't been any open conflict. We avoid family conflict. It's happier that way. There are no things to get upset about.

When I was growing up, my grandparents subsidized our family financially. But Christine and I have prohibited financial subsidy. Not because they didn't offer. We were just convinced there would be very big strings attached. I think we would be expected to have closer relationships than we wanted to. We don't tell her about important decisions in our lives and she doesn't get involved in them because she doesn't know. It would have been impossible without the geographic separation. We would have had constant contact, visiting the grandchildren from a very young age, spending a lot of time over at the grandparents. It just didn't look attractive.

Our calls are very ritualized. They last a certain length of time and then people run out of things. What do you hear from the grandchildren? Do you still like your job? The calls in most instances have come from them. We call when something unusual comes up. In part it's my inability to communicate on the phone. I have never been able to communicate without seeing the person. Calls don't allow me to feel affection because I just don't relate to such communications. I'm usually pretty curt on the phone. My mother usually dominates and I respond. Probably I am insincere. We give excuses for not coming to visit that are not fully true. I'm not frustrated during calls. But I'm glad when the call is over.

We never resolved visiting arrangements. After I was married we visited and they visited us. Our summer place in Maine was a kind of venue for relations to visit. The other two grandparents live in Pittsburgh too, I mean my wife's parents. Both of those couples got along fine. They are also at the university. And that also was one of the real problems going to visit. When they had their houses they lived four miles apart. Fifty percent of the time always seems greater when you're at the other place apparently. So there was always this hassle. They would say, "Well, you don't want to spend time with us because you're always spending much more time with them." We tried the two nights in one, two nights in the other, but it seldom worked. There's a lot of time when we're at neither place, just seeing the town, or going in between. We stayed at one place or the other but we weren't going to be shuttling back and forth. So the last few times when they were all living there we just stayed in a motel. It was unpleasant.

The relationship was different when we got married than when we had children, obviously. With the children there were more of us and both sets of parents tended to relate more closely to their own child. This was always a problem. They'd start up conversations advising their child how to do something. It was annoying. I think both sets of parents had genuine interest in what both of us were doing. I don't think it was conscious to talk only of their child. Our children didn't notice it as much. They've gotten along with them all. They're all spread around now that they're all grown up. And they keep in telephone contact with their grandparents.

75

It was awkward when my father was dying because in such circumstances one always thinks that there is more the doctors can do. I was frustrated at what seemed to be nothing going on in his treatment. I suspected they were withholding information when he was in his final illness. That was one of my problems at that time. I was angry too. Looking back on it there's no reason to believe I was correct or accurate. I was convinced they were withholding information then.

He had been ill for some time. But he had been mobile and going around being treated, and he visited us. At first it was prostate cancer; then it was bone cancer. I could never get in touch with the doctor. I called many times. But I never spoke to the doctor once. My brother and sister were there presumably handling things, as well as my mother.

We visited about once every three weeks while my father was sick. We were actually pushing it to be able to get there that often. It was hard because it was extremely busy here. It was over a four-month period. I probably didn't assist her when my father died. I imagine she did have a need. But we think she got plenty from my sister. She wanted us to be down there constantly. After my mother was widowed . . . well, she was helpless. She never learned how to drive. She never wrote a check in her life. And she never traveled a lot, so she finds it very difficult to travel except when my sister takes her somewhere. So she doesn't visit.

The cases presented in this chapter identified and described three voices of emotional attachment to distant parents: the displaced, the well adapted, and the alienated voices. Closer examination reveals that these voices differ with regard to three main themes in the participants' relationships to distant parents: (1) memories of past relationships, especially adolescence; (2) the use of routine communications and contacts with distant parents, especially telephone calls and visits; and (3) perceptions of lifecycle transitions of distant parents, especially health and social-status transitions in old age. The following chapters elaborate these themes, paying particular attention to differences and similarities in the expressions of displaced, well-adapted, and alienated voices.

Memories of Leaving Home

In this chapter we will look at the external and internal forces that influenced the decisions made by displaced, well-adapted, and alienated children to leave home and live far away. The memory of such forces still affects distant relationships with parents, particularly for alienated children.

For most young Americans the initial decision to leave the parental home and set up a separate household does not necessarily lead to distant living, because a separate household is established near their parents' home. A young adult child is able to return home again, though the experience of living as an independent adult in the outside world makes it undesirable to return to the previous status of emotional and economic dependency in the parental household. Of young people between the ages of eighteen and twenty-five who are not married, 60 percent live with their parents (Glick 1975). Many parents of those who have delayed marriage and child-rearing have to accommodate themselves to this divergence from cultural norms. Most redefine their expectations so that they feel it is all right when their children fell outside the norm (Spense and Lonner 1972).

Distant children recall that their decisions to live far away were influenced on many different levels, including the conscious and unconscious, rational and emotional. Some made decisions alone, others decided in collaboration with parents or peers. Some decided after much deliberation and planning, others decided impulsively with no consideration of consequences.

Both external and internal forces influenced decisions. External forces include the desire for upward economic and social mobility, which defines distant living as a necessary and desirable prerequisite. Internal forces include factors related to individual psychological growth: the self, life-cycle development, and the need for young adults to prove they can be self-reliant, self-supporting, or live alone. This early adult decision lays the groundwork for the development of relationships many children will later maintain with their distant parents, including visits and telephone patterns, the ability to give and receive assistance, and expressing feelings of frustration, satisfaction, affection, and family solidarity.

THE EXTERNAL FORCES

The desire for economic and social mobility pressures young adults to move away for educational and occupational advancement, marriage, or other opportunities. In addition, core cultural values encourage them to accept distant living as normal and natural. American core values regarding the child's normal life-course development include a strong belief in self-fulfillment, autonomy, and separation of the generations. Both the child's quest for self-reliance and independence and the parents' desire to help the child attain them are considered normal. Beginning in early childhood, the American parent-child relationship is permeated with a strong motivation for individual achievement, success, and personal fulfillment. Most Americans believe a young adult needs to be away from parental influences at least for some undetermined period.

George DeVos (1965) draws attention to a contrast between middle-class American and Japanese achievement stories in which a young man leaves home to strike out for himself. The Japanese protagonist differs from the American first in that he does not *want* to leave home, and second, if he does leave home to study and work elsewhere, the story often ends with his return home. American children are indoctrinated by their parents to want to leave home, at least for some time, in order to develop their potential skills or special talents, seek their fortunes, achieve their dreams, and thus attain independence, self-reliance, self-fulfillment, and social recognition by attaining high status and wealth. The requirement to return ultimately to parents and family is conspicuously absent in the American stories.

In addition to core values that support distant living, economic an social forces play an important role in the decision young adults make to live near to or far from their parents. Social class is very important in predicting the geographic mobility of young adult Americans. Between the ages of eighteen and twenty-five, the greatest mobility is in the middle class. With far fewer opportunities for higher education and occupational mobility, most young working-class and poor Americans remain closer to their parents and families; they share economic responsibilities and formal patterns of mutual exchanges, which become an incentive to live nearby.

Middle-class Americans achieve economic mobility mainly through formal education, which is also the major reason for migrating from one's family. The more resources a family has to send a child to college, the greater the likelihood the child will travel some distance from home (Cicirelli 1981); and the more skilled and specialized the education, the fewer the educational centers where it can be achieved. Thus, the higher one's educational level, the more likely it is that it was obtained away from home, over a period of time. Moreover, America's corporate occupational structure favors the selection of individuals who are oriented toward high mobility and achievement, and encourages them to relocate perhaps several times in their careers, often to great distances away from their natal families.

Those who are perhaps not so highly trained or motivated and have no clearly defined or specialized career goals may decide to return to the town or city where their families live, sometimes to live at home or sometimes to take a nearby apartment. But for some the temptation is great to relocate to a larger or different city with more job opportunities, or to the East or West Coasts "where the action is" and where more chances for travel, leisure, and romance are available. In recalling their early stages of distant living, sons and daughters typically emphasize core cultural values of independence, youth, separation of the generations, and a high level of individual achievement interwoven with career, education, adventure, seeking one's fortune, and marriage. Most distant children left home for the first time to go to college. But these early memories vary according to the different voices of emotional attachment.

Displaced children typically emphasize the emotional difficulties they and their parents experienced during separation. One son says:

> I think my parents were initially unhappy emotionally about the distance and separation even though they could intellectually accept the reasons for it. They made statements like "I wish you didn't live so far away." My mother used to do something else too. She would have a long laundry list of things that had to be done that only I could make the decisions about whenever I came. That list was in part a conscious or unconscious message that I should be there. She could have made those decisions herself. But she was using this as a way to say there are so many things we need you for.

Displaced children indicate, in retrospect, that they might have tried harder to stay closer. A son muses:

> I haven't lived in Texas since I left originally to take a position in Kentucky. We always remained in contact. I was concerned to look for a situation that would be best for my career. I would have given greater weight to being closer, if not to the exact locale. It would have been easier in terms of access and problem solving.

Such statements about early graduate experiences reveal that displaced children are homesick for their parents. They acknowledge the economic necessity of geographic mobility but often declare a preference for remaining in one place, as one displaced son explains:

> I left Cleveland in 1973 to go to graduate school at Berkeley. I guess I'm the sort of person who likes to be in certain places and stay there for a while. Berkeley was one of those extraordinary places where people do everything possible to stay. Well, we had a group of about twelve people and we spent a lot of time with each other. Now many of them have stayed on in Berkeley. They've also

started to have kids and they live in a similar community except it doesn't have grandparents. In my fantasies one thing I'd like to do is find a way to spend about six months in Cleveland and six months in Berkeley. Now there would be a perfect world. And probably down the road I would find a way to have my parents and Marlene's parents come there too.

In contrast, the well-adapted children's memories of leaving home to attend college include several reasons that are in harmony with American core values. A son recalls:

> Leaving home did seem so much like a natural, educational career thing. Well, I went away to college up in Minneapolis, which was far enough away to really start to separate myself, and from there on, it was just kind of a natural transition to other farther places.

Some left home to see the world, find adventure in new places or simply because it was the expected thing to do. For others, family traditions of leaving for college justified their actions. A daughter remembers that her parents were academics and it was understood that academics go where the job is. Other children recall parental pressures to leave home and attend college. As one daughter says:

> There was no deliberate intention to leave. I went away to college, which is something they wanted me to do. The only time geographical independence was communicated to me was how important my mother made it seem that I go away to school. The idea was it would cheat me if I didn't get this important college experience. It was that you need to do this in order to become independent.

An only child recalls that she, her mother, and her father each wanted her to leave, but for different reasons:

> Very clearly, I wanted to leave for emotional reasons. I went to the University of Wales in part because it was one of the campuses farthest away from any relatives. I chose not to apply to universities

that were near them. It was not smart in retrospect but that was my reasoning then.

My father encouraged me to travel and said very directly I should certainly get out of that town. My father had a fear of my getting sucked into the family the way he thought my mother had been sucked into helping her family. My father was emphasizing independence much more to get a job so you can choose what you want to do. I think my mother believed my chances of finding a suitable husband were greater if I went to the university. So her ambition for me was not career-oriented as much as it was making a good marriage.

Several children felt pressure to leave from their friends. A daughter remembers:

I went to a Catholic high school in Chicago and there was a lot of direction in the high school to go to a Catholic university. The nuns would have preferred that I go to a small girls' college. But my two friends and I, the three of us, chose Marquette.

Others left on a quest to find their careers, as a son recalls:

It was an occupational quest. Seeking some occupation that I would feel comfortable in. I was doing engineering research. It was boring, something I couldn't live with. I went from engineering to returning to school, to management theory. Then after I got my M.A. I felt I still didn't know what I wanted to do, so I went on for a Ph.D. Then when I started teaching I realized that's where I belonged."

Not all left their home or city to attend college. Several children remained at home for college, then left home later to attend graduate school. A few well-adapted children call attention to emotional difficulties they and their parents experienced when they left for graduate school. This is especially true of daughters who were the first women in their families to pursue a career. Fathers in particular seem to have had a very difficult time saying good-bye. One daughter remembers:

They supported my leaving for college but there was some resistance to my staying for my M.A. degree. I was twenty-four when I got my M.A. and took a job in Virginia. My father was very grieved. He said good-bye to me as though he were losing me, as if he'd never see me again. I think they accepted it a little more after they came out to visit me. Once they saw the place where I was it didn't seem quite so removed. That was my major separation from them.

Only one well-adapted daughter recalls leaving as a high school senior under very stressful circumstances:

After my mother remarried I moved out in my senior year because I couldn't stand living in this stepfamily arrangement. I moved to my girlfriend's house because there were too many siblings from my stepfather and not enough space. It was horrible, yeah. I couldn't do it anymore. My mother wasn't happy, no. I mean, she had a whole breakdown.

In sharp contrast to the sense of normalcy conveyed by well-adapted participants, most alienated sons and daughters left home under great stress and with emotional problems in their relationships. An alienated son recalls:

I was very excited to be going off to graduate school. The whole point of going off to graduate school is to get away from the scene, to verify essentially the way that I was in opposition to my parents. At the time I left Houston in 1968 I was on bad terms with both my mother and my father, and on less bad terms with my stepfather, because none of them wanted me to go. Basically, I left the whole kit and caboodle, including my girlfriend. I wanted to leave my problems behind. Let's put it this way, that's what I wanted. But it didn't work out.

They did not support my decision to go to UCLA. I think they felt I was a drug-crazed hippie who was running away from home. Make no mistake there was a commitment to my profession, but at twenty-one my life-style was more important. They were against my going to graduate school in the humanities, against my becoming a university faculty member. They really didn't have much regard for it. To them the whole thing was scatterbrained.

Several distant children recall a time shortly before or after graduate school when they considered getting a job closer to home

83

and family. Sometimes their parents discouraged them from taking a job close to home, as a son remembers: "My parents did not encourage me to accept a job there. I remember distinctly that my Dad was very relieved when I took the job here and not there. He felt it would be too stressful there and that Michigan State was more appropriate." Most children claim that rejecting an early job offer near their parents had little to do with their relationships but was due to the career advantages of the job itself. Some older well-adapted and displaced children express regret that they did not pursue a closer job because of their continued separation from parents. A displaced daughter recalls:

> I think after I finished my doctorate, there was some talk of getting a job in the South from a person who actually worked at the university. I didn't feel regret about leaving the city but about leaving my family. Because of the closeness and the contact, and the kind of enjoyment of just being together and the activities that we engage in. I miss that part of it.

Younger adult children resemble displaced sons and daughters since they are still looking to find a position closer to home. A son describes his first job as transitional and expresses a preference for living closer to his parents:

> I applied to USC last year. I don't know if I would have taken it, and my parents didn't want me to because USC is in a bad part of downtown. My father is sufficiently impressed with my abilities to think I can eventually get a job in Santa Barbara or Irvine or San Diego, the better places to live. They occasionally ask if there are jobs open in the West. It's not preferable to live far away.

Yet regardless of emotional attachment, in most cases career opportunities set the stage for continued, prolonged distant living in conjunction with higher education and career advancement. A well-adapted daughter from England recalls her original plan to study in Canada and the changing career track that led her to remain in the United States for higher degrees and job opportunities:

> They didn't intend it to go beyond the B.A. level. Then I was supposed to stop. After I had earned my B.A. degree I came to Can-

ada, theoretically for one year to get my M.A. degree. That was how I perceived coming over here. My parents were encouraging. My father very directly. My mother would rather I hadn't left but didn't make a big to-do out of it. I thought I would go back after a year. But once I was in Canada I wanted to see the United States. Then they offered me fellowships. So I stayed, finished, and came here.

Some well-adapted children recall a certain amount of stress in making job decisions early in their careers. The prevailing cultural value, however, places career mobility and job satisfaction over living close to family. A well-adapted son reaffirms this value in emphasizing that his parents made it a point not to interfere with his decision:

When I finished my Ph.D. degree one of the jobs I was offered was back in Brockport, New York, in the state system. The people were very nice and it looked like a lively department. Everyone was very excited about it. But I could not make myself take it. I really didn't want to go back. As I look back I wasn't very clear about it. I remember thinking that it was a real bleak landscape. Actually the job I took here was a better job. This was a more lively institution and I could do better things here. My parents would have made a point not to interfere.

Most alienated children did not seriously consider jobs near their parents. When such opportunities arose they rejected them, as this son recalls:

I had another opportunity to live closer. I could have taught at the University of Texas and certainly at a small college nearby where a relative was chairman of the department. I didn't apply systematically even where I had connections because I didn't want to be there. I've often wondered. I've constructed alternative scenarios as to what I could have done to have stayed in Texas. The upshot was that I was unable to imagine how to do that at the time. In retrospect I think I did the right thing; I don't regret that I left. I think it's remarkable that I could leave.

An alienated daughter with a job opportunity close to home notes her parents' displeasure with her decision to continue in higher education and her growing sense of independence:

When I graduated from Wisconsin I had an opportunity to teach in a high school near my parents' home. And almost at the same time the chair of the math department asked me if I would be interested in staying on to do an M.A. degree with an assistantship. I decided to do that instead. My mother was not pleased with that decision. I finished college and here I could have a job. But instead I continued being a student. There was some conflict at that time. I don't know if I even convinced her. Had I decided to take that position my mother could never have understood my taking my own apartment. She would have expected me to live at home because that had been the pattern in my family. My cousins had lived at home until they got married. I was the odd person in the family.

In some instances alienated children express guilt or ambivalence for not moving closer when they had a chance. An alienated daughter examines her reasons for rejecting a job near her parents:

I came very close to getting a job in Chicago after I had already been here. My decision not to pursue was, well, my friends said, "You withdrew because you don't want to live close to your parents." That was not in my consciousness, although I wouldn't deny that it wasn't operating on some level. I turned it down because my relationship with Peter was just starting, and I thought that it would be good for me to stay here with him.

Marriage is often important in determining where people live. Those who marry local sweethearts have two natal families to consider, while those marrying partners from other places soon become aware that juggling contacts and demands of their separate parents and families has some impact on their own marital relationship. Certainly after the birth of children the emotional and financial-support role of extended families becomes even clearer.

Anthropologists have studied a wide variety of postmarital residence patterns. Newlywed Navaho Indians believe they should reside, and often do reside, in the same household with the bride's mother, called uxorilocal residence. Among traditional Chinese and rural peasant farmers in India, it was customary for newlyweds to live with the groom's parents, called virilocal residence. Because of the cultural diversity characteristic of contemporary America, it is not possible to identify a single postmarital residence pattern; small enclaves of Americans practice any number of them. Yet most Americans desire a neolocal pattern in which the newlyweds set up their own household apart from either the bride's or the groom's families.

Career and marriage strongly influence people's decisions about where to live. The pursuit of one or both partners' careers might encourage a couple to live in a particular city where career opportunities exist. Or one partner may agree to leave home and family for the sake of the other's career. It is not fashionable for a well-educated woman to say she moved to a certain location because of her husband's career, but it still happens more often than a husband following his wife.

One well-adapted daughter explains how she started out close to home in a conventional marriage to her high school sweetheart. Her decision to leave her hometown developed in an unconventional way:

> My first husband and I went away to college, but we came back to the town we grew up in and lived there till he died. A year after his death I decided I was being smothered there in that town. We were high school sweethearts who married a year out of high school. We never even considered whether we loved each other. Our marriage wasn't what we wanted to do, it was what we would do. We lived happily ever after.
>
> Basically, their idea of my going to school was, "Well, it's a nice thing for you to do as a woman. And it's a great thing to fall back on if you ever need to." But their hopes and dreams were that I would be a mother and stay home and raise a family and do the same things they'd always done; "a housewife is God's calling for a woman." They didn't encourage me to be independent; they encouraged me to be dependent.
>
> I began to have a feminist awakening at about age twenty-eight. I discovered that we had grown in very very different ways and, while I loved my husband, probably we would not have chosen each other had we been adults. We had thought we were alike as teenagers think they're alike. He was captain of the football team and I was captain of the cheerleaders. What more alike can you be?
>
> I was already starting to not be happy in my marriage. My mother already knew that. But I think she didn't pay any real atten-

tion to me until after he died, when she began to give me this advice to find somebody to marry immediately. The night he died she told me that I should remarry as quickly as I was able to find Lonny a father, because it wouldn't be good for me to raise him alone. I said, "Mother, right now the way I feel I will probably never remarry. I've had it with men up to here."

After he died, they didn't ask me to move back into their home, which I would not have done, but they started keeping their thumb on me all the time. I had been away from home for over ten years and all of a sudden they were checking on me every five minutes. If I went out of the house, why hadn't I called to let them know where I was going? If I was out more than twenty minutes after dark they screamed at me. I began to go away on the weekends. Ted and I would get in the car and go wherever we wanted just so I could have some space.

Then I moved to Georgia to go back to graduate school. That created tons of problems for my parents, but even more problems for my late husband's parents. They were very upset at me for taking their grandchild away. And I couldn't get them to understand how much I needed to get away. I just would never be able to have a life of my own.

A final external factor influencing distant living is the degree of urbanization of the natal community. Proportionally more rural than urban children live outside their parents' community (Bultena 1969). Young adults from rural areas leave town because their native communities do not provide adequate economic opportunities. Adult children in the rural working and farming class live in nearby towns. Only the exceptional family has more than one adult child living nearby in the hometown location itself.

A young adult may decide to relocate out of devotion to a leisure-time activity such as skiing, surfing, theater, or art. An individual's life-style may also influence that choice, as in the case of a homosexual who moves from a small town to San Francisco to find anonymity and community. An individual on a spiritual or religious quest may leave home for a large city or a rural commune to live at the center of his or her spiritual world rather than on its margins.

Several well-adapted and alienated children remember being dissatisfied with their hometowns. The principal difference is that well-adapted children restrict their unhappiness to the location, whereas the alienated children are unhappy with both the location and their relationships with their parents. A well-adapted daughter explains:

> I wanted to leave to get away from the kinds of smallish big-town classmates I had there. Everyone was going to Iowa and I simply didn't want to be in the Iowa context anymore. So I came to Michigan to school. It was getting away from the small town business.

An alienated daughter says:

> I don't regret leaving. I was glad to go. It was just a very xenophobic little town. They didn't like change, didn't like outsiders. I was suffocated there. Recently my mother had this fantasy when I visited, "Oh, wouldn't it be nice if you could stay here." I said, "No. I couldn't have become who I am if I had stayed here."

And an alienated son recalls:

> When I was an early teenager I had a very strong feeling that I wanted to get out of there. I felt the Midwest was a cultural wasteland. I was living in a community where my interests and gifts just didn't have any kind of value put on them. I have lots of memories of finding ways to leave. One of my fondest memories was when my parents drove me down to Indiana on the way to college. I remember settling back and thinking to myself, "Only a few more hours and I'll be gone from my family." I wanted to get away from all those values.

THE INTERNAL FORCES: THE SELF AND LIFE-COURSE DEVELOPMENT

Clearly, external factors play a considerable role in the decision to leave one's hometown. But external factors do not operate in isolation. Rather, they must be seen in combination with internal forces that deal with questions of internal growth, the self, and individual life-cycle development.

Life-course development theorists believe the major task in

young adulthood is to develop role identity, to find adult social roles that are both psychologically satisfying and socially acceptable. In making the decision to stay or to live far away, the individual's place within the family setting is of primary importance. Birth order, family dynamics, siblings' careers, parents' age and health, the nature of emotional attachments to parents, and roles in the family all play a part in the decision. Decisions of this kind often culminate in adolescence, the stage of development that focuses on the search for autonomy (Thornburg 1982) and is often the source of much parent-child conflict.

Both parents and children create unspoken or even spoken contracts regarding the adolescent's future. Simultaneously the adolescent develops a picture of himself or herself as an adult based on self-image, prior role models, and the processes of differentiation and integration. Part of the problem is whether or not the young person can thrive living close to parents and family. In many cases, it requires leaving.

The goal during this adolescent transition is to break the infantile ties that children enjoyed during their earlier years, and to develop alternative relationships. Adolescents are often unable to break their early emotional bonds with parents logically or objectively. They become rebellious, emotional, or hypercritical in order to persuade their parents that they are different now and must be independent. Such behavior has the potential of breeding alienation and the beginning of generational differences.

Psychologist Daniel Levinson (1978) characterizes leaving the family as a period of emotional separation, a transition between adolescent life, centered in the family of origin, and entry into the adult world. A great deal of diversity exists within this pattern, but in general it can be considered a normative pattern for both men and women.

Leaving one's family ordinarily occupies a span of three to five years, starting at about age seventeen. It is a transitional period in the sense that the young adult is half in and half out of the family, making an effort to separate, to develop a new home base, to reduce dependence on familial support and authority, and to regard himself or herself as an adult now living in the adult world.

In its external aspects, emotional separation from the family involves changes such as moving out of the familial home, becoming financially less dependent, and entering new roles and living arrangements in which one is more autonomous and responsible. In its internal aspects it involves an increase in self-parent differentiation and in psychological distance from the family, though these processes start earlier and continue well beyond the leaving-the-family period. According to Levinson, there is roughly an equal balance between "being in" the family and "moving out." The "leaving home" period ends when the balance shifts—when for the most part separation from the family has taken place and one has begun to feel comfortable in the adult world.

Gaining independence is a normal developmental process. As the adolescent increasingly becomes a distinctive individual, earlier ties to parents are replaced by a more mature relationship. Researchers have determined three essential goals that young people strive for in the course of this process: (1) behavioral autonomy, (2) emotional autonomy, and (3) value autonomy (Douvan and Adelson 1966).

Behavioral autonomy is the earliest type sought by the adolescent. It is especially sought in regard to dating, employment, economic resources, and in the choice of leisure-time companions (Douvan and Adelson 1966). The most obvious behavioral shift is in dating, followed by a drop in the percentage of time one interacts with parents. In general, behavioral autonomy satisfies the need for independence before emotional autonomy such as detachment sets in later in adolescence.

Emotional autonomy reflects the degree to which the adolescent has managed to cast off infantile ties to the family (Douvan and Adelson 1966). Adolescents need to give up childhood dependencies and learn self-control and self-reliance. Emotional autonomy is more difficult to accomplish than behavioral autonomy. Many adolescents never want to let go of the security found in childhood ties and therefore never become emotionally autonomous. Some parents invest so much emotional energy in a child that they become reluctant to relinquish the earlier relationship.

Value autonomy generally develops in late adolescence or in

young adulthood, after major educational, occupational, and marital goals have been achieved and a workable degree of self-identity is attained.

Adolescents tend to think that accepting parental values will put them out of step with their peers, and this period of an individual's life is notably difficult for the parents. Adolescents may feel their parents do not try to understand their problems (Rallings 1969). They interfere with their parents' privacy; they stay up later at night, join their parents' conversations, and are attuned to their parents' sexuality. Nevertheless, parents and adolescent children will go to great lengths to maintain their family ties. Hagestad (1979) found that many use "demilitarized zones," make pacts about what not to talk about, and Troll (1972) observed an analogous strategy of being careful about what they fight over. College students and their parents both claim that they fight over hairstyles and clothes—relatively trivial issues—rather than over serious moral or core values.

In some cases the individual decision to leave is made long before adolescence. It is not actualized until adolescence because that is the time when leaving becomes socially acceptable. The decision to leave may be connected to many aspects of the parent-child relationship, such as wishing to leave the role in which the adolescent is a helper to the parents in the practical requirements of everyday life or serves as an emotional confidant to a parent.

Distant children discussed three significant internal forces at work when making the decision to leave home: (1) parental supports and expectations toward the child, (2) conflicts between parents and children; and (3) the resolution or persistence of conflicts after adolescence.

Most distant children recall parental supports during their process of separation. The way they express it reflects their varying voices of emotional attachment. Displaced and well-adapted children remember a great deal of parental support, both financial and emotional, when they first established distant households. A well-adapted son recalls the importance of his parents' confidence in his ability at a critical moment in his career. Their support meant a great deal to him, since his parents were not well educated and were initially reluctant to have him leave for graduate school:

I had mixed emotions about going off and living on my own. Mostly I was happy. I felt it was about time. But there was also some trepidation. Could I make it? They had a hard time understanding it. But I think they were proud of me in their own strange way. I talked to them about my fear whether I could make it in the department there. It was a really hard experience. I almost quit after two or three weeks. They said, "Oh, you've always done it before, you can do it now too." They meant it. They were supportive. They would have felt bad for me if I wouldn't have succeeded. They wanted me to do what I wanted to do.

Well-adapted daughters freely acknowledge their parents emotional support for their careers. As one says:

They always were supportive of the kind of work I wanted to do. When I wanted to study mathematics they were supportive. When I wanted to change as a senior to the humanities that was also supported. I was worried about that change leaving mathematics, what I had been doing since the seventh grade. Still, they said you should do what you're good at and what you want to do.

Another son from a well-off family also needed and received his parents' emotional support to break ranks and leave the family business. He explains:

They realized I would not be back and involved in the family business. They saw me going off on my own and accepted it. I am different from my family. They never put pressure on me to move back there. But they thought it would be so much more advantageous to me to work with them because I would have so much more money. But they pretty much gave up on me twenty years ago. I've been away since 1961, almost thirty years. But it began when I was eighteen and went to college.

Well-adapted and displaced children express gratitude for the financial sacrifices their parents made to help their careers. A daughter notes that without their financial support she would not have been able to do the Ph.D. A son remembers proudly:

My father really sacrificed to put me through school. In my family one never talked about it. I noticed after I graduated that all of a sudden my father started buying clothes. And he could never afford clothes. He bought these sport jackets and I was shocked. It took me a long time to understand he hadn't been able to do that. He was very generous in that way.

Some well-adapted children remember their parents' assistance when they moved to begin their academic careers. A daughter remembers that even though she had a full scholarship her widowed mother still supplemented it. A son recalls that his parents bought him a car to commute to his first academic job. Another well-adapted daughter from a large family explains that her mother and stepfather created a system of financial support to help all the children start careers by giving them loans but at the same time develop financial independence. As one of the older children she felt a moral obligation to repay because the education of her younger siblings depended on it.

In contrast, alienated children typically claim their parents were not supportive of the college they went to or the subject they wanted to study. One alienated daughter stresses her parents' inability to help financially or provide emotional support for her career:

> I never heard anything. I don't think she knows what social work is. I don't know that I care or not. I never thought of that. I really don't know how she feels about that. I can remember they didn't like the idea of social work at all. I didn't get a lot of recognition for anything.

Another daughter feels guilt about her career choice: "If I feel guilty about anything, it dates back to my career choice and the fact that my parents were unhappy about my career choice and my sister's, generally. We've both got Ph.D.s. But they wanted us both to be lawyers." Alienated children express more independence from parental supports even when they acknowledge it, as one son says:

> They never helped me. I went through UCLA completely on scholarships. My father paid room and board and some spending money each month. My stepfather and mother didn't pay anything.

In graduate school I was 100 percent self-sufficient. I was very lucky to get scholarships.

Alienated children often mention parental inconsistencies about financial support. One son complains that his father gave him money whenever he needed it but never showed him how to budget it. An alienated daughter complains that her father promised to supplement her grant, then suddenly withdrew his support. Another alienated daughter acknowledges parental support but even then she understood that her relationship with her mother was not healthy:

> They supported my going off to college. My mother had this understanding. She always wished I could live ten blocks away. But I think she sort of knew we really couldn't be too close together. In fact she even said to me one time that she thought it was probably better that we were far away since she didn't know what I was doing so she wouldn't be upset by it.

Turning to the issue of conflict between parents and children, well-adapted as well as alienated children recall significant conflicts focusing on issues of independence and autonomy in adolescence. Well-adapted daughters often recall conflict in social relationships, dating, and sexuality. An unmarried daughter says sex is an area where she could not talk openly with her parents. Another well-adapted daughter remembers a serious conflict with her mother:

> There were conflicts about normal things that I wanted to do, like date. I could never bring up sex. They did an excellent job of raising me on guilt. I felt guilty about everything I ever thought I wanted to do. I'd been told a million times this is wrong. My mother had this wonderful saying about whenever you're out with a boy, anything that you think you want to do just ask yourself, if Jesus were in the back seat would you do it? So you can imagine what I felt like with this thing on my shoulders.

Frequently, well-adapted children call attention to conflicts their older siblings had with their parents. Having experienced such conflicts vicariously, they and their younger siblings did not have to experience them directly. One son, a younger brother, resolved at an early age to become financially independent by getting fellowships to study. Another well-adapted son recalls:

> My older brother was more rebellious and had most of the major conflict. He had a conflict about having a car and how he used his car. And he had conflicts over his relationships with girlfriends, his desire to marry young. I had no conflicts at that time.

Several children remember that their parents accused them of taking drugs. A few claim their mothers were domineering and controlling. Well-adapted children often recall one main conflict before breaking away from their parents' authority. The eldest daughter of a large family remembers:

> My last big conflict with my father came when I was in college. It was about where I was going to work for the summer. When I said what if I work in the summer resort anyway even though you say not to, that was a major step. Do I run the risk of not going home if they say, "Well then you're out." They didn't say that. They said they'll call me back tomorrow. Until I could make adult decisions I accepted their authority but with lots of kicking and screaming and back talking.

In contrast, alienated children remember that angry conflicts with their parents dominated their separations and made them miserable. An alienated son recalls an old conflict with his parents about distant communications:

> She spends time going through the family drawers, things that have accumulated in the house over the years. She found a letter I wrote to her and my father in an angry vein saying, "You've got to stop this business of trying to make me feel guilty for not getting in touch with you. If you don't know what I'm up to or how I am, then get on the phone and call me. But stop accusing me of not being a good child because I don't keep you informed of my health and so on."
> I remember that conflict had gone on forever, when I was an undergraduate too. I did my graduate work at Berkeley and when I

drove out there they didn't hear from me for the first two months. Finally I got this panic telephone call. My father sounded like, well, I thought somebody died at home. He said, "Oh my God, we've finally found you. You really are OK."

It was crazy. They could have called three weeks before they did. They waited for me to call because as far as they were concerned I was supposed to keep in touch. They did the same thing with visiting. They had a lot more time. But they wanted me to pack up the family and come and visit instead of coming here. They came but that was an extraordinary event.

Recalling their separation experiences and careers displaced children often mention difficulties, but never with their parents. A typical displaced son reports:

No major conflicts in adolescence. It was the kind of conflict any parent and child might have then, but it wasn't substantive. As an adolescent I was quite independent. I had a tremendous amount of trust. They did not restrict me very much. I suppose it was a relationship that worked because I didn't give them any reason to doubt me.

On the other hand, well-adapted and alienated children recall difficulties with their parents during separation. The chief difference between them is that well-adapted children relegate such conflict to the past whereas alienated children feel such conflicts persist in their present relationships. Typically, a well-adapted son in his middle fifties notes:

As you grow older there's a kind of forgiveness in the relationship. You forget the problems of your youth and get on with your life. I think the question pertains to adult children who are younger. Can you imagine somebody in their fifties still having these problems with their parents?

Many well-adapted children speak of conflict resolution with their parents as a period in their adult lives in which they consciously set out to resolve adolescent conflicts. In their narratives both they and their parents have changed for the better. A son reports his father is more mellow now, not as critical as in the past, and willing to consider an alternative view. Another well-adapted son recalls a major resolution:

He's very different from me. He's really good at making stuff, fixing mechanical stuff. Well, I think it's harder for me to separate myself or to differentiate myself from my mother. My father and I resolved our real conflicts only when I was in my thirties, after I had a job as a professor. That made a lot of difference, when I was financially independent. It's been possible for him to see me as a real person who's really somebody.

We had great reconciliations and long serious talks. I was definitely my mother's kid. I was the baby of the family. I'd had a serious back problem when I was little. She had to take care of me for years. Reading, you know, all that. He resented it. He's told me all this stuff. It was to his credit because he's not the most self-conscious person. He's willing to talk now and he really is genuinely aware of what's inside him. So that's a change from the past.

An unmarried, well-adapted daughter claims her mother is pleased and doesn't worry about her anymore because her life has not been filled with trauma or tragedy. The theme of independence appears again and again as well-adapted sons and daughters report that their relationships with parents have been resolved or improved now that they are on their own and grown up. A well-adapted son explains:

I think my relationship with my parents has gotten a lot better since I left home. There was a lot of friction, especially in high school, about things they didn't want me to do. Now that I'm on my own they have no control over that. They're starting to recognize that I have a life of my own, that I really don't do things that they were afraid I'd be doing. So our relationship has improved. I think it's adult to adult now. And in the past it wasn't.

Well-adapted daughters often note their parents have changed for the better or that they are able to accept their children's point of view now even when they couldn't in the past. A daughter says:

My father is a lot more easygoing. He thinks other people should grant their children more freedom. He claims that he was too strict with us. And he feels sorry that he didn't let up a little bit. I feel really great about this. I agree they should have done it forty years earlier. I was an adolescent in the sixties too and there was an awful lot going on. For example, when I went to march on Washington I had a lot of conflict with them. Now looking back on it, my dad says I really admired you for what you did even though I didn't understand it then and I gave you such a hard time about that.

For well-adapted children such conflicts did not persist into their adult relationships. A well-adapted daughter typically says:

> I remember much conflict but none of it has remained. Also, at one point my parents were very strict with us. They never gave us enough personal freedom to be out with our friends. They were afraid. They always had to know where are you going and who are you going with? It isn't always easy to explain because you may not know where you're going with a group of kids.
>
> My sister was younger and I think some of her conflicts managed to survive. She still resents that she married right out of college, that she's never had a chance to sort of go off on adventures. In my mind that was her problem. I could always stand a little more adventure. But I really feel like I got past that and it hasn't survived as a problem.

In contrast with the conflict resolution characteristic of well-adapted children, alienated children complain of conflicts that persist in their present relationships. Their problem brings to mind a line from one of William Faulkner's novels. "The past isn't dead," he said, "It isn't even past." Frequently, alienated children trace conflicts to a time when, as young adults in transition, they decided to separate themselves from their parents and establish a distant household for the first time.

Alienated children have a major problem distinguishing the past relationships from the present, in part because distance offers fewer opportunities to reinforce new identities and keep parents in tune with changes in their lives. Memories of the past may be confusing and sometimes painful for everyone. In conversation with an adult child anticipating new employment, an aging parent may recall the child's behavior on the first day of kindergarden or the child's early attitudes toward new foods. Or, in anticipation of a transition, an adult child may recall how her mother treated her when she was sick, sad, or angry. If the distant relationship is not renewed and reinforced through adequate communications, memories can dominate it.

In one conversation a daughter complains symbolically that her mother's Florida condominium contains no photographs of her beyond her seventeenth birthday. She believes her absence all these years was partly responsible for her mother's inability to allow her to grow up. For her, the fact that her mother was unable to watch her mature into adulthood calls attention to the negative impact of distance. A shy, introverted child may become an outgoing, sociable adult. A child whose room was always a mess may grow into a compulsive housekeeper. By the same token, parents may change dramatically in adapting to old age (Cohler and Lieberman 1979). A mother who never joined organizations outside the home when her children were little may become active or return to college after her children leave. Significant personality and behavioral changes must be communicated so that children and parents can put the past in perspective.

A common fear of alienated children is that past conflicts with their parents will transfer to their own children. A daughter remembers that her mother imposed unattainable standards on her. She then worries that she may be doing the same thing to her own adolescent son:

> My mother always had very high expectations for me. But I never met them. Somebody could always do better. I was a very good student. I'd say, "I got 98 on my chemistry test." And my mother would say, "That's good. What did Kate get?" And my best friend Kate always got 99. So I was always compared to her. The greatest conflict is just knowing that you never quite measure up. My mother is a very insecure person. And if she doesn't feel good about herself, how can she feel good about something she produced?
>
> My older son accused me of the same thing, having too high standards. He'll say he just had a great interview and it really went well and he's really excited. And I'll say, "That's wonderful and I'm glad to hear it. Now remember to write a thank you note." And he'll

say it's never enough. No matter what, you're always asking something else.

Another alienated daughter has resolved to respect her adolescent son's privacy because she resented her mother's intrusiveness when she was an adolescent:

> One of things she was oppressively notorious for was every time I had any sort of reading material that I could have learned anything from about sex, she pried in my things, found those things, and promptly made me take them back to wherever I'd gotten them or throw them away. So I didn't read much because my mother was a real snooper.
>
> As a result, I am incredibly determined not to pry in my own children's things. When my son brought his middle school annual home I wanted to look at it. And he said, "No Mom, there are things written in it. You know, people sign it and I don't want you to read that stuff." So I didn't. He put it in his room and I never looked. Then one day I was having a conversation with my husband and I said something about things kids Brad's age know and my husband said, "He knows these things, I've read his annual." And I said, "What? You read it. You snooped in his things after he asked us not to do it?" So I told him how I never would do it because I was so infuriated when my mother snooped in my personal things. It can really be detrimental. At least it was with me.

An inability to communicate effectively with parents or solve problems as a family may linger to undermine the possibilities of comfortable relationships between children and distant parents in the later years. Since they did not develop skills to address these problems in adolescence, the problems continue.

Some alienated children have found help through therapy, which encourages them to seek the sources of their dissatisfaction through a reconstruction of their adolescent relationships and perhaps try to communicate their insights to improve relationships with their parents. An alienated daughter in her middle fifties believes her conflict with her mother began in early childhood:

> Many of my adolescent conflicts survive in some form. I've always had real negative feelings toward Mother. Even when I was a

little girl, if she would hug me or kiss me I can remember turning away. I always felt guilty about it but I couldn't understand why. I think it went all the way back to when I was born.

Six years ago we spent a year in Japan. Just before we left I found out that years ago Dad was headed to be a missionary in China. And they didn't go because they had a sick baby: me. She said we had to stay home and care for the baby because there was no medical care for it in China. The sense I got from the discussion was that she had been very frustrated with me for having been born and for having stopped Dad from doing that. And it helped me realize where my anger came from. I can remember as a little girl being really frustrated and angry, and never trusting my mother. I'd like her to understand this. Perhaps she could.

Memories of adolescent relationships are packed with deeply felt emotions, especially ambivalence and guilt. An alienated daughter remembers why she lacks a confidential relationship with her parents:

I remember feeling aggrieved, being blamed for doing something I hadn't done. They wouldn't believe me and I could not explain myself. I had a sense that I should have been doing different things and trusted them more. I was not popular in school. I was very studious and didn't have any dates. In some way I never became fully engaged with adolescence. I just had this sense of feeling dissatisfied and misunderstood.

Parental dependency clearly influences an adult child's decision where he or she will live. Parental dependence on a college-aged son or daughter may take many forms. In fact, the death, disability, chronic illness, or divorce, remarriage, and widowhood of a parent may either constrain or provide an added incentive for a young adult child to leave or stay. A college-aged child whose parent needs him or her to work or perform domestic services cannot consider distant career opportunities in the same way as someone whose parents are well and independent. Any family trauma of significant proportion would more often deter an adult child from considering a career and life in a distant location, though in some cases such traumas may become an incentive to leave.

The memories of alienated children are filled with emotional trauma, sad family lives, and a great need in early adulthood to escape from emotionally dependent parents. Invariably, children who describe their parents as emotionally dependent are alienated. As a result of the past, present relationships are characterized by a lack of emotional closeness. An alienated son traces his conflict with his parents to his father's abandoning him and his mother when he was very little, and the neurotic dependent relationships that his mother developed afterwards:

> My mother depends on her ex-husband for many things. But she is basically very self-sufficient even though her heart is not good. My mother is currently living with my stepfather who is her ex-husband. She divorced him formally but they continue to live together. It was a significant step in their relationship for them to be divorced officially but go on living together. She is not capable of breaking away from that dependency. She is psychologically counterdependent. She attaches herself to people who are dependent on her as a way of assuring her control over them. Once you get that concept down, it changes the way you see people's relationships. She assumes this posture of kind of sublime self-reliance and gives the impression of self-sufficiency. The reality is that she is compulsively dependent on people who are dependent on her, like my stepfather for example, like my brother, but not like me. I was the one who walked away from her.

An alienated daughter explains how her mother's alcoholism has created emotional dependency in their current relationship:

> Well, my mother's an alcoholic. And she has been since my sister and I can remember. So that is probably the source of everything that's problematic in our relationship. She was abusive. Probably the emotional abuse was worse. The physical abuse was very sporadic, like throwing things. Inappropriate behavior, ranting and raving, making demands that are unreasonable. By the time I was seven years old I already knew my mother acted strangely sometimes. My mother is not a very independent person. As it stands right now, it's very difficult for her. She doesn't like to drive by herself. She doesn't like to go out by herself.
>
> My mother can vary, hot and cold, enormously. In some of my

deepest, darkest moments, I could call my mother and she could help. And sometimes I could call her and she'd be passed out. It's so completely variable, not dependable at all. Sometimes we can have very long and involved conversations about emotions and things that are going on, feelings she has or things that are happening to both of us. And I can go to her for advice. But sometimes it's almost worthless to talk to her; she'll lecture to me how everything in my life is wrong.

Under certain circumstances her personality changes after she drinks. But she's denied it all through the years. My sister and I always say that we'd spent half of our lives trying to get away from there. Mostly because her drinking dominated everything. Well, if my sister and I brought up the fact or said as boldly, "Ma, you've been an alcoholic, you're an alcoholic," they would be very annoyed with us. Or they would be sad or upset with us for having stated it that boldly. The denial about my mother's drinking problem is so highly charged. Two years ago my sister got married and turned thirty in the same year. We went out to dinner on both of those occasions, and during my sister's wedding my mother got drunk for the first time in several years. And then it was really awful, very inappropriate, it was terrible.

She draws all the attention to herself. She's loud. She's abusive. She says cruel things, all the things that you keep deep down inside that sometimes you don't even think come out. So she did that at my sister's wedding. Then she did it again at my sister's birthday party. So, within the space of six months, two occasions to celebrate the transitions in my sister's life, she diverted attention away from my sister to herself. And these occurred so much out of the blue and so connected to my sister, that we were both very disturbed by them. My sister, in fact, forbade them from staying at her house several times because she was so angry with my mother.

Alienated children also suffer from the long-term dysfunctional effects of conflicts between their mothers and fathers. Such conflicts play an important role in their own lives and contribute to a lack of emotional closeness with parents. One daughter draws a connection between her parents' conflicts and her emotional repression in childhood:

We were socialized as children to be emotionally repressed. As adults we learned it's better not to repress our emotions. Then we either can come closer to our parents or not. I always perceived my father as undermining my mother, picking on her, as kind of cruel to her in public. I think it camouflaged his own feelings of social inadequacy. She was a classic victim. Now I noticed the last few times they were here that she does that to my Dad. I had not noticed before. When I was a child I identified with both of them: the victim and the victimizer. I mean I would side with my father sometimes when he would pick on her. But at the same time in seeing her victimization I learned what it meant to be a female. I learned that role of being victim.

Anger and emotional conflict with parents tends to survive especially when alienated children remember a deteriorated home environment, as an alienated son recalls:

> I went to the university to get as far away as possible. They fought so badly that the police had to be called several times. Physical distance was a way of getting away emotionally as well. I didn't reject any opportunities to live closer. I have no regrets. I left deliberately.

In recent years running away from home has become an increasingly serious problem in the United States, although it still affects only a small proportion of the adolescent population. In 1980 over one million teenagers between thirteen and fifteen ran away from home; more than 10 percent had been ordered out by their parents. Over half returned within four days of leaving (Brennan 1980; Jorgensen, Thornburg, and Williams 1980).

In general, adolescents appreciate and care for their parents, have a good understanding of the parent-adolescent relationship, and are not interested in leaving the home environment prematurely. What seems significant about teenage runaways is the clear linkage in their minds between geographic distance and their growing need for emotional autonomy. One does not know for sure whether teenage runaways will later leave permanently by forming different households or stay when they make the decision in young adulthood.

Leaving home prematurely is related to conflict between parents and children and represents an adolescent expression of behavioral and emotional autonomy. Most runaways are upset or angry enough to prefer the obvious risks of running to staying at home. Usually they are fleeing a distressing home situation rather than seeking adventure. The most common reasons are: parental conflict including abuse; parental problems over which adolescents have no control such as alcoholism; school failure; emotional disturbance; drugs; and desire for adventure (Gullotta 1978; Munro and Adams 1978; Orton and Soll 1980). Some evidence indicates that parent-child interactions may be the key precipitation.

Another study (Jorgensen, Thornburg, and Williams 1980) concludes that many teenage runaways have a need to escape their home environments temporarily but are still within the range of normal adolescent development. Most runaways come from intact homes, but these adolescents felt that their needs for individuality and emotional support were not being met at home and that communication problems were a major source of conflict.

None of the well-adapted or displaced children in this study ran away from home during adolescence. But several alienated sons and daughters ran away or reported that their siblings ran away. One alienated son ran away as a result of the tragic consequences of his mother's divorces to his father and stepfather:

> When I was in high school I got involved with narcotics and was arrested. I had dropped out of school before that. At sixteen I was sent to a reformatory in New Jersey. I was in a repeating pattern. Then at seventeen I went from the reformatory to a federal narcotics hospital in Tennessee, then at eighteen to a county jail. At nineteen I wrote bad checks and I left my mother's apartment when the police were after me.
>
> From sixteen to nineteen I was institutionalized. Clearly, the break from my mother was unusual. It wasn't as though I had decided I had had enough and was going out and getting a job and taking care of myself. Instead I fell into a life of crime on the street. I went back to live with my mother. My stepfather left her. He came back and took his boys. When I came home from school they were gone. At that time my mother was in her own world and so was I. My mother is a heavy beer drinker but she had no formal alcohol treatment.
>
> I got sick. I was a public health hazard actually, because I devel-

oped T.B. I was in New York on the street and not feeling well. I stopped in a chest-X-ray clinic and found out I had T.B. I couldn't get any money so I had to go to the sanitarium. The staff lived in dread of me. I was not a model patient. I would run alcohol into the hospital. The head nurse took an interest in me and persuaded me to take a high school preparatory class. I passed the exam. Then she persuaded the dean of the local college to admit me.

An alienated daughter whose mother is an alcoholic did not run away herself but remembers that her younger sister ran away during their first years at college. She and her sister have kept this secret from their parents all through the years. This reveals one of the most important characteristics of alienated children: they do not trust their parents:

She was nineteen and already a freshman in college. I was twenty-one, and I was actually living at college that summer. She had decided to live at home, and to work, but unbeknown to my parents, all through high school, really from the time she was four- teen, my sister was having a very unfortunate affair with a man who was twenty years older than she, one of her teachers.

It was really disgusting. He was the band director, and my sister was a very talented musician. I think it had to do with the fact that it was really unpleasant to go home. My mother was an alcoholic and our lives were miserable at home. So my sister would hang around the school. And she got to know this guy. He was just a sleazy character. He was about thirty-five and he was married.

Well, she became very promiscuous because of this. She would get involved with other people so that she wouldn't appear peculiar, and he would become very jealous and sometimes he even abused her physically. This was a very sick relationship.

It continued on for five years. She transferred from one college to another to be closer to him. My parents didn't know that was the reason either, and that summer she wanted to spend more time with him, but my parents were very demanding. They wanted to know where she was. It wasn't, "Don't stay out, or don't go out." It was, "For safety reasons we want to know where you are going to be, and when you are going to be coming home." If she didn't come home at night, that disturbed them. She resented the restrictions they were placing on her time. She said, "I'm an adult, I'm working for

my own money. I want to come and go as I please. So I'm leaving."
To this day my parents still don't know why she ran away.

I found out about it that summer. So I am my sister's confidante.
She went to live in his house. She lived with him for three weeks.
Then she went back to college. Well, my parents and she had met a
couple of times to negotiate things, and I called a lot from Boston,
and actually came down once.

I had no idea that she had been carrying on this affair. But I knew
he was a close friend of hers from the band. So I called his house,
"Is Kim there?" He said, "Yes." I spoke to her, and then all of a
sudden, it started to click in my brain. So I confronted her, and she
admitted what had been going on.

I understood the implications. I thought it was horrible, and I
told her exactly what I thought. But I said, "I'm not going to judge
you." I was afraid that she would cut me off too. So I said, "You can
talk to me about anything and I'm not going to tell Mom and Dad
anything you don't want me to tell them. But I feel like you should
get out of this relationship. It's terrible." It lasted another year.

For alienated children adolescent conflicts with parents spill over
into the present. This same daughter whose sister ran away speaks
about her current emotional relationship with her parents as a legacy from this trauma, when her parents and sister were locked in
conflict. Yet in some ways she feels more distant from her parents
than her angry sister:

I try to avoid being the peacemaker, my role in the family. It's
just too burdensome. I think my sister is more connected to my
parents than I am, despite the fact that, emotionally, their relationships are more problematic. She is much more angry and her relationship is much more volatile. She's more affected by the things
that they do and say than I am. They can hurt her more than they
can hurt me. She's also more secretive and withholds more from
them than I do. She doesn't respond out of a sense of duty. She'll
rebel. She said, "I would never let Mom live here. I would go out of
my mind." But I say, "If I needed to and she needed it I would take
on that obligation." My parents don't feel like they get enough of
her inner emotions. She doesn't share with them.

But you know, my feeling is that she's actually more emotionally
connected to them and it's too painful for her. And she has to do

that out of a sense of protection. Whereas with me, I'm not as connected, so I can tell them I'm blue or I'm sad and I don't care what their response is.

Distant living and prolonged separations aggravate and intensify relationships with parents in the past, the present, and the future. All sons and daughters evaluate their present distant relationships in light of their memories while separating from parents and becoming adults. Such memories focus on childhood events, adolescent conflicts, brothers and sisters in the family dynamic, and the circumstances surrounding their first distant households. For some, memories of past conflicts may detract from emotional satisfactions in current relationships with distant parents.

In this chapter we looked at the external and internal forces that influence the original decision in early adulthood to establish a distant household. The different voices of emotional attachment shape memories of the past. Displaced children do not remember any significant adolescent conflicts with their parents. Well-adapted children remember conflicts in adolescence but such conflicts neither shaped their determination to live far away nor persist in their current relationships. Alienated children had conflicts with parents that lead to distant living and persist in their present relationships.

CHAPTER 5

Reaching Out and Communicating by Phone

In this chapter we will examine the frequency, length, and content of routine telephone calls and letters of displaced, well-adapted, and alienated children. We will look at miscommunications and the problems of telephoning and identify several factors that influence a satisfactory telephone call.

Since regular face to face contacts are unavailable to children and distant parents, the most distinctive characteristics of distant relationships emerge directly from patterns of contact, mainly through letters, telephone calls, and visits. Each form of communication has its own limitations. Letter exchange, for example, is the least interactive communication form since the writer must wait for a reply. Moss et al. (1985) suggest the contact itself may reaffirm the bond in addition to relaying content, and serve to define the relationship (Ruesch and Bateson 1968). Gifts and packages sent through the mail should be considered an important symbol of affection and mutual assistance.

Adult children and their distant parents communicate most often by telephone. Such routine communications often evolve over a long period. An unmarried son in his fifties explains:

> We've been talking over the phone thirty-nine years, since I went off to college. It's been our major way of communicating. I can't remember everything, but certainly over the last ten years there's not been anything that's been unresolved.

Children and their distant parents visit routinely and frequently over many years for vacations and holidays such as Thanksgiving and Christmas, and for family transitions such as graduations, birthdays, anniversaries, weddings, and funerals. Such visits become the main context for face-to-face interactions throughout the developmental cycle of the family. Routine visits often begin to decrease when elderly parents' health declines, since traveling becomes more difficult for an ailing parent. Gradually, often imperceptibly, routine telephone communications take on greater significance in perpetuating relationships with distant parents.

For many years, distant telephone communications serve to reinforce bonds of affection. As parents confront the normal life-cycle transitions of old age such as widowhood or retirement, telephone communications increasingly begin to focus on questions of assistance. Few children are consciously aware of the frustration, stress, and guilt they experience in telephone communications as their distant parents' health begins to decline.

ROUTINE LETTERS

Though letters may have been traditionally used to communicate ideas and maintain discourse, modern-day Americans have substituted telephone calls for letter writing. Only a quarter of the distant children and parents write and receive letters once or twice a month or exchange cards and gifts on special occasions.

Many circumstances influence letter exchanges. A daughter with a small child claims her parents like to send her coupons for diapers. Another daughter says she can write about her work but cannot discuss it over the phone. A recently married son claims his wife corresponds with his widowed mother. One son said his father used to write but cannot control his hand anymore because of the deteriorating effects of Parkinson's disease.

Well-adapted and displaced children say letters enhance their telephone communications. A divorced daughter and an unmarried son exchange conversational letters about everyday life with their distant widowed mothers. The son says:

> My letters include topics on family affairs, my work, my life. Since I don't have a family of my own I'll write about friends, if anything is going on at work, my students. She talks a lot about her life. If she's got a cold or a mild problem she writes about that and her social activities since she's still physically active; she plays volleyball once a week. Also, Mother is the contact person for a lot of other people in the family so I'll get information about the health of a lot of others too, what my relatives are doing.

In general, alienated children are not satisfied with letters because of continuing stress in their distant relationships. A daughter in her middle fifties says:

> She writes every week. I write regularly. Her letters are always about two pages and they say the same things. I went to church on Sunday. Then I did various activities with friends, keeping busy and active. It's all pretty superficial. She doesn't ever include anything of substance, what she's thinking. My family represses a lot of what we're thinking and feeling.

Typically, alienated children claim their parents are not satisfied with letters either, as another daughter explains:

> She writes more than I do because they don't use the phone as much. I'm not satisfied with the overall contact. I'd like to be closer to them emotionally. She's not satisfied either. She'd like me to write all the time. She'll say, "Don't you know that Helen's daughter writes every week?"

When the distance between children and parents is so great that frequent telephoning becomes too expensive, people depend more on letter exchanges to reinforce their family bonds. Children who live farthest from their parents report an increased dependency on letters. A son in his early fifties whose father lives in Puerto Rico says:

> We exchange newsy letters about what's going on in the family. I write and he responds. I try to let him know what's going on in my life, including personal things about me. It tends not to be personal though, most of the time. He never complains. My father likes to write letters. I must say that. He says the trouble with the telephone is that it's killing the art of letter writing. And he loves language and the written word. I never can respond when he says he's depressed. I'd like to be on the same land mass. I would like to see him more frequently than we do.

ROUTINE TELEPHONE CALLS

Most distant children prefer the telephone to letters. A son explains that calls are more personalized because his mother sends the same official family newsletter to him and his brothers every week. A daughter from a large family claims she has her mother's complete attention on the telephone because so many people distract her during visits. A daughter who lives very far away feels closer emotionally on the telephone:

> Telephone calls affect my well-being but not self-esteem. I felt so isolated for so many years not being able to talk with them, being dependent on letters. Really, literally to hear their voices even if they're not doing very well makes me feel better, makes me feel much closer to them.

Only one child in my study claims he and his mother prefer letters to telephone calls because they can deal with more important issues:

> We correspond once a week by letter. For some reason we've never gotten into a phoning pattern. It's more important that I exchange these letters than that I go to see them. We deal with important decisions more in letters. We also have a tendency to wait if possible until we have personal contact.

A well-adapted daughter claims she prefers the phone because she wants to keep close touch with her mother's health condition but her mother prefers letters, "so she can read them over again."

Distant children and parents must deal with several inherent limitations of telephone communications. First, telephone calls exclude the visual component of human communications; all forms of nonverbal communication, body language, touching, gesture, and nuance so basic to the intimacy of parent-child interactions are absent (Climo 1988). That catchy slogan of telephone commercials, "Reach out and touch someone," is indeed interesting for it is the one thing telephone communications can never accomplish.

Second, since a phone call is such a focused communication event, it may also limit the exchange of details of everyday life. Many calls are too brief and too intense to include all the important daily events. One must take turns and wait for a spoken reply to know how the other person has responded to an idea or question. Many people feel unsatisfied with telephone communications without knowing exactly why. People may get on the telephone, chat for a while, hang up, and only afterwards remember why they called in the first place.

Finally, telephone usage varies by generation. In general, the older generation seems more reluctant to speak for a long time or chat in a leisurely mode. Most parents prefer to use the phone as an instrument for exchanging important information and feelings but not for visiting. They want to end the conversation as soon as possible, perhaps partly because of the cost.

Such generational differences make distant communications difficult even under routine, relaxed circumstances. Understandably, however, these normal problems become highly intensified during a family crisis. Emotions and needs tend to dominate thoughts and feelings under pressure, thus detracting from the children's capacity to express themselves clearly or listen sympathetically to their parents.

Three modes of intensity dominate most distant telephone communications. The routine mode is the least intensive, allowing both the child and his or her parents to reinforce their bonds of affection through the contact itself rather than through the substance of its messages. Routine communications focus on mutual experiences, current events, and basic expressions of affection.

Many children report that routine long-distance calls yield a strong sense of emotional gratification. A sentimental telephone commercial which ran for a while on television illustrates the importance of intensity on the telephone. A very maternal older woman answers the phone and is slightly surprised that her son is calling. She asks a series of nervous questions without waiting for answers, while her elderly husband, sensing her concern, moves toward her and the phone to listen. "Are you all right, are you ill?" she asks. Then she bursts into tears, and, turning to her husband, she says with maternal happiness, "He just called to say I love you, Mom."

A second mode of intensity involves problem solving or decision making. Since problem-solving is often interactive and families differ greatly in their ability to solve problems, telephone communications may not suffice and face-to-face communications become necessary. Problem-solving activities are generally high in emotional intensity, often revealing deeper levels of conflict in the relationship.

During the crisis mode of communications, visits and telephone calls take on great emotional intensity. Strangely, during the intensity of a crisis relationships appear either very rigid or very flexible. People are either more open to change their perceptions of one another, or prior conflicts surface. In response to the fear that crises generate, both children and distant parents communicate very often.

Distant children and their parents commonly talk about a wide range of subjects, including family and related issues (100 percent), recent personal events and travel (97 percent), health (87 percent), work (85 percent), news events (80 percent), plans for future family visits (54 percent), financial issues (45 percent), personal problems (43 percent), politics (41 percent), planning reunions with friends (35 percent), and purchases (15 percent). Parents and children who talk about a wider range of subjects bridge the distance gap better, are more involved in each other's lives, share more information, and feel closer emotionally.

For a few children, the ritual of telephone communications is far more important than any of the information exchanged. Such rituals lock people into habitual patterns with little substance. Rather than encouraging spontaneity or the exploration of ideas, such patterns may be stagnating, serving only the minimal function of re-newing bonds of affection. Having little real substance the contact itself becomes the message, as a typical well-adapted son reports:

> It's a way of keeping a dialogue and just hearing their voices when there's really not much content. There are certain questions that seem to repeat. It's just a communication. It is without a clear message. Just to find out how they're doing. It doesn't have to do with anything in particular.

Most children claim their telephone calls have an important in-formation component such as the need to express love and caring, news about the family, or anything of mutual interest. A displaced son in his late forties reports different kinds of information exchange:

> A good deal of our conversations are ritualized. Calling would be a staying-in-touch gesture on my part, a means of substituting for the distance that separates us. The medium isn't the only message though. I would say before my father's death there was a greater mixture of purposes. We also had to resolve substantive issues like home repair and advice. These were things that I would provide input for them. Ordinarily we would speak on a weekly basis.

A common area of information exchange involves planned visits or travel. Many children mention the importance of keeping their parents apprised of their travel plans. A typical well-adapted daugh-ter says:

> Occasionally we've exchanged important information such as when I'm getting ready to visit, particularly if I'm flying, giving her dates, times of arrival, that sort of thing. I just have to remind her a lot and ask her to please write it on the calendar because she won't remember that kind of information unless she writes it down.

A well-adapted son lets his parents know when he goes out of town for meetings:

> If I'm going to be out of town for a couple of weeks I'll call them ahead so they'll know how long I'll be gone. If I'm at a meeting, I'll

tell them where I'm going to be. If it's just over a weekend usually I wouldn't even mention it. But if it's for a week, I'll tell them where I am so they could actually get a hold of me if they needed me.

THE FREQUENCY OF CALLS

The frequency of distant communications is less important than its emotional meaning to the individual (Gelfand 1982; Adams 1968). Since distant living limits face-to-face communications to occasional visits, children and their parents place more emotional importance on telephone contacts. Well-adapted children feel close to their parents and are more likely to say they call because of enjoyment. Guilt and a sense of filial obligation mobilizes alienated children to call since they do not feel close.

Frequency of contact explains little about the quality of the distant relationship. Telephone contact may be very frequent even when aid between older people and their adult children is largely ritualistic, "based on obligation which is devoid of warmth and closeness" (Wood and Robertson 1978) or based on the dependency needs of aging parents with little emotional satisfaction gained on either side (Horowitz 1985). No positive correlation has been found between the frequency of contact and the morale of elderly parents.

The frequency of telephone communications can vary within the same family. The average distant child speaks with parents about once a week. About 45 percent speak once or twice every week and 10 percent speak two or more times each week. About 25 percent call every two weeks and 20 percent call once a month or less.

A principal of generalized reciprocity governs routine telephone use rather than holding either the child or the distant parent primarily responsible. In most families initiating calls is roughly equal under normal circumstances. Nevertheless, neither children nor parents keep close track. Moreover, many mitigating circumstances may cause either child or parent to call more frequently without upsetting their perception of balance. About half the children say they and their parents call equally, a quarter say they call more often, and another quarter say their parents call more often.

Younger, displaced, and well-adapted children report more balance in initiating calls. A well-adapted married daughter in her early thirties says:

> We're on the phone usually in the morning. They're both on the extension at the same time. I call about once a week and they call me as often. There is nothing that says you must call or I will look forward to your call. It's just because I feel strong affection toward them. We usually don't take turns but we both call.

Some children initiate more calls than their parents. A daughter from a large family calls more often because her mother has to divide her calls among ten children. Another daughter claims she calls more often since her mother became ill because her mother's need is greater. Some children claim they do not call as often as they would like because of busy work schedules, child-care responsibilities, or guilt. A well-adapted daughter explains:

> I'd call more often if I had more time, money, and energy. But by the time I get my kids to bed I just sit in the garbage and read the paper until I crash. I'm too tired and there's not much to say by the end of the day. I call a lot. Well, because they're getting older and time is running out.

A well-adapted son in his fifties also calls more often:

> They don't call me a whole lot. They're more concerned about catching me. I'm not home as much as they are, so it's come down to, pretty much, me calling them. Although now I have an answering machine at my house, so they'll call and leave a message once in a while. But mostly, they're a generation where they still don't make long-distance calls as freely as I do though much more than they used to.

Several children claim their parents call them more often now than in the past because they have more time or because they've developed a more tolerant attitude toward the telephone over years of prolonged separation, as a son recalls:

> Actually I can recall maybe twenty years ago, when they were more hesitant to use the phone. They've actually changed their at-

titude about cost. Phone calls used to be only every month and they would almost always make some comment about how expensive this was, but they just wanted to call to double-check. But over the last ten years it's been more like every couple of weeks or so.

Another son says his father calls more because he feels it is his parental duty. Some parents call each week at the same time and the same day by formal arrangement, as a daughter says:

My mother calls me more often, always on Sunday morning after she gets back from church. If I'm going out on Sunday I'll call her. Or if she's going out of town like this weekend she won't call. But if she doesn't call every week I get somewhat concerned so I call.

Several factors influence the frequency of telephone calls, including distance, parents' age, marital status, health status, and cost. As distance increases, the frequency of telephone conversations decreases: three-quarters of those living closest (200 miles) speak one or more times each week compared to only one quarter of those living more than 600 miles away. Children living farthest away were far less likely than those living closest to speak once a week. On the other hand, children living more than 800 miles away all report that they and their parents would call more often if they could. When distance is very great, routine calling is so expensive that families may be limited to one call a month or even less.

Age and marital status of distant parents also influences the frequency of telephone calls. As the parents' age increases, the children's desire to call decreases. Also, children with married mothers and fathers report a greater desire to call than those with widowed parents. But this pattern is typically reversed during the year after the death of a parent; phone calls to recently widowed parents increase markedly.

Parents' health status also influences the frequency of telephone calls. Children with healthy parents report more reciprocal calling. But when parents show signs of disability or illness, notions of reciprocal calling quickly give way to increased child-initiated calls. A typical daughter reports: "I call once every few weeks. But during the time my mother was sick I called and spoke to them every few days." Children also report a greater desire to call when their parents have a health condition that limits their activities.

Cost influences the frequency of telephone calls for many children and distant parents. Older adult children frequently report high phone bills because they speak to their own distant children as well as to their parents, as one daughter says: "I would call more if it weren't so expensive. We call so many other people too: our children, Bill's dad, his brother, his sister, my sisters. We call our kids at least once a week. And our daughter calls us probably equally from Virginia." When both generations can afford it, the caller usually pays. In most instances, a mutual understanding of financial differences prevails and the generation most able to commonly pays for very expensive calls. This is also symbolic of current directions of familial assistance.

Typically, children believe their parents desire more telephone communications than they do, but they are also more concerned about costs, as this son in his fifties says:

> I think it's short because they're concerned about the cost. Now it's 50/50 sharing. They just don't like to spend money no matter whether I'm spending it or they're spending it. It's a generational thing. Now they're just sort of, "Hello, how are you? What's the weather? Some neighbor's ill but now they're OK." You know, just the briefest contact.

Several children say their fathers are more concerned with cost than their mothers, as a daughter notes: "Sometimes Mother will call when my father's not there because he worries all the time. He'd be very gruff, 'Don't spend so much time on the phone. It costs money.' But my mother would talk for hours." But expense is not a major factor for everyone. One son reports that his father charges his calls as a business expense. In other families children and parents share the cost when calls become expensive. One daughter claims nobody ever thinks about costs because in this world of credit cards you don't pay for it till later.

The length of phone conversations is also highly variable, depending on custom, the time of day, whether something important is happening in the family such as illness or a family crisis, or the different telephone attitudes of the generations. Calls are longer when family custom dictates that each member speak briefly with every other member. Other families put everyone on the phone at once. Needless to say, such calls are certainly more chaotic. The average long-distance call lasts about fifteen or twenty minutes. But a quarter report frequent calls of thirty minutes or more.

PROBLEMS AND MISCOMMUNICATIONS

Most children derive satisfaction from telephone contacts. Calls renew bonds of affection with parents and maintain positive feelings of family solidarity. Nevertheless, children report occasional problems and miscommunications that evoke frustration, anger, or stress. Such emotions conform to their voices of emotional attachment.

Several factors contribute to telephone problems and miscommunications. The first is the inherent ambiguity in the language. The dictionary includes about thirty different meanings for each of the most common words in English. Even the simplest messages can be interpreted in many ways. The chances that the intended meaning will be the only one received are often quite low. The second factor is selective perception, which results from ambivalent feelings about what children or parents want to hear rather than what was actually said. Even if children say exactly what is on their minds, communication may still break down, for what they say may not be what their parents hear. Finally, unsolved problems that already exist in the relationship may surface on the telephone.

Unrealistic Expectations

One problem in distant telephone conversations arises when one or both generations set unrealistic expectations. Nothing leads to failure like the expectation to fail. When failures from the past relationship dominate one's thoughts, behavior may actually help bring about the feared outcome. An alienated son, for example, may fear that his parent won't accept his explanation for not visiting, or an alienated daughter may fear that her mother will criticize her if she reveals problems with her own children. When one expects that nothing positive could possibly emerge from the conversation, it is likely that both parties will put up defenses and failure will result. Alienated childen commonly express self-defeating attitudes with regard to planned visits, behavior of parents during ilnesses, their own parenting skills, and their attempts to solve serious problems or share feelings. A theme emerges of repressed emotions and an inability to express true feelings. As one alienated daughter in her fifties says sadly:

> I never have expressed my feelings with her. Never. It's probably why I became a social worker. I've worked on it all my life as an adult, how to express my feelings and not keep them repressed. It's not very easy, especially when you learn as a child all the techniques of denying and repressing them.

A related problem appears when expectations are set too high. Here a child's expectations become the equivalent of wishes projected onto the parent. They can be confused with realities and result in disappointment and a negative impact on the distant relationship. When distant parents or children expect some assistance, emotional support, or reassurance for ongoing problems, their disappointment can be very great when the other party does not respond accordingly. One area, fraught with expectations and misunderstandings, is travel plans and visiting. A well-adapted son says of his widowed mother: "Sometimes information is misinterpreted. Especially when I say I'll get there, the timing will be confused. She thinks I'm going to arrive sooner. That's very common. And it's solved very quickly." Children may hold such expectations of their parents too. A well-adapted daughter expressed frustration with her own parents because they could not visit on an important occasion:

> I don't feel frustrated in the sense of angry. But we had Andrew's mom visit from Florida and I wanted my parents to get acquainted with his mother. I thought it would really be nice if my mom and dad would drive down here, have dinner with us, and when I first mentioned this to my mom she said oh that sounds great. But then she said they couldn't do it. My frustration was that I thought of course you can do it. But I know it's very difficult for them.

For most well-adapted children these misunderstandings are temporary and quickly forgotten. A more serious problem arises when parents insist that their child relocate to live closer. An un-married, alienated daughter expresses frustration at the pressure she feels from this unrealistic expectation:

> When my father called me for my birthday last weekend, he said, "Hello, why don't you apply to the University of Connecticut? I just read that there were some openings there." Not, "How are you? What's happening?" Oh, I try to explain to them what the academic job market is all about and that you can't just apply like to a factory. And I told them that I would prefer to be in the northeast but that just won't be possible for the next few years, if at all. And sometimes my mother will say, "You're going to probably spend the rest of your life there. I know it." And I say, "Well, Mother, there's no way I can know." So that's how I try to address those concerns, by explaining to them exactly how academics can move or not move and that I would prefer to do it. I would like to be there, but there's nothing I can do about it. I don't feel guilty about that conflict. Really, that's out of my control.

Domination and Patronization

Several telephone problems relate to the children's and parents' capacity have to communicate their emotional needs on the tele-phone. Telephone communications can easily go out of balance when one party dominates or patronizes the other. In dominating a conversation one party has much to tell but little ability to listen.

Many children allow themselves to be overshadowed because they want to keep the conversation going smoothly. A well-adapted son in his early thirties accepts one-sided conversations because his mother is widowed and lonely:

> The main thing I do for my mother is, I'm an ear for her. She lives alone and she needs someone to talk to. She doesn't provide an ear for me. She talks, I listen. She dominates the conversation. Since she calls me once or twice a week I usually don't call at all.

Good listening is essential for success in distant telephone com-munications. Another well-adapted son in his late fifties makes a point of listening carefully to each parent:

They tell me more about their lives than I tell. I kind of like it that way. For one thing, I know the whole cast of characters there better than they know it here. So my social life is more easily summarized because I don't have to tell them every person who was at a party or something.

My father likes to talk about how he's feeling and his routines to keep himself feeling good. He's a pretty good listener. He wants to know what's going on and how I am. My mother talks about what she's been doing, who she's been seeing, who she talked to of our mutual friends and relatives, and how they all are. She talks about her feelings, but she takes a little more prodding. My mother is a very good listener. I usually give them a much briefer account of what I'm up to, and my kids, and Janet.

Some children become frustrated when a parent does not respond to their comments or questions, as another son reports:

My father is not a good listener at all, although I remember him as a good listener when I was a kid. He has become very self-centered. He'll ask you a question and before you reply he'll bring up something entirely unrelated. I don't know if it's a symptom of Parkinson's or an inward-turning, but I'm sorry to see it because it's very unpleasant. He doesn't appear to do it intentionally and it isn't a deliberate attempt to insult or injure. But it's a problem.

In general, mothers dominate calls even when fathers are on the line at the same time. Half the children who have both mothers and fathers said they communicate more often with their mothers, a quarter communicate more with their fathers, and a quarter converse with both parents equally.

Several children say their father is more difficult to talk to. An alienated son whose parents were divorced when he was a young child calls his father only on special occasions but speaks on the phone regularly to his mother. A number of well-adapted children have difficulties conversing with their fathers, as one daughter explains:

I don't talk to my father at length. That one is ritualized for sure. "How are you doing? Are you taking your medicine?" I may even want to pursue the conversation longer, but before I get a chance to do that, he'll say, "You want to talk to your mother?" So that's the end of it.

Several children say their fathers depend on their mothers to do the communicating. An alienated daughter complains that her mother dominates:

I try to talk to my father. But my mother is a talker. I've become more pointed over the years because I realize that I may not have an opportunity to communicate with my dad unless I interfere directly with my mother and say, "I asked Dad this question." She has the tendency to answer for him or interrupt. He's willing to talk but someone has to call and ask him a direct question. But I am holding my own these days.

When one parent is ill, the other one usually dominates phone conversations as in the case of a son whose father had a stroke several years ago:

I mostly talk to my mother on the phone. My father will get on the phone for a couple of minutes. Since he has a difficult time talking sometimes, he gets embarrassed and frustrated when he can't say things that he wants to. His mind is all there. He knows what he wants to say. But there's something skipping in the link between his brain and mouth.

Rarely, a father dominates the conversation, as one daughter describes:

He has things he wants to say and says them. His voice is so strong it drowns out mine. He says, "Now I'll give the phone to your mother but we've already talked for a long time." So he tries to control with whom I speak and for how long. The pattern is to get the business done, which means whatever he wants to talk about. Then I'll ask my questions, particularly now since there's been so much in health and he's been taking care of her.

One son actually prefers talking to his father because he talks more honestly about his mother's health. Several children say neither they nor their parent dominate regularly, but the situation determines who talks more. Only one son said he dominates the conversation with his widowed father.

A second kind of off-balance conversation results when one party patronizes or treats the other insincerely, wherein one person talks to another as if he or she were less than functional, or explains things that do not need explaining. Patronizing may result from an effort to try to simplify information and being afraid of the other party's response, or because of a difficulty in expressing deeply felt emotions. Some parents patronize their children out of long-standing habit, while some children think this is the way one talks to an older person. The result is often problematical; only a few children say that neither they nor their parents patronize each other on the telephone. A well-adapted daughter may not actually like what her mother wore during a visit, but she will tell her she did. A well-adapted son in his early fifties pretends to involve his parents in important decisions:

> I discuss important decisions in a sham sort of way. I might ask them what kind of car I should get even though I don't intend to take their advice. I mean, I wouldn't totally ignore or do the opposite just because they said it, but it also wouldn't weigh more than anyone else.

A well-adapted daughter has learned not to take her mother's compliments quite as seriously as she used to,

> Sometimes she'd tell me what a good daughter I am compared to my sister, which is really patronizing, given all the problems I had with her over the years. I mean my older sister was fashionably addicted to valium at one point. So for a while she was the black sheep. Then when I eloped and married a man so many years younger, I became the black sheep.

Some children patronize their parents when they complain of ill health. A well-adapted son provides a measured response to his mother's health complaints so he doesn't alarm her:

> My mother would be concerned about upsetting me and I would feel the same way. If something were wrong, I would try to say it

moderately and not express it completely seriously. I would communicate the problem but not exaggerate its importance because my mom would tend to exaggerate it even more.

One divorced son claims his patronizing is the result of prolonged separations and divergent life experiences:

I try not to patronize her. It's important to at least make sympathetic noises about things that I have different opinions about. I'm not part of that community anymore. But I once was clearly part of it. And I've retained my interest and involvement. But it's really just for her sake.

Withholding Information

The need for control in telephone communications reflects more fundamental emotional issues of dependence and independence in the distant relationship. Children or parents who hold back rather than reveal must continually avoid turning the other party's attention to this sensitive area. In concealing, one's attention is divided between accurate communication and camouflage. Some part of the individual wants to share information while another part fears the consequences of disclosure.

Parents especially do not tell children about possible health problems. Children do not tell parents about sexual, marital, financial, and health problems or about problems with their children. Only a few older children said neither they nor their parents withhold information from each other; most say that both they and their parents have indeed withheld information.

Everyone can think of a situation that justifies concealment. Yet withholding information invariably carries with it a judgment that the distant parent or child is not capable of knowing something they have a right to know (Edinberg 1987). Children and parents almost always justify concealment as a desire to protect, that somehow the knowledge would hurt them. It seems logical to assume that in withholding information, children and parents also hold back psychological involvement to protect themselves from the other person.

As parents become ill or anticipate greater dependency, they may try to conceal health problems simply to confirm to themselves that they are still in charge of their lives. They may feel that to confide in their children would add a burden of stress in their children's lives. Since they believe their children cannot help them anyway, they conceal their health status to protect their children.

As we might expect, displaced children have a great deal of difficulty concealing information. A displaced son describes his stress when he concealed his wife's illness:

> I concealed from them with this one big big issue of Andrea's. And it was a very peculiar experience for me because it was the one instant in my life where I didn't tell my parents what was going on. I was always having to stop conversations before I would have to reveal it to them or lie about it. Or say we're not going to talk about that. It wasn't my decision. Andrea didn't want to reveal it and that's fine; it's her disease. It was very strange, something I'd never experienced before. In a sense it really wasn't about me. If it were about me it probably would have been painful. But it was something I'd never like to have to do again.

His wife explains very clearly why she didn't want her parents or her in-laws involved:

> My parents were wanting to give more advice than I wanted to hear. As an adult I didn't want that kind of advice. They were saying get another diagnosis, see another doctor, because they wanted to hear something else. Or, it was my impression that it was a lack of faith in my ability to evaluate my own health situation. I knew once I was willing to accept the diagnosis I would adjust to the extent I had to but no more.

In contrast with displaced children, most well-adapted and alienated children report incidences in which their parents concealed information from them. Some say their parents confide certain kinds of information in their near-living sisters and brothers but not in them because they live far away. A well-adapted daughter explains:

> There's a kind of "let's not burden them with the details." A kind of secrecy, she consciously doesn't share as many of the things that

are going on. She has different medical problems that I think she shares with my sister at home more so than with me. If I were at home, she would share more. She doesn't want me to be bothered with that kind of detail.

A well-adapted son recalls that his mother tried to withhold information about her health so he wouldn't worry about her at the time of his wedding:

My mother withholds health information. I have to pry it out of her. When I called I asked her how her annual physical went and she started to cry. She said, "Why did you have to ask me that?" I said, "I want to know." Well, the doctor found something suspicious on the mammogram so she had to get more tests. She was very upset. She wasn't going to tell me unless I asked. She didn't want me to worry about her, especially around the time of my wedding.

A few well-adapted children are unhappy when their parents withhold. A son in his fifties sadly describes his widowed father's extreme self-sufficiency:

I am not happy with this situation. He's very closed-mouthed. Once I got a call from Rochester, New York, from a surgeon. He said, "You know your father was operated on today and I noticed there were no family members here." So this nice guy had called me up to see what was going on. My father had a gall bladder attack in Puerto Rico, got on a plane to go to Rochester to have his gall bladder removed and hadn't said boo. It certainly fits that he returned to the U.S. for important medical problems. He says medical care is not as good in Puerto Rico as it is in Rochester.

But most well-adapted children are not upset when their parents withhold information from them. Several refuse to be judgmental. A number have accepted their parents' withholding as part of their personalities, style of communicating, or upbringing. Well-adapted children respect their parents' wishes to protect them in situations where they could not have helped anyway. A well-adapted daughter recalls that her mother was in the hospital last year but waited until she knew what the problem was before calling. The daughter defends her mother, saying she wasn't deliberately concealing. She knew her daughter couldn't help. One well-adapted daughter takes the responsibility on herself for not asking more questions:

> She doesn't want to burden me with a lot of things that are going on in her life. If my mother is not willing or ready to share some information, then I won't push it. I don't have negative feelings about it. I think the burden is on me to ask and pursue it further. I figure when a person's ready to reveal some information, he or she will.

One well-adapted daughter claims she conceals information from her mother about her financial circumstances or problems she is having with her children. Another daughter says:

> We did conceal from her when the negotiations for my Yugoslavian trip got hot and heavy because she's been pretty open about not wanting us to leave the country for a year, and especially having to do with Yugoslavia, although no country would make her happy. So it wasn't until they actually made an offer that I told her about it.

The primary reason any distant child gives for withholding is a desire not to worry or to alarm. A well-adapted daughter explains:

> If it's a problem she needs to know about, then I'll let her know. But basically, I don't want to worry her unnecessarily. For example, last year I had a lump and was not sure what it was going to be. So before I found out I really didn't want to tell her. I knew she would get hysterical. After I found out it was OK then it was OK to tell her.

In sharp contrast to the tolerance of well-adapted children, alienated children describe their distant parents as always concealing information or never telling them what is really happening. When alienated sons and daughters discover that information was withheld, they usually react by feeling depressed, angry, or betrayed. An alienated daughter describes her anger when she became aware of a problem after it had been resolved:

They withhold lots! My father had an operation and we were planning to visit on the day that he was scheduled for prostate surgery but we didn't know that he had it until we got to New York. We had driven all day. We were going to visit for almost a week with lots of things planned. We had talked about them for weeks. I walk in the door, there's my mother, "Hello, how are you?" Kiss, kiss. And, "Where's Dad?" "Oh, we didn't want to worry you, but he just had surgery this morning. You can visit him at the hospital tomorrow."

We had to readjust everything! And I was less upset about canceling the plans than I was that they had duplicitously made them over the last month. "Oh yes, we'll go in and see this play, and we'll go to that exhibit, and we'll go and do this and that," knowing all the while that they were actually not going to do any of those things. Oh, I was furious!

Response to Criticism: Avoidance, Confrontation, Argument

Many deeply felt emotions spill over into telephone communications. When parents are critical, children may confront or avoid them. Avoidance maintains a surface level of peace and tranquility; children and parents talk about unimportant issues while avoiding confrontation. Some feel guilty for postponing an inevitable confrontation. Or they may feel satisfaction that they are able to maintain peace in the midst of family problems. A well-adapted daughter who lives very far away fears that confrontation could destroy the fragile phone contact she has worked so hard to develop:

> I'm afraid to fight with them on the phone because it's such a new and tenuous connection and it's so very important to me to have access. I don't want them to feel it's an intrusion that's going to be a negative intrusion. The conflict is about the housekeeping and the gardening. I'm biding my time like with the telephone. They'll eventually have to get help.

Most children avoid direct confrontation on a variety of sensitive issues, mainly when parents are critical of them or of other family members and in-laws. Children recall parents' criticisms for not visiting enough, for not formally practicing religion, or for not buying a house properly. An alienated daughter explains how she avoids discussing the subject of her new house:

They were always telling me that we weren't going about it the right way. Now if my mother brings that up, I'll say, "I've explained to you the reasons already why we've made this decision and those haven't changed. This issue is closed. So there's no point to talk about it."

Another major area of avoidance centers on the distant child's marital life. An unmarried alienated daughter recalls:

Oh, God. They're critical about everything all the time on the phone. When Brian and I decided not to get married that was a big one. Every once in a while, my father still takes Brian aside and gives him a good lecture about it. Now, when my father gets on my back about not being married, I usually just say, "Let's move on to the next subject. It's not worth talking about this anymore."

Parents also criticize children for eloping, for marrying the wrong person, for divorcing, and for not having children. A son in his middle forties recalls:

The only thing that my mother never adjusted to was the fact that we never had children. She felt that it was wrong and she blamed us both. Just before she got sick she could be pretty direct and unpleasant about it. She would make comments like, "My friends wonder why I don't have grandchildren." It just made her unhappy. And I was sad that she was unhappy. Well, I didn't get into it. I tried to avoid the subject.

Many children experience conflict when distant parents are critical of their siblings, nieces, and nephews. Yet well-adapted children avoid direct confrontations about these issues on the phone, as a son says: "We don't disagree on the telephone. I avoid those issues. I listen politely when I have to. She is critical of my brother's children. But I won't get into any discussion with her about it." When parents criticize siblings, children feel uncomfortable even when they agree. A displaced daughter avoids engaging in the discussion:

I am reluctant to get into a discussion when my parents call to complain about my sister or my nephew. My nephew is constantly

on the verge of dropping out of school. My sister is very irresponsible about money. They tell tales about her using their phone for
long-distance calls when they're away and not telling them. I just
say, "Now, now . . . I would rather not be in the middle of that."
There are times when it's really fierce and justifiably so. I mean I
agree with my parents.

Another displaced son joins his parents' complaint against his
sister-in-law:

My brother didn't and won't have children. He married a woman
who doesn't believe in children. In some very important ways she
doesn't fit into the family at all. So they bought a dog. My dad calls
it "the grand-dog." My brother would probably like to have kids.
Sometimes I feel he'd really like to spend some time with my kids
but because of his wife he feels constrained.

Few children feel capable of confronting their parents on the
telephone. Most postpone confrontations for face-to-face visits.
Nevertheless, several remember some telephone confrontations
with their parents. An alienated son indicates he can confront his
father in defense of his nieces and nephews but he must do so very
carefully:

Deep disagreements between us aren't very subtle but they are
veiled. For example, my sister has complained to me that my father
has not paid attention to her children, that he's not visiting or looking after his grandchildren. When this happens I will call my father
and raise the subject with him. Occasionally I've been direct in saying he ought to see his grandchildren more often. It almost never
leads to anything unpleasant. The conversation just tapers off.

In another example, a well-adapted daughter confronts her
mother in defense of her sister-in-law:

My criticism is mostly about Mother interfering with my sister-
in-law. I have communicated that to her. She tends to write Betty's
problem off as somebody who is lazy because she sees depression as
a moral rather than a psychological problem. I suggest that my

brother do a little bit more to help his wife out. And my mother immediately comes to his defense. He's a lawyer and he doesn't have time to do any of these things. She'll say, "That's what Betty should be doing."

Husbands generally defend their wives against their parents' criticisms, as this alienated son says:

When she criticizes my wife I will occasionally argue with her on the phone. She's not crazy about my wife. My wife is not good enough. My mother doesn't like the fact that my wife is not very demonstrative toward her. In fact, my wife can't stand her because she sees right through her, that my mother worked her over when I took her down to see her in Texas the first time, and my wife has never forgotten it.

Stepparents are in-laws of a sort. As such, children criticize them, as a daughter says:

Our conflict is over my stepfather. He and she make decisions together having to do with how to treat my younger sisters. If my stepfather answers I ask him to get my mother. He and I don't have lots in common to talk about. Maybe he's not interested in what I'm doing and I'm not interested in what he's doing, but one way or the other there's no chit-chat. I feel bad only because it might hurt my mother.

Telephone arguments between children and parents are especially problematical because issues of dependency and independence surface from past relationships. Most children and parents will go out of their way to avoid arguing on the phone. But when disagreements deteriorate into arguments, most children find a quick way to end the conversation. An alienated daughter in her early thirties is exceptional in reporting frequent telephone arguments with her parents. Significantly, both parties are quick to reestablish contact:

Selling their house was extremely stressful and they actually didn't want to call me because they didn't want to talk about it. They were on hold for a month until this guy had his affairs in order. For a while my sister and I would call on a regular basis: "Has he gotten the mortgage?" They were so annoyed about us constantly pumping them about it: "No, we haven't heard. There's no news. Don't talk about it anymore." So my sister and I decided not to call them about it anymore.

Then, when I finally did call two weeks later, my father said, "You don't care about what's happening. You never call," and he actually hung up on me. I think they were still on hold, but now they felt so abandoned. They said, "Nobody wants to have anything to do with us because we're leaving the community, and nobody calls anymore." My father's hung up on me and on my sister, we've hung up on him and my mother. We're all very angry. The interesting thing is that most of the time, somebody will call back right away.

Self-Esteem

Maintaining satisfying communications requires self-esteem. For many alienated children feelings of low self-esteem, regret, and guilt often dominate telephone calls. People with low self-esteem feel unlovable. Their lives can become a desperate search for safety, security, and the approval of others. For well-adapted children, parental praise or expressions of affection on the telephone make up an important component of their relationship. They feel high self-esteem when parents are proud of their accomplishments or have heard something good about them. A well-adapted son says:

> My parents make me feel good about myself. I'm very proud and appreciative of my parents as good people and extraordinarily good natured and healthy. I respect them a lot in comparison to other people who are getting old. They don't feel sorry for themselves, they embrace life, they have some real vigor. I feel very grateful for having people like that behind me and in me. I don't take it for granted. I also feel pretty much that I've done what I can for them.

Children with low self-esteem expect and fear rejection, so they devise communication strategies based on self-protection. Constructive comments may be taken as put-downs and immediately denied, as one daughter recalls:

Early in my remarriage I took issue with things they said that maybe they meant in a more loving way. I thought it was critical. There were times when it would have been better to see each other in person. The same thing happened in letters. I would write things and she would take them the wrong way. Or she would write things that I would take the wrong way.

Alienated sons and daughters often feel low self-esteem. One daughter traces her feelings of low self-esteem to feelings of powerlessness she learned from her mother:

> I often feel uncomfortable about the way my mother continues to claim that my father won't let her write letters to the editor or call a cleaning service. It is primarily a function of perceiving my mother as a victim and identifying with that. I have a theory that women really do learn a lot of self-hatred from their mothers if their mothers don't like themselves. So when I see these weaknesses in my mother it effects my self-esteem because I identify with that. I have fought hard to overcome it but it's such a large part of my life that it still affects me. I ask, Why do women allow men to have this power over them? So as a woman I feel demeaned.

Children with low self-esteem take it badly if their parents criticize them. Alienated children repeatedly raise the theme of repressed emotions. A daughter in her late forties complains that her mother always communicates her feelings indirectly:

> She called and left a message on my answering machine that she had gotten some books I sent her. I didn't call her back because we were so busy. Then later in the week she called and said, "I called you four times this week and I began to wonder if you were out of town." It annoys her because if she gets the machine four times she has to pay for four calls. Her indirectness really gets to me. She wouldn't ever say "I'm unhappy" or "I'm concerned." She doesn't express her emotions because it scares her. She doesn't like me to either.

SATISFACTION AND DISSATISFACTION

One might assume that, all in all, children and distant parents are satisfied with their communications—that letters, telephone calls, and visits are adequate to maintain familial bonds of affection. In fact, a substantial number of children are not satisfied. A majority claim distance detracts in some significant ways from satisfaction in their relationships. When asked about the ideal distance between children and parents, a majority said between one and four hours, and 20 percent said less than an hour away. More than 60 percent chose ideal distances that were closer than their actual distance, reflecting the belief that if they lived closer, they could visit more often.

Many children would like to be able to visit and return on the same day. Some noted the importance of spontaneity in visiting, but without being overwhelmed—close enough for personal growth and independence but with limits to obligations and expectations. Some said they would like the grandparents to be closer to their children.

A majority of children are satisfied with distant telephone contacts. Yet a third claim they need more telephone calls; they would like to call their parents and would like their parents to call them more often. The most common problem children mention is the absence of frequent opportunities to communicate the details of daily life in a face-to-face relationship. As one daughter says, "I really miss having coffee and talking with my mother." Grandparents cannot watch the grandchildren grow. Parents and children are not present to share important moments in life together: the loss of a job, a successful promotion, the expression of a child's happiness when something exciting happened at school, or a health crisis. Distant children cannot easily perform needed routine services. Ironically, children cling tenaciously to an ideology that holds them responsible for such services.

Most children believe that their distant parents have accepted their distant living without great objection, and that only a minority of them continues to hope their children will one day live closer. In truth, most parents want to see their children more often, to live closer, and to maintain more regular communications. Thus patterns of telephoning reflect conscious communication strategies to overcome limitations and conflicts that arise at different stages of the family cycle.

It is significant that each voice of emotional attachment expresses both a positive and a negative side to telephone communications. In general, well-adapted children are satisfied while displaced and alienated children are dissatisfied with telephone communications because of unresolved conflicts and unfulfilled expectations.

Displaced children claim they need to call more to exchange daily news because their parents are getting older and there is not much time left. Some say they want their parents to speak more with the grandchildren. Still others say their parents are lonely and more calls are needed for their sake. They are unhappy about geographic distance but are grateful that the telephone allows them to maintain contact, plan future visits, and hope for ultimate reunification.

Children living the farthest from their parents resemble displaced children in their great frustration with the telephone, though they praise it as essential. An only child, unmarried and in her thirties, describes her difficulties and satisfactions with telephone calls to her parents in England:

> They resisted having a telephone ever since I can remember. I really scraped the bottom of the emotional barrel and I said, "Your only child is thousands of miles away. Don't you want to be much closer? Suppose I need you?" He said, "Send a telegram."
>
> But this Christmas when I went to visit them I surprisingly arranged to have a telephone installed. I didn't have the courage to tell them until the evening before I was leaving. My father said, "Terrific idea. We should have done it before." So now we do phone.
>
> It's just knowing I have access to them in a way I didn't. It's a toy that's so new. Now that they have the telephone we're able to exchange snippets of news, nonessential but those things that make up life. I feel another kind of bonding is taking place. They volunteer weather information, health, and about their garden. They're likely to volunteer good news, not health deteriorations.
>
> At this point I initiate the phone calls, probably two or three times a month, depending. When my mother was having knee surgery it would be at least once a week because I wanted to know what was going on. At first she was in the hospital. Then she came back

and was disoriented and exhausted for a while because of the anesthesia. Those phone calls were horrible. I felt estranged. There's been a marked change in the last four weeks where I finally feel she's talking to me.

They have called once or twice. But they're very frustrated if I'm not at home. And my schedule is so much more erratic. I like it when they phone me. But I'd have to have a very regular schedule because it's a six-hour difference. Cost is important. I've decided it's worth it because I've been starved of the opportunity. My father said he wants to share the cost. So far we have not had any miscommunication on the phone. It helps my feelings of affection.

Telephone conversations reflect the problems of great geographical distance for a son whose father lives in Puerto Rico. He feels emotional emptiness in his inability to communicate more meaningfully:

He doesn't like telephones because they interrupt him. We exchange very little on the phone. We're talking about one or two calls a year from Puerto Rico through his neighbor's phone. But it's so frustrating during the year to speak so rarely to him. He doesn't see my point of view.

I'm generally satisfied when I call him. I like just the human exchange, the contact with him. The frustration is the silence of not knowing what he's caring and feeling, that I'm losing out on our relationship. It's the loneliness.

But I also accept that's the way he is. I view it as a kind of eccentricity that's sort of sad. When I write to Puerto Rico I can just say things, but I really have to have something important to say when I call there; our conversation is very businesslike. A little chatty, then he's like "time's up." It might be a generational thing. I remember from when I was a kid we never used the telephone much.

In general, well-adapted children are satisfied with telephone calls because they include the expression of affection and family solidarity, as a daughter explains: "I'm satisfied because we remain in contact, involved in each other's lives. It's almost as though we'd see each other . . . well I'm sure we'd see each other more if we lived in the same city. Calling reinforces my feelings of affection."

At the same time, well-adapted children may worry about their parents' health and sometimes feel frustrated and powerless. A son becomes frustrated when his father procrastinates about seeing the doctor. A daughter explains:

> I used to not be satisfied because of me. Now it really depends on her. If she's disoriented I really get worried. I don't get frustrated anymore in the sense of why didn't she remember this; I just told her five minutes ago. She's seventy-five and has all these things wrong with her.

In contrast, alienated children are generally not satisfied with telephone calls; such contacts reflect yet another facet of unsatisfying relationships. One daughter in her late fifties sadly describes her feelings of emotional distance and low expectations:

> Either I'll call or she will. I just call to talk, without a clear message. I feel no frustrations. Our conversations are superficial in the topics we talk about. It's always been that way and will continue that way. We are not insensitive because we don't talk about anything sensitive. My mother is not a good listener and not sincere in responding.

An alienated son in his late forties is frustrated by the limits of conversations with his mother:

> I'm not generally satisfied when I hang up. That's a long-standing problem. The kinds of things that I like to talk about are not generally talked about in my family. It's not that they don't like to. It's just that they don't think to do it. I get frustrated because there's a real limit to what you can talk about. We run out of topics and then we stop.

On the other hand, some alienated children are satisfied that they live far away from their parents because they are free to choose when they call, as a daughter notes: "I'm occasionally frustrated but mainly satisfied. I get along better at a distance. It worked out better that they're farther away. I can pick the times I want to interact. I think my mother probably would want to call me more."

Adult children and distant parents communicate mainly by telephone. For many years long-distance calls have been serving to reinforce bonds of affection and family solidarity. Yet telephone communications are often distorted by a number of inherent technical limitations, including the absence of visual and nonverbal communications, generational differences in telephone use, and varying modes of intensity in intimate family relationships. Most children speak with distant parents about a wide range of subjects, and most claim their conversations include important information exchange as well as emotional satisfaction in the ritual contact itself. As distant parents confront the normal life-cycle transitions of old age, telephone communications increasingly focus on questions of assistance and support.

The frequency of calls is less important than its emotional meaning and explains little about the quality of the distant relationship. The question of who initiates calls and how often varies greatly within a framework of generalized reciprocity over the family cycle. Several factors influence frequency, including distance, parents' age, children's and parents' marital status, health, and expense.

All children and distant parents experience problems and miscommunications on the telephone, especially unrealistic expectations, domination and patronization, withholding of information, criticism, and questions of self-esteem. Yet children's interpretations of such problems with regard to their relationships reflect their satisfaction with telephone contacts as well as their voices of emotional attachment. With some qualification, well-adapted children appreciate the phone for enabling them to maintain strong bonds of affection over great distances. Displaced children remain frustrated by the lack of face-to-face contact yet acknowledge that the telephone is far better than letters or no contact. Alienated children generally remain dissatisfied with the telephone because of more fundamental problems in their relationships with distant parents. Their only satisfaction comes in the knowledge that they live far away and can choose when to call.

CHAPTER 6

*F*ace-to-Face Encounters in Routine Visits

Distant children and parents engage in two kinds of visits: routine visits during vacations and holidays, which comprise three quarters of all visits described; and transition visits, which take place during health and social-status changes of family members, when most assistance takes place. In this chapter we will focus on the frequency, length, and substance of routine visits, also described as rituals of renewal in five stages. We will see that the three voices of emotional attachment influence the degree of satisfaction with routine visits.

Shanas (1979) found that 84 percent of elderly parents had seen at least one of their children within the last week. Often visits by near-living children and parents involve no more than brief conversations, "catching up on the time of day." Visiting very old parents may be a kind of monitoring, to see that all is well, but often includes face-to-face services such as shopping, domestic help, recreation, or religious activities.

Visits of distant children and parents, however, differ in at least three ways. First, because distance requires travel and staying for a while, such visits necessitate planning ahead and making arrangements. Second, since most routine distant visits take place during vacations, they are not spontaneous, "just dropped-by" events. Finally, routine distant visits last longer than visits of near-living children; most last two or three days and many last several weeks.

Here we will address several little-known aspects about the meaning of visits in distant relationships. For example, how are children's and parents' visits alike and how do they differ? To what extent do distant routine visits reflect current needs and circumstances instead of past patterns of emotional attachment? When conflicts and ambivalent emotions emerge during visits, how do parents and children handle them? How do patterned family activities during routine visits change through the distant-family development cycle? Are most children and distant parents satisfied with their visiting arrangements? Finally, to what extent do routine visits provide an opportunity to help family members in need?

Because most children work, children (68 percent) more than parents (15 percent) will visit during their vacations and holidays, especially at Thanksgiving and Christmastime. Some parents and children alternate holiday visits. Most parents are not working so their visiting schedules are more flexible.

When parents are widowed, holidays are increasingly celebrated either at the distant child's or a sibling's home. The location of holiday visits is negotiable in many families and varies with circumstances and the family cycle, as a divorced son suggests:

> We have a fairly good tradition that Mother would come here for Thanksgiving. She helps me cook the dinner. My brother's wife's mother comes too. My mother and I might go to my brother's for Christmas. She doesn't host big dinners anymore like she used to.

A married daughter enjoys hosting Thanksgiving for her parents and her husband's parents, then likes to return to her mother's for Christmas:

> I've been big in pushing my parents to come here for Thanksgiving. Mark planned to go to his parents in Farmington. But I said I want to invite them to our house for Thanksgiving so we'll just combine the whole shebang. It was tons of fun. We had about twenty-five people because it was my whole stepfamily and their spouses.

We will definitely go to my mom's house for Christmas. That seems to work fine for everybody and she depends on us coming. I tried for many years to put less emphasis on the ritual of serving these meals but she's just consumed by it. You can't stop her, so I help.

THE FREQUENCY OF ROUTINE VISITS

The frequency of visits is governed mainly by the children's desire and feelings of responsibility. Most children visit distant parents far more often than parents visit them. The typical child visited twice in the last year. The range was one visit in three years to twelve visits in one year. A third of the children visited once a year, while another third visited three times a year or more. Only 10 percent had not visited in more than a year, either because they lived very far away or were alienated emotionally.

In contrast, the typical parent visited far less often, slightly less than once a year. The range was no visits over ten years to three visits in one year. A third visited once in the last year, another third visited once over two years, and a quarter didn't visit at all over two years.

Several factors influence the frequency of routine visits, including time since the last visit, distance, parents' health status, responsibilities to other family members, work and retirement, and children's age and marital status. Children who had not seen their parents in more than six months were more likely to say they are not satisfied with the frequency of visits and experience positive emotions anticipating visits. As an adaptation to the high cost of travel, many very distant families have infrequent but longer visits rather than frequent, brief, but regular visits.

The disadvantages of distant visiting are many. There is an intensity when in close quarters with those who may not enjoy the same activities and events. Conflicts are difficult to resolve. Moreover, one party is not in his or her home environment and may feel out of place and uncomfortable. Yet many children who live very far away feel delight in being able to visit at all. Given the potential for conflict, it is surprising when a six-week-long visit from a mother in England, for example, goes so well. After the visit, a certain exhaustion sets in along with the profound sadness of know-ing that almost an entire year will pass before the next visit.

Several children who live farther away now than before visit less frequently, whereas those who live closer now than before visit more frequently, as a son reports:

> I live closer now than when I was in Pennsylvania. It's four hours now, it used to be close to ten. I still go home on all the same holi-days. But now I can throw in a couple of extra visits; this year I went home during the summer and spring, for my brother's ordination, and in October for a baptism, then for Christmas. That's five times this year. If they aren't for special occasions, I would just take a weekend and go in.

Illnesses can inhibit or encourage visiting. Usually, parents do not visit when they are ill and parents in institutions never visit. As driving becomes more difficult for parents, the frequency of their visits also decreases, as a daughter explains:

> They drive in at least once a year. But I think this is going to diminish now. My mother made a comment that she didn't think my dad ought to be driving these distances any more. She drives part way, maybe a hundred miles of it, a certain stretch through Illinois.

On the other hand, distant parents often expect children to visit them when they become sick in the hospital or at home. Many children visit ailing parents frequently. One son at first stopped vis-iting as often as he had when he had lived closer. But when his parents became frail he consciously began to visit more often:

> I visit them more now than before, like I go back at Thanksgiv-ing, Christmas, and in the summer. When I first moved up here it dropped from more frequent visits to once a year. But in the last five years it's been twice a year. I'm coming more to the realization that they're not going to be living for all that many more years, so if I am going to visit, I should do it now.

Another son whose father's health is failing rapidly expresses a growing need to visit more often:

The decision to go to Florida was their decision. They have always believed they would not want to live with their kids. I hadn't thought it necessary until recently. Now it seems every time I see my father I'm not sure I'll see him again. And it's partly also that they both need the emotional lift and distraction that visits from family give them. So I expect to visit them more frequently now.

Responsibilities to other family members also encourage or limit the frequency of visits. A well-adapted daughter explains that her mother and stepfather moved away from Michigan but visit frequently because all her siblings and stepsiblings remain in Michigan:

This is really a case of my parents picking up and moving away eighteen years ago. We didn't go anywhere. I think they come to Michigan more than we go to Connecticut. Of course, they have five kids here. And then there's my two stepbrothers, Ed and Bill. So everybody's in Michigan. Each time they come they can see five people. My stepfather's mother also lived outside Detroit.

In a remarkable family situation, a well-adapted daughter explains that after her widowed mother remarried, her younger sister fell in love with and married her stepbrother. At first both parents tried to discourage them with the insightful warning: "We're afraid because if you hurt each other you will not be able to leave each other." Nevertheless, her sister and stepbrother visit her parents very frequently because they have both parents (and parents-in-law) to visit.

Another well-adapted daughter reports that her parents are primary caregivers to her maternal grandfather who lives with them. They generally do not travel because they can only get away on rare occasions when someone comes to stay with him. Another daughter in her late forties reports that since her children are grown, she and her husband are now free to visit their parents more often:

Now that we don't have children's schedules to work around we can visit more often for shorter times. The problem wasn't leaving the children or taking them. They were involved in a lot of important activities and the problem was missing their activities. We've

146

missed some of the aunts' and uncles' funerals and I missed a couple of my nieces' and nephews' weddings. I look forward to seeing them more now. We can take off on a Friday night after work and drive as far as Illinois, then stay overnight there, go on the next day, and come back on Sunday or Monday. We'll initiate more contacts now, absolutely, especially now with my husband's father ill.

Like family obligations, work obligations also limit children's ability to visit frequently. Some children fly rather than drive because of the time pressures of their work. At the same time, retirement does not necessarily permit parents the expected leisure time to visit their children more often, as a daughter explains:

> I think they need to get straight that they should visit more. My stepfather retired, but now he took on another job that is turning out to be just as monumental a commitment, and we're like lost in the shuffle. They were supposed to have more time because of the retirement, but now it turns out there are all kinds of other commitments.

Whether children are married and have children also influences the frequency of visits. Children did not mention this factor in interviews, but it emerges from the data in conjunction with gender and the absence of grandchildren. Elderly parents rarely visit sons and daughters who are unmarried and living alone. Only one mother visited her never-married daughter one time. The remaining parents never visited five distant children who were unmarried or married without children. Visiting grandchildren is an important albeit unconscious motivation for parental visits to distant children.

Unmarried and childless adult children respond to parental visiting neglect in different ways. Well-adapted children generally accept the situation and compensate by visiting their parents more often. An unmarried son in his middle forties explains that his mother stopped visiting after his father's death. Then, he adds without complaint, it has turned out to be more convenient for him to travel there. Consistent with this theme, the daughter who visits the most, twelve times in one year, is divorced, without children, living alone, and her parents have never visited her. This displaced daughter had lived and worked close to her parents for many years. She explains how her pattern of frequent visits evolved:

> When I first got this job and came out here, my husband stayed in New York. So at that point I went back once a month and stayed with him and I also stayed whole summers and all Christmas vacation. It was a commuter marriage. But my husband being my husband, even when I went back to stay with him I spent most of my time with my parents and friends. So when we got divorced I didn't see any reason not to, and I think my parents would have been very hurt if I'd stopped.

Not everyone willingly accepts visit neglect from their parents. One alienated daughter, married, without children, complains that her mother visits her brother and his family more often. She appears to rebel, fighting for some principle of reciprocity in visits:

> Mom is going to drive up with Jill, my sister-in-law, because we all got dragged down to my niece's wedding in South Carolina. And I had said that I would never visit them again unless one of them came up here. I was sick and tired of being dragged every place they've ever lived and nobody ever coming to visit me. I said, "I'll never see you again until Mother's funeral because I've had it." So Jill, being a good trooper, said she and Mom will drive up and visit us.

Another unmarried son complains that his parents don't visit enough:

> I'd like them to visit me more often too. That would indicate to me that they view me as an adult. It's not really a point of contention. But it's just upsetting sometimes because I know they traveled to go see my other brothers whenever they lived elsewhere. I always felt that I was always the student and always the baby of the family. They've gone to Texas a number of times. My other brother used to live in Kentucky and they went there. The first time they ever went to visit me anywhere was when I was here in Lansing. They never came to visit me in Philadelphia when I was in graduate school, and no matter how often I invited them to stop and see the campus and meet my teachers they never did. That bothered me.

An unmarried displaced son balances his unhappiness that his parents don't visit with his feeling that he probably will eventually relocate to be closer to them:

> I'm sure my mother would love to see me more but that's the way mothers are. They keep saying they're going to come here to see me. Although their idea of coming here is to fly to Chicago and I have to go there for a weekend. Lansing wasn't high on their list of places they had to visit again except for seeing me. I would rather be in the Southwest anyway just because my research is down there and that's where I'm from.

THE LENGTH OF VISITS

Several factors influence the length of routine visits. First, length varies according to expectation and circumstance. Some families expect and have long visits. In other families length may be problematical because children and parents perceive the visit differently. The average child's visit lasts four days but ranges from one day to six weeks. Two thirds stay for five days or less, one third stay between one and two weeks. Children also stay longer when they or their parents are ill, except when parents are institutionalized, in which case they usually stay no more than a day.

Second, as distance between the generations increases, the frequency of visits decreases but visits last longer. Children and parents travel by plane rather than car. Those living farthest away often stay the longest because of the cost and the difficulty of traveling frequently. A daughter explains why she now visits less frequently and for a shorter time:

> When you live very far away, staying longer when you visit makes it more stressful. I used to go home every summer for at least six weeks. Now I stay more like three weeks. I probably won't go next Christmas either. Last time my father really lost his temper and exploded. He emphasized he wants me to come in the summer. He just doesn't want Christmas.

Finally, children stay longer when the visit takes place in a family vacation home. In three cases sons stayed from two to five weeks with their widowed mothers in such family cottages or homes.

The typical parent visits for five days. Visits ranged from two months by a retired father visiting from abroad to four hours from parents who met their alienated daughter while they were driving through the city. About half the parents stayed four days or less, the other half five days or more.

Many children and their parents perceive the length of the visit as part of the planning process, which involves the schedules of both generations. Many children juggle their work routines to make free time. One daughter notes that her visits are shorter since she started working. Length can become problematical when it is not negotiated and agreed upon in advance. A son complains that his father simply informs him when he is coming or going with no sensitivity toward his feelings or schedule. A married daughter without children explains that her lifestyle demands short visits:

> What I know is that I want to spend time visiting with her because we love each other and we need to see each other. I find that a two- or three-day visit is just about right. If we spend too much time together we get on each other's nerves. She's starting to stay longer because it's getting harder for her to travel. We never tell her she's staying too long. But I think she understands that she would drive me crazy if she stayed too long.
>
> The life-style gap between me and my mother is a major issue. Arnold and I live by ourselves, and when you are used to living by yourself and you suddenly find more people in the house it is disruptive. We're just very stodgy and set in our ways. If we get upset we're really very traumatized.

Some children can deal only with short visits. If they or their parents visit too often or stay too long the potential for conflict increases. An alienated son believes visits should be short to avoid conflict:

> First, there haven't been many visits, but a good visit is invariably a short one in which there are a lot of activities that take up time. One doesn't know what one's going to get into in conversation. On the third day, if we haven't yet found at least one issue in which we don't see eye to eye, we probably will then.

THE FIVE STAGES OF ROUTINE AND HOLIDAY VISITS

Children and distant parents regard visits as rituals of renewal that reestablish their affectional bonds. A routine distant visit consists of five distinct phases: (1) preparation and planning; (2) travel and greetings; (3) adjustment; (4) settling in; and (5) separation and departure.

Preparation and Planning

Long-distance visits require preparation, planning, and organization. Telephone calls increase shortly before a visit as parents and children prepare themselves psychologically, make arrangements for the reunion, plan important events, and discuss real and potential obstacles and the logistics of travel. Many visits are initiated on the telephone, as a daughter illustrates:

> She called and said, "What are you doing for Thanksgiving," and I said, "Oh, we'll probably go to Mark's family." And she said, "Well we don't have any plans." I said "Oh," and I didn't think anything and then finally about two minutes later I went "Bing" and I said "Oh, do you . . . would you like to come here for Thanksgiving?" And she said, "Yeah, we would." So she called back about a week later and said, "I think I'll take you up on that. We would like to come."

During the period of preparation and planning, adult children experience a wide range of feelings and emotions corresponding to their voices of emotional attachment. Half say they feel positive emotions, such as pleasant excitement about looking forward to seeing their parents. A third report mixed emotions, ambivalence, or an uncomfortable sense of responsibility in combination with other more positive feelings. The remaining 15 percent report negative emotions, such as anxiety, nervousness, or conflict, when anticipating a visit.

Displaced children experience great happiness in anticipation of a visit, as a daughter describes:

> I feel delight and eager anticipation of visits. There's always a flurry of activities, phone calls, and present exchanges just before a

visit. We talk about who's bringing what before we leave. My family is big on plants. I also feel some frustration though because there isn't enough time in the visit to do more things together.

A well-adapted daughter feels good anticipating a visit but at the same time notes that visits home are impersonal because her family is so large. Well-adapted and displaced children express positive feelings when anticipating visits; the planning process is enjoyable in itself. They enjoy their parents' company, report that they can talk openly and share common activities and interests. They also emphasize good relationships with in-laws, feel glad their parents are healthy and can come and go independently, and feel their parents approve of them, their spouses, their children, and their life-styles. A well-adapted son symbolically reflects on his positive experience anticipating a visit: "I'm driving there with my family. I start humming. Ellen tells me I'm humming. I didn't even notice it. Will the visit go well? I don't know. I'm just happy to be going home."

Planning visits can be stressful, however, when children and their parents' life-styles differ and when they are interested in different things. About half the children experience some stress, nervousness, or anxiety deciding activities and events during the visit. Alienated children feel sad or guilty because they would like to visit their parents more often or because they are visiting out of duty rather than desire. One alienated son warns his mother in advance not to make a schedule for him and his family. Some children say it is harder to decide what to do after they arrive, so it is important to plan ahead. Several daughters clean house before their parents or in-laws visit so their housekeeping doesn't get criticized. The key to the successful visit is often in its planning. As one well-adapted daughter says: "We're glad to go there and glad to come home before we get on each other's nerves. If we're busy, we can make it for two weeks. But if we're around all the time, in three days we've had it."

Alienated children express anxiety when anticipating visits. A common theme is that their mothers treat them like children. "After a certain length of time," says one woman, "we revert to a relationship we had before I became an adult." Parents can be critical of their children, in-laws, and grandchildren. Or they can be controlling. Alienated sons and daughters fear that their parents will try to tell them how to do things. In some cases mothers try to feed and watch over their daughters. The result is intense anxiety, as an alienated daughter says:

> I feel anxiety. It's an opportunity to expose them to something that they might enjoy, as well as the fact that I might fail. It's mixed feelings. Following a visit, there's a question: "Will I do this again?" "Not for a long time." In other words, I've had a dose of a lot of negative stuff too.

Few children express only negative emotions. But unresolved issues generate stress. An alienated daughter feels she sees her mother too often and anticipates visits with a great deal of anxiety:

> Just before a visit I feel excitement but in my heart I know I'm going to be disappointed and angry. The pattern is always the same. On arriving at my mother's condo in Florida she greets me warmly, then apologizes for the cramped space in the condo. She begins by saying how great I look, then rapidly turns to the subject of how much weight I need to lose. I feel I am being reduced to an object, not a person. I'm intellectually aware but I'm never emotionally prepared.

Infrequent visits from those living far away may rekindle conflicts between parents and other members of their nuclear family. Some children feel stress about conflicts between their parents and their spouse. Several sons expressed anxiety when their mothers criticize their wives. A few daughters are hurt when their parents have conflicts with the grandchildren or criticize them as parents. One son expressed his fear that his children won't be respectful toward their grandparents.

A crucial by-product of most planned visits is that they lack spontaneity. This tends to encourage some formality and ritualized "guest-host" patterns that often detract from satisfaction in the relationship. This is not to suggest that spontaneity is always desirable. Indeed, spontaneity may itself become problematical, as reflected in the story a son told of a ninety-year-old man who had a heart attack following his poorly conceived surprise birthday party. On the other hand, the lack of spontaneity in parent-child relationships may encourage ritualized contacts, rigidity, and insincere communication that comes from of a sense of duty rather than from the heart. The relationship may lose the spice and currency of affection that everyone seems to crave. A well-adapted daughter recalls a spontaneous visit when her husband's business trip was suddenly canceled:

> We had planned to go to New York but now that was out so I said, "Why don't we fly to Jersey and visit my mother?" She wasn't expecting us, but when I called and said we were coming she practically fell off her chair. And I'm telling you it was without question the best visit we ever had.

This daughter remembers that her mother treated her like her long-lost best friend and never once mentioned her weight or criticized the children. Certainly, in many cases spontaneity may improve the quality of visits.

Travel and Greeting

Most adult children travel long distances willingly and without complaint about the journey, though traveling is especially difficult for those who live the greatest distances. Adult children with very young children sometimes report difficult and taxing journeys. Finding time to leave work and saving money to travel are common problems. Most children (63 percent) and parents (53 percent) travel by plane, the remainder by car. Some children make travel arrangements for their parents and some parents meet their children at the airport.

A displaced daughter who visited her parents twenty-four times over a two-year period describes her rigorous travel routine with much pleasure:

> Normally, I go home to New York to visit my parents at least once a month. I'm very lucky. I'm beginning to see my friends go through real trauma with their parents. Aside from the distance my situation couldn't be better.
>
> I teach till Thursday afternoon. I leave class at 2:40 P.M., then

drive to the Detroit airport, where I fly to New York. My parents pick me up at LaGuardia. Thursday night I'm pooped, but I've got two full days to visit, Friday and Saturday. Then Sunday after they drive me back to LaGuardia I go home. I'm ready to teach Monday. It's a satisfying routine.

I also go in for a weekend in June. Then I drive in for a couple of weeks in August. I bring back a year's worth of stuff that's too heavy to carry on the plane; canned goods from my mother's garden. I see the city in November. But in the spring and summer I'm with them in the country.

In contrast, an alienated son recalls his holiday visiting pattern to his divorced parents in two distant locations:

At eighteen, I was already dividing up holidays between my real mother and my real father, who live very far apart. When you have to divide up the holiday, that's one level of problem. But it's very frustrating when there's so much distance between them and you spend time traveling.

Before I was married and before my father died, both my parents wanted me. I would find myself driving Christmas afternoon for five hundred miles. Even if I tried to alternate the holidays, it wasn't good. So the best thing to do was to see them both. Usually I would come the week before to see my mother in New Jersey. Then late Christmas morning I'd jump in the car and drive to North Carolina to see my dad. I'd be there by late evening. Then I'd spend four or five days with him. I guess I paid a big price. But at that time it never bothered me and I didn't feel I let them down in any way.

Children often express concern over their parents' difficulties traveling. Cancelations of planes due to bad weather, unforeseen delays, sudden illness, and even accidents along the way cause anxiety. In addition, the journey itself may be arduous, especially for older parents. On arriving, parents may be tired and need time to recover, as a well-adapted daughter explains:

My mother gets really excited about traveling and so you always know that if she comes in on Wednesday she'll have a headache on Thursday. For Christmas, my mother's getting in on Thursday and we don't plan to do anything on Friday because she'll have a headache. Then Saturday we'll do something. It's the stress. I find it irritating. It's so predictable.

Greetings are filled with expressions of affection, delight, and happiness. Children experience positive emotions when they see, hug, and kiss their parents. In the first minutes, parents and children exchange impressions of how they look, about their health, the grandchildren, and any events that occurred along the way.

Half the children and their parents made arrangements in the last two years to visit at some location other than where either of them lives. Many visits take place in summer homes during family vacations together. A son explains that his father stays in his summer cabin when he comes for extended summer visits from Puerto Rico. A well-adapted son spends the summer with his mother and hosts many extended-family relatives in the family summer cottage:

> When my dad died I inherited the family cottage. I'll spend a couple of nights in my mother's house, then drive her shopping and on errands. Then she comes and stays at the cottage, which is nice for her to get out. There is an extended family gathering at the cottage every weekend. When I was younger we used to have about fifteen people overnight every weekend. As young children we slept on the floor with big heavy quilts. I have fond memories of that kind of relationship with my brothers and cousins.

One divorced son recalls traveling with his widowed mother to pick up his daughter from college for vacation. A married daughter without children describes the evolution of her annual international travels with her mother:

> My parents had always traveled. It took me forever to finish graduate school. They were always saying as soon as you get it finished we'll do something together. As luck would have it my father died first. So she and I started traveling every year internationally. We've gone to all these places, to Italy three times. I've only been married six years. My husband stays home. It's my vacation with my mother, my tie.

A large majority of children (75 percent) and parents (88 percent) visit in each other's homes. A few stay in motels or hotels, however, depending on the availability of space and the reason for the visit. On special occasions such as a wedding or anniversary, lodging is more variable. Sometimes younger, unmarried children feel uncomfortable because their apartments are too small. An alienated daughter believes visits will be more reciprocal now that she bought a house:

> It is starting to be more even. I visit them, they visit me now that I have a house. Before that it was kind of a problem when they came to visit. They could stay in a hotel, but it wasn't very pleasant. Now they can stay and relax.

Married couples with both sets of parents in the same location often feel pressured because they must coordinate their efforts to ensure that parents on both sides are visited equally, as a daughter explains:

> The time is split equally no matter how many people we see. My husband's mother died the first year we were married. So we spent equal time with his dad when we were there because he's alone. It's very difficult to change those patterns after they're established. He's not a joiner or a participant. Now he's eighty-two and ill with terminal cancer. He's still active. But it's a matter of time now.

A displaced daughter outlines the advantages and disadvantages of having parents and in-laws living close,

> My husband's parents live about six blocks away from my parents. When we visit I usually stay with my parents and my husband stays with his parents. This arrangement other people find strange. But we find it works very well because we mostly want to visit with our own parents even though we see each other's parents too.
> Our parents are also very good friends, which has been both an advantage and a disadvantage. It's an advantage because they keep track of each other. In the event somebody got sick or had an accident and couldn't get a hold of my brother, they would probably call my husband's parents. And we would find out very fast too. It also has an advantage that we see both sets of parents on one trip. And our older daughter moves back and forth; she thinks it's great to stay

one night in one house and the next night at the other. The younger daughter usually stays with me because she's still in the crib. But I suspect she'll want to move back and forth like her older sister.

We also try to get out to dinner by ourselves when we're there. And when we went in for that wedding, my husband's parents were invited, mine weren't, so my parents could babysit and that was extremely convenient. It's inconvenient in the sense that they tend to talk with one another and worry about things when they get together."

As parents age and find it more difficult to host visits, children stay with near-living siblings, as a daughter says: "My brother is married and has a family in Minneapolis, about four hours' drive from my mother. Mom and her sister took a bus just a week ago to see them for Thanksgiving. That's where I go now too. I don't go anymore to her home." The same pattern occurs when parents move into retirement communities. Although many communities have accommodations for visitors, children generally do not enjoy staying there with distant parents. Several take their parents to a sibling's home.

Adjustment

The first day or two is a period of adjustment. Discussions focus on living routines; when, where, and what to eat; sleeping, bathing. The visitor unpacks. Children and parents visit, tell news events, talk about themselves and other family members, and perhaps exchange gifts. They provide information about health and the status of planned events.

Conflicts make their first appearance. An alienated daughter complains when her mother criticizes her weight. A well-adapted daughter whose mother was widowed two years ago experiences a sudden emptiness in her stomach, which she recognizes as a longing for her deceased father. Far away in her own home, she could accept her father's death without feeling so much pain. On an unconscious, irrational level she had been telling herself that her father still lived with her mother, far away. Now, sitting in her mother's apartment, she suddenly feels a deep anxiety, the reality of his death.

Adjustment also involves joint activities that renew the old bonds.

A well-adapted daughter claims that she and her mother always re-connect through a ritual they both love—shopping:

> We go shopping, my mom and I. I love to shop. Yes, that's our thing together, the best. I think it's how we connect back to each other when we haven't seen each other for a while. Well, when you only see somebody two, three times a year, there's a lot of distance. You need a gentle way of getting back in touch with one another.
>
> Oh, she still buys . . . yes, and my little girl whispered to me the other day in the car, "Mom, Grandma still treats you like a little girl." And I said, "I love it. You know, Janet, it'll be the same with you. You'll probably always be my little girl. You know, there are some special things in life."
>
> My mom will buy me all kinds of things: "Oh honey, this looks cute on you. Let me get that for you." She's generous, and very nurturant in the context of shopping. That really provides an opportunity for us to get together and renew our relationship.

Activity-level and life-style differences create frustrations early in a visit. About a quarter of the children complain that their parents' daily routines are out of sync with their own, especially when their parents are not active enough for them or their families, as a son reports:

> They're not as energetic. They've slowed down and they seem to sleep more when I'm visiting, but I think that's just their physiology. It's not a problem. Both of them used to work and a great deal of their life was revolving around their job, which of course they now don't have. I also sense that they may be slightly more lonely, which was certainly not the case when I was growing up.

A daughter says:

> I've stopped asking if we can take little day trips and do things. Now I wait for them to suggest them because I've felt that was putting some kind of pressure on them. They're not that active. They have had a really nice garden. It's getting out of control now.

And another daughter says:

> I'm often frustrated by my mother's lack of independence when she's here alone. She is not accustomed to suburban life. We need a

car where we live and she can't just hop a bus the way she does at home. She's bound to the house too much. It's a forced dependency that I find frustrating.

Speaking about her visits to her widowed mother, another daughter suggests:

> Maybe my visits are too long. There are only so many days I can just visit and sit around. I'd like to be more active and she'd like me to stay longer. My mother's activities with her friends aren't what I like to do—cards, going to the theater on the premises of the retirement center.

A few children, however, complain that their parents are too active for them. One daughter says: "My mother likes to do everything herself. That's part of the conflict. Also, they pack too much in. They're always on the go, and don't allow any quiet time. I find it tiring. No time for contemplation. They never sit down and read a paper." Another daughter in her early thirties says:

> They're very demanding and they're hyper. They require a lot of attention, and so they're draining, exhausting, to be around. When they were here for a week, about halfway through the visit Brian sent them out. Go, go take a walk. He sent them away. He said they were exhausting us so much. Because we just needed some time.

A recently married son presents a mixed review of his mother's high energy level:

> My mother is very independent, high-strung, the archetype liberated woman. One has to be able to keep up with her. My wife finds it very difficult; she is much more relaxed. When they went to the mall she had so much to do and insisted that my wife meet her at such and such a place at exactly that time. It was very stressful.

One of the most frustrating experiences during visits comes when activity-level conflicts arise between grandparents and grandchildren. Many adult children are caught in the middle when their parents' and their children's routines collide. Grandparents frequently get impatient with the demands of young grandchildren whose routines are disrupted by visits. At the same time, even older children may be bored when their parents and grandparents have not planned for their specific requirements on visits. An adult son finds it irritating when his mother becomes impatient with his young daughter or criticizes him as a parent. A daughter who is sensitive to conflicts in daily routines comments: "I wish we had more structured activities when we visit my mother. She gets going late in the day and she runs late into the evening. It's very difficult with a young child whose routine is almost the exact opposite."

Some children are clearly put off by the influence of their parents' routines on their own children. A son complains that his parents are TV addicts, which sets a bad example for the kids. Activity-level conflicts between in-laws may also arise, as a daughter reports: "Getting my parents up and out is most frustrating. My mother is late and slow. My husband is punctual and fast. The most frustrating thing for me is avoiding conflict between my mother and my husband."

Life-style conflicts may arise from generational differences in values and interests. The theme of a lack of shared interests emerges again and again. Several children become frustrated when their parents are unable to acknowledge or accept their life-styles or do not show enough interest in their work. A son wishes his parents understood academia more. Another son becomes frustrated because his widowed mother criticizes him when he can't visit for the holidays. A daughter says:

> I like to do needlework and she would like me to paint. So she doesn't appreciate the needlework. It's important to me and I resent that she doesn't appreciate that I do it well. If it's not important to them, they're not interested. We're on different wavelengths and they can't accept that we're different.

Many children become frustrated when their parents criticize their work. Daughters in particular are concerned when their mothers respond negatively to their jobs. One daughter says:

My mom's not happy about my job. I get friction because she doesn't think I spend enough time with my family. I get frustrated when she gives me mixed messages about my job. She'll say, "It's great you have a career. Shouldn't you be at home more?"

Some children criticize their parents' life-styles. A son is critical of the retirement community where his parents live, saying it encourages dependencies. Other generational conflicts are related to socioeconomic differences. When parents are better off financially, adult children complain: "My father won't let me pay the bill when we go to a restaurant." Other children are critical of their parents who are too tight with their money. A son claims his parents maintain a "depression mentality," suggesting they are preoccupied with costs even when they can afford things. An alienated daughter expresses anger at having to search for "twilight specials" in second-rate restaurants when visiting her mother. But some parents consume beyond the means of their children, as one son reports:

We get tense because my mother gets judgmental and loses her tact under stress. Joan and I are frugal and not spendthrift. My mother says to buy things for the children and I'll say Joan and I don't want it or need it. It makes us feel anxious and angry.

Life-style differences may also be related to education and social competence. One daughter clearly relaxes more when she visits her mother than when her mother visits her:

When I'm in Columbus I can spend more time with her, take her shopping and places. But she doesn't feel comfortable with my friends. If we have people over to dinner she just sits and listens to all of us talk; she never enters an intellectual conversation. I can still talk to her about my feelings. But I don't expect her to understand my sensitivities or needs. We're just very different people.

Because we don't have children and we live by ourselves, we have a very structured life-style, everything is always in its place. My mother feels she would mess up if she didn't do things our way. And she's justified because in certain ways she's not very competent. For example, she was home by herself and I had forgotten to take a carton of tomato sauce out of the freezer to defrost for spaghetti for supper. So I called her from work and said, "Why don't you take the tomato sauce out of the freezer and if you put it in the oven it will start to defrost." Well I came home to the back door and there was a carton on the back porch, smoldering. My mother had put the carton in the oven and turned the oven on and it had caught on fire. So now we just assume she should sit in the living room, let us make the dinner, and we'll call her when it's ready.

Some children complain when their parents ask them to spend time with extended family. They feel that rushing around to see everyone detracts from their chance to see the city or visit with their own friends. One daughter says simply, "I don't like spending time visiting people I don't want to see." Others feel grateful when their parents agree to babysit so they can go out with their spouses. As one daughter explains:

For many years now we've visited both families together. We stay with one set of parents for three nights, then the other for the next three nights. In Chicago, we spend most of the visit running back and forth, seeing both sides of the family and making sure the children get to play with all their cousins. I'm always on the phone trying to call my mother's brother's wife or my father's sister so they won't be hurt that we were in town and didn't see them. Chicago is a really great place to visit. But we never get to see the city because we're so busy with family obligations.

A number of children are happy that their parents' social networks and communities are intact. Others speak sadly about their parents' loneliness or lack of supports. A daughter in her late forties contrasts her father-in-law's social isolation with the strong social supports her own parents still enjoy:

I see such a contrast between my husband's father and my dad. They're both from poor farm families but so different. One of the great differences is my folks' support system, the church. And my dad has been active in the Kiwanis Club and he has an informal network of friends uptown. My dad's siblings and he get together when somebody has a birthday.

163

My husband's dad really has no support system. His wife, my husband's mother, died the year we were married. He has no brothers or sisters in the same town. My father-in-law is a cantankerous man, one of those people who can be extraordinarily unpleasant to a waitress. He hasn't been actively employed for many years. He has a place in the country with several acres and he just putters around, but it's in very great disrepair now.

My husband's second cousin cooks and makes her home with him. She has no family. She works as a seamstress in a store. It is very difficult for her to transport him around. He wouldn't say she takes care of him but she does. He had colon cancer two years ago and had major surgery. Now it's in the liver. He has a hard time getting along.

Settling In

The heart of the visit takes place some time around the third day. Both planned and spontaneous interactions characterize the settling-in period. Children report a variety of activities with parents, including talking, recreation, and going out to restaurants (80 percent); shopping and day trips (70 percent); and attending family affairs, engaging in child-oriented activities, attending religious services, and visiting friends and relatives (40 percent). Most children (60 percent) say reestablishing emotional bonds with parents by being together is the most satisfying aspect of a visit. Physical proximity itself helps renew parent-child bonds of love and caring and generates strong feelings of attachment and meaning in family life. Several well-adapted and displaced children comment that they feel loved and wanted. As one daughter explains:

> I just like the joy of being together and feeling like a complete family. I really feel connected and I think she does too. She loves coming here because she loves the laughter and feeling she is around people who care about her. I enjoy it because I know she doesn't feel lonely. For me the most satisfying part of the visit is being with my mother who loves me. She's there for me no matter what and I know it.

Sons also express a sense of personal history which adds to the importance of their relationship, as one says:

I like the idea that ancient child-parent bonds are still active. It's not a tangible thing that happens but a real historical marker in my lifetime; that the lady who gave birth to me is still around and interested in me, that she loves me. It's really nice.

And another son says: "I like to see them. I've know them for forty-five years. I like them. They're generous, warm people. If I'm not happy they make an effort to please me. They try because they care about me."

Many children derive satisfaction when their parents interact with their children. Several have made a deliberate effort to cultivate strong bonds between their parents and their children, commenting that satisfying interactions between grandparents and grandchildren are particularly important because they only get together a few times a year. The grandchild-grandparent bond also reflects their own bonds with their parents. One daughter says proudly that her mother is warm and loving to her children and they respond very affectionately toward her.

Well-adapted and displaced children commonly identify a special activity that gives them satisfaction during visits. A daughter notes:

> When they come my father enjoys fixing up the house, which is wonderful. He paints, fixes drawers and all those things that you keep saying that's not terribly important and it doesn't have to be done right now. My father also enjoys the kids quite a bit. When my brother's children were babies he was still working so he didn't have much time to spend with them. He didn't even change a diaper. But with my kids since he's been retired he's done a lot of that. He's been surprised actually how much work having children is.

Another daughter claims she enjoys visiting her mother alone because she likes going to the beach, taking a ride, or going out to lunch. For some well-adapted children the highlight of a visit comes when their parents admire their accomplishments or successes. One son says he enjoys mealtime because everyone engages in pleasant conversation. Another son enjoys showing his father around the university campus. An alienated son comments on the satisfying visiting relationship he has developed over the years with his stepfather:

> I don't talk with my stepfather very often. But there's a lot of good strong male bonding. When we get together here we go over to the gym and lift weights. He's been consistent in my life for thirty years. He's like a big brother to me. He does not replace my father in any way, shape, or form. And he's very smart, he never tried to replace my father. I've realized that the person in my life who matters to me most, the great love of my life, is my father, as it is for most boys, especially if their father abandons them.

In many cases no special activity highlights the visit. Instead, these children are satisfied when the visit is free of conflict, when they enjoy themselves generally, and when they know their parents are still healthy, independent, adjusting well to old age and in control of their lives.

Separation and Departure

Some time after the third day, children experience a conscious or unconscious awareness that the visit must end soon. Some report an intense desire to go back to their work routines, to seek privacy, or to return to the familiar surroundings of their own homes. Occasionally the host, either child or parent, feels a need to escape from the many responsibilities involved in the visit.

Separation often takes the form of anxiety or nervousness. In familial interactions it takes shape in arguments and conflict between parents and children or between spouses. Both children and parents develop a clear awareness of the other's problems. About half the children report problems interacting with their parents. Both well-adapted and alienated children sometimes feel their mothers cannot deal with them as adults. A typical alienated daughter says:

> I feel a terrific awkwardness interacting when my mother comes to visit. It's as if my mother has never really figured out how to deal with adult children. My mother still worries that I'm not eating properly or that I'll catch a cold if I don't dress warmly enough. It's

almost as if she believes that if she sits long enough I'll become four years old again.

In contrast, a well-adapted daughter believes her feeling of reverting to childhood around her mother is really not her mother's problem but her own:

I feel restricted. It's just reverting back to being a kid. It's probably all in my mind. I just feel somehow that I have to be on my best behavior. As it turns out, when she's there I don't really do anything any differently. I just feel that I don't have the option to do it. When she leaves I feel I can do what I want to do.

An alienated daughter in her late fifties attributes her mother's criticisms to old patterns:

Mother is getting older and forgetful. Being in an institution, when we get together she just talks and talks, mainly about having friends and then they die. She doesn't have younger friends available to her who could counterbalance it. Despite the fact that I'm a grandmother she remains the critical mother. She continues to give me unsolicited advice, telling me what I should do and how I should do it. When she finally found out this last summer that we no longer attend church, her first response was, "Shame on you, that's not what I would do." I said, "Well, Mother, I could have just said yes and lied to you and then you'd have to guess."

A son avoids open conflict with his father but relives disturbing patterns of interaction from the past:

This morning I was going to put up the birdfeeder up at the cabin. And he kept climbing up the ladder. I said let me do it. But the whole time he was pushing me out of the way so that I wouldn't do it, telling me about all the dangerous things involved in it so that I should be careful. And while I was doing it he also notices a nail on the tree that I should be sure to remove because somebody ever sawing it down would get hurt. This is an old pattern; if he wants to take over something he begins to point out the dangers. And I've gone through this my whole life. But I still feel humiliated from my adolescence. I see the pattern but it still affects me.

An alienated son reveals the deep sources of food conflicts with his mother:

My relationship with my mother is very contentious. I'm troubled by food. My family is fat on both sides. On one side, a brother, on another side, a sister, grotesquely fat. Both sides of the family are heavy feeders, gross feeders. Again it's probably cultural. Down South people put on the pork, they don't think anything about that. They're also physically big. Many of my cousins, female, are over six feet tall.

They tend to fight over turf. When we get together with my mother's sister there are fights over who does the cooking. And the food is all heavy and rich. They don't cook well, but they cook a lot. This gets into incredible scenes. Partly as a reaction against the excesses of my mother's preoccupation with food, I became a good cook. That's what I do for recreation. I love to cook.

My mother controls through the kitchen. So our gambit is to insist on cooking Christmas dinner. This is always a problem but we win because it's our condition of going down there. If we say, for example, we don't want stuffing, we want rice, we get stuffing because she just can't hear us, she checks out. She goes through this kind of self-absorbed schtick. And it's so unpleasant.

The food fights are incredible. Mother is always trying to feed us. We're always trying to say no and she always tries to make sure we can't say no. If, for example, we don't want to eat lunch she takes us out to the Cajun seafood bar where she knows we can't say no. The whole point is eat, eat.

In many ways her food-service trip is a substitute for more productive kinds of exchange in a real relationship. I'm very worried myself since I realized I was substituting food for more significant kinds of exchanges with friends out of a sort of suppressed fear that I wasn't good enough. As soon as I could identify it, everything suddenly got simple. All I had to do was to get off the food trip and I was all right.

With one of my brothers we joke about the fact that she talks all the time about losing weight but never does it. My youngest brother takes my mother seriously. It's funny because I'm the serious one in the family, he's the joker. But I'm the one in the family who got through this. He will never figure this out. He thinks my mother is a little crazy but basically normal. I think my mother is absolutely insane. She's liable to kill us if we don't figure out where she's coming from. And John just doesn't get it.

Many children claim their relationship with parents is not intimate, repressed, or too superficial. A well-adapted daughter feels visits are so packed with activities that her parents seldom express their true feelings: "I'd like my mother to share her feelings rather than talk about daily events and routines. Sometimes after the kids are in bed and we can talk, she'll tell me more about what's going on, how they are managing now that my father is retiring." Other children want a frank discussion about their childhood relationships. A well-adapted son explains why he generally feels unsuccessful in his bid for closeness:

> I was born in Poland and was a child survivor of the Holocaust, though I was too little to remember anything concretely. My parents are Holocaust survivors too and to a great extent our relationship seems to be permeated by Holocaust memories. Whenever I plan to visit them I experience strong emotions in the hope of possibly discussing things in the past or their feelings about the war or their childhoods in Europe. I have a great desire to break down the generational barriers between us. But they always resist when I try to probe my roots. It is difficult because at each stage the discussion involves different members of the family who were killed. Soon they reach their limit and my questions always go unanswered.

An alienated daughter feels her parents are rejecting:

> I feel a great deal of guilt and want a deeper investigation into the relationship without each of us being so defensive. I don't make much of a contribution to her psychological needs because I'm too subjective and emotionally involved. In my heart I'm sad and angry about it, that my mother sees enough of me even though she says publicly that she'd like to see me and her grandson more often.

And another alienated daughter recalls the childhood source of her repressed emotions interacting with both parents:

Historically, my mother would protect my father. He worked at home but he worked very hard, constantly. She felt she had to protect him from a lot of minor emotional events of the children because her husband was so busy working. So she became a shield in between him and his daughters. My sister and I both have a good deal of trouble talking to him. He doesn't like to engage in small talk. He doesn't make an effort. It's been difficult for both my sister and me.

I feel anger, depression, and sadness. It's sad when a group of people who share the past and still share a lot of values can't talk about the things that matter. My mother has used hurt feelings and crying as a defense. If she is frightened of something or a criticism, she cries. Where she protected my father she now expects me in some unspoken fashion to protect her from realities she doesn't want to face.

So I feel I have to be careful about what I say, about myself, the deep things that really matter. I don't have to be careful about casual things, work, or politics. At home I couldn't express my emotional side. I had to protect my mother on the one hand and my father wasn't accessible emotionally on the other. It was a sad childhood.

Another alienated daughter points out that her parents are demanding and insensitive. No matter what she and her sister accomplish, her mother is never satisfied, it's never enough:

I feel guilty and angry that I can't get close to my mother. When I visit with her she does all the talking and she generally talks about who's dying and tragedy. Or, her other theme is how good somebody is to their mother. There's a hidden agenda there, other people. I don't know if she does it on purpose. She doesn't say, "Look at the way you treat me." But if I try to brag about my children, she'll say, "Did I tell you about so and so's son who did such and such." She always translates that to someone else. She's just a very self-centered person. And she's insensitive to my feelings.

During the separation phase, distant children don't like to hear their parents complain to them about their siblings or try to put them in the middle of current disagreements. One daughter gets annoyed when her mother criticizes her sister's children while praising her children. Another alienated daughter does not like to hear her mother criticize her sister:

> My sister has to drive for an hour to get to work. And they have a daughter who is a senior. But my mother complains that Shirley doesn't spend enough time with her daughter. I say, "You know, Mother, this is for Shirley and Louis and Beth to work out and it's nothing for you to interfere with." And she would usually stay out of it. But when she was visiting with Shirley she would complain directly to her and they would have a fight. She's just a hard person to be around.

Separation and departure may become frustrating when a parent's personal problems or personality interferes with successful communications. One son complains that his widowed mother is preoccupied with her health, while another claims his mother has become too dependent on him following his father's death. In a few instances, declining health of a parent foreshadows future family problems.

Many children refer to a kind of debriefing following the frenetic energy expended visiting their extended families. Though visits are enjoyable and children are pleased to be near people they love, visits can be tiring because the group itself generates a great deal of emotional energy. Several children note that the presence of in-laws and small children changes the tone of the visit, sometimes taking away opportunities to converse openly with their parents. When visits focus on the larger extended family, children and parents may forget to discuss issues of mutual concern. In such cases either one or both generations may end the visit feeling a lack of completeness, that their bonds have not been renewed satisfactorily.

Following separation and departure, many children note that their sadness in saying good-bye is ameliorated by plans for future reunions. About half have mixed feelings immediately after a visit—sadness along with satisfaction. Only two alienated children report feeling only relief without any positive emotions. Displaced children are often frustrated that visits are too limited in time or space. A displaced daughter says:

It's so intense to get together because of all the planning and everyone rushing around in the same space. We can't get anything done. "Uh oh, I say, we never got to talk about cousin Susan!" I'm not satisfied. I wish I could be more spontaneous and relaxed; I would be if we lived in the same city.

A well-adapted son muses:

The time before my wedding, I was a little nervous because that's the first time they'd ever come to visit me here. I felt sad after the visit because whenever I leave I see that they're getting older and maybe their health isn't always the best. But it's part of life.

A well-adapted unmarried daughter sheds a positive, realistic light on the visit: "After such visits I feel close to my mother. I generally accept my blood kin the way they are. I am not looking to change them. Each one in the family is so different. And I feel affection toward everyone."

Typically, an alienated daughter expresses regret and depression:

Mother always wishes we could have stayed longer, could have done more. And it never gets done. We clear out this drawer or that closet or visit those people. The regret is that you can never do everything. It's the same thing as a child. When you're trying to get your kids to bed the child just never did enough during the day.

During departure children focus on assessing the success of the visit. Some feel frustrated if visits are too infrequent or too short relative to family expectations. On the other hand, if the visit is too long, life-style differences assert themselves and result in conflicts. A number of children make a distinction between visits during vacation times and work times. Vacation-time visits are better because the normal stresses of work are absent and both generations can enjoy leisure-time activities together. About half the children claim they are not satisfied after a visit, and more than half say their parents are not satisfied.

Displaced, well-adapted, and alienated children express different levels of satisfaction. Displaced children are uniformly dissatisfied with visits because such brief face-to-face contacts highlight their larger problem of living so far away. Typically, they express regret, as one son says:

> I regret the distance and the separation, the complexity of trying to maintain a satisfying family relationship over great distance. It wasn't so much that I had a desire to live in that physical location, but more that I felt the years are going by. The gravity of that starts to come home when you start to realize your parents don't have many more years left and that everyone has missed out.

A displaced daughter regrets that her mother doesn't have enough daily contact with her children: "I think we have had more regret in recent years. Now I feel that we should see each other more. It's frustrating that she lives so far away. I would love for my kids to have more Grandma contact. They adore her." And another displaced daughter says:

> Distance is very difficult to deal with in our lives. When you're with a young child you have a lot of open-ended time. But you don't have the closeness of dropping by. When you live so far away, if you want it to happen you have to make a plan to visit, interrupt one thing to do something else. What I would like to make just an every-day life thing. My family should come over for a piece of pie then go away again.

Displaced children believe more visits would bring greater satisfaction. But those who visit more frequently are not necessarily more satisfied. For example, a displaced daughter feels a strong lack of satisfaction with visits because her father's health is failing and she could help her mother cope better if she were near her parents. She feels guilty and helpless. Although she visits very frequently she remains unsatisfied.

In contrast with displaced children, a large majority of well-adapted children say both they and their parents are satisfied after visits. They describe routine, satisfying though highly diverse patterns of visiting. They convey a lack of emotional stress and a sense of control in their relationships with parents. A theme emerges of self-confidence in their ability to keep a healthy emotional distance from their parents' problems. Their strength rests first in their ability to reveal only what they know their parents can handle, and second in their willingness to accommodate to parents' wishes during visits without feeling threatened. For example, many parents are satisfied with visits but still feel they would like more visits, as a recently married son reports: "I think they understand that I have things to do and that I visit when I can. They're satisfied in that sense. But more is always better."

Several well-adapted children admit their parents say privately they would like to have them live closer and visit more, but such expressions do not undermine their own decisions to live far away, as one well-adapted daughter explains:

> Occasionally she laps back into saying, "I wish you lived closer to home." But in public at least, particularly when I'm there and I go to church with her and when she introduces me and tells what I do, she's very proud of that and you can see it on her face and hear it in her voice. And people in those small rural communities are so accustomed to having everyone live in the same town they grew up in, they say to her, "How can you stand for her to live so far away?" And she tells them I went to school for a long time to be able to do this and I have a good job. And she's very happy for me that I can do that. I even heard her tell one person who doubted that I could love her when I lived so far away: "She loves me a lot. She drives all the way down here. It takes her three days to get here and she comes two times a year."

Other well-adapted children say being satisfied means being realistic, as a married daughter explains:

> We love to visit my parents. They live in a beautiful, beautiful location. That's why we've visited so often in the last few years. We would go wherever they live because I like to visit them. But it's an added bonus because we can spend time at the beach and it's gorgeous.
>
> They are satisfied with the contact they have with me except that if we lived next door to them they would enjoy dropping by. I'd like to live in the same town but it's not realistic. I'm willing to accept things the way they are. It would be nice to be helpful to each other. I especially would like a mutual babysitting service. I could stay with my grandfather and they could stay with my son.

Well-adapted children report their parents are also realistic. A well-adapted son in his fifties explains that his parents have learned over the years to accept the distance between them:

> They are proud of me. When they introduce me now they think that's great that I'm here. They would like to see me living in the same town they're in. Not in the last ten years, but when I first came up here they would say, "Why don't you check into those job opportunities at Texas?" I didn't do it. Well, that university is not that great but it was in the same town. I liked it here. I wasn't interested in moving back.

In sharp contrast, most alienated children say neither they nor their parents are satisfied with the content of visits. An alienated daughter in her early thirties identifies parental pressure as a major source of dissatisfaction:

> My parents want me to be near them. They're never satisfied, never. I'll give you a perfect example of that. When we were in New York in August, we all went out to celebrate my father's birthday. Later, he said, "Now Pat, if you lived near here, we could do this every Sunday." And that's what he would like, to have the whole family together about once a week.

A few alienated children become unhappy when their parents initiate too many visits. But most are satisfied with the frequency of visits because distance gives them a sense of control; they can maintain the necessary psychological distance from their parents. An alienated daughter explains:

> Distance makes me sane. It keeps me sane. It allows me an excuse in a certain sense to distance myself from some of these demands and some of the obligations. Because I know, even if I lived a block away, there would be something wrong about the way I was interacting with them. It would never be satisfactory.

And another alienated daughter says:

> Living farther away from my mother helps me remember positive interactions. I feel if I were closer it really wouldn't be as good

for me. It would be harder to keep my emotional distance. My mother is just a very judgmental person. She's very imposing and lacks any sensitivity to my feelings. I say I don't care when she behaves badly. I should be angry, right? I have to ignore her. But I do listen and try to be helpful to her. Many of these things get to me.

Several alienated daughters believe their mothers are dissatisfied with distant visits because of their own family histories:

The circumstances between my generation and my parents' are not identical but certainly analogous. They left home forty years ago and moved far away. I honestly don't think my mother ever recovered; she still regrets that. Her family didn't have much money and wouldn't call. They would write to say her grandmother had been buried a couple of days ago. She felt really cut off. As an adolescent she despised them. She always felt hated when she lived there. I remember she felt very bad about it when I was a kid.

And another says:

She'd like us all to live closer. But then I think that desire also has a context. She wishes we had more time as a family together again. I don't think it was ever really like that; it was always a fantasy. The family she came from was more cohesive, probably because they went through horrible years together in the Depression. Her father and one of her younger sisters died young, and that family pulled together. She and her brother being the two older children helped the other three get through college. So in her background there was that cohesiveness where our family doesn't have it.

Routine visits, examined as rituals of renewal in five distinct stages, are important to relationships between adult children and distant parents because they represent the major opportunity for face-to-face contact. Emotional attachments along with several other factors influence the frequency, length, substance of interactions, and satisfaction during such visits. In general, well-adapted children express satisfaction with the frequency, length, and content of interactions during routine visits with parents. Although conflicts arise, well-adapted children minimize their importance and resolve them quickly and confidently. Displaced children are happy to spend time with their distant parents but express frustration; routine visits resemble a tasty appetizer followed by an announcement that the main course has been canceled. Alienated children remain angry and unsatisfied with routine visits. Past conflicts continue to surface in any face-to-face contacts and remain unresolved.

Patterns of routine visiting may continue uninterrupted for many years. Ultimately, however, life-cycle transitions force a reconsideration of the quality of the distant relationship. The next two chapters examine relationships with distant parents during important life-cycle transitions. Transition visits and calls differ from routine contacts in two important respects. First, many life-cycle transitions cannot be planned, especially those involving health changes such as acute illness or death, or social-status changes such as widowhood. Parental decline into chronically ill health may happen suddenly or gradually. In either case, contacts change from routine patterns to patterns of crisis and emergency. The second difference is that during transitions one generation requires assistance from the other, whereas assistance during routine visits is normally not required.

CHAPTER 7

*H*ealth-Status Transitions in Old Age

In this chapter we will consider children's responses to their distant parents' health transitions. Even though health-status transitions and social-status transitions are treated in separate chapters, it is important to note that they often occur together. For example, when a spouse and parent dies of an illness, the status of the surviving spouse changes to widowhood. Moreover, shortly after a spouse dies, the surviving spouse may change housing, remarry, or become ill.

Increasingly, adult children find themselves coping with situations that have few precedents. No tradition has yet been passed down that explains how to deal with life-cycle transitions from a distance. Yet children and their distant parents often make courageous efforts to visit, telephone, and help each other during such transitions, interpreting their contacts as important expressions of family solidarity.

Many social-status transitions of old age, including voluntary relocation, remarriage, and retirement, do not require more than emotional support from distant children. Transitions to widowhood may require more help, though before the appearance of a significant illness, distant parents are still living independent, active lives with little need for assistance. Some crises, such as acute illness or death, may be handled by an emergency visit or by getting on a plane and traveling once or twice a year to help out. But problems really become serious when aging parents become frail or chronically or terminally ill. Then relationships change from visiting every year to visiting every week.

Distant relationships become increasingly difficult for both generations. Increasing dependency on one's spouse or child creates strong feelings of ambivalence, anxiety, and anger in many parents who wish to remain independent (Hess and Waring 1978). Distant children also feel ambivalent. On the one hand, they feel responsible for providing face-to-face care, while on the other hand, since distance does not allow them to be there, they feel guilt, stress, and frustration. Children also experience emotional stress, anxiety, and feelings of helplessness resulting from their long-distance efforts to arrange health care or housing for their elderly parents. Additional problems include the tremendous financial expenses, the disruption in the lives of working children, and the miscommunications and misunderstandings that arise.

Three major factors influence the distant child's capacity to help his or her distant parents during transitions: (1) stage in the life cycle; (2) distance; and (3) voices of emotional attachment. Even at very different stages in the life cycle, some transitions bring similar problems, common experiences, and a convergence of needs. For example, both widows and adolescents suffer from problems of loneliness, role loss and grief, and the need to prove one's ability to be self-reliant and independent. In a sense, the emotional problems resulting from transitions to widowhood and adolescence converge, making individuals experiencing such transitions compatible and capable of helping each other at this moment in their lives. Programs that put teenagers together with grandparents owe much of their success to such convergence. Another example of life-stage convergence is found in the phenomenon of "social-age peership," in which both the parents and the children are students, workers, retirees, and even parents of young children at the same time

(Hagestad 1979). A strong degree of mutual understanding and assistance can develop between generations in such circumstances.

One can imagine a situation in which life-cycle transitions cause a divergence that leads to incompatibility and an inability to provide effective assistance. When parental needs for help during health and social-status transitions conflict with the needs of nuclear-family members, the stage is set for divided loyalties, stress, and frustration. Difficulties in providing help can also be triggered by a distant child's own transitions, as in the case of a daughter who is in the process of divorce while her mother becomes widowed. The self-absorption of each generation in such circumstances can limit helping the other and generate resentment.

Robert Butler (1975) terms the "life review" a period when many older people begin to think seriously about the events and meaning of their lives as a kind of psychological preparation for death. Death becomes a recurrent theme in their conversations, since they want to confront it directly. Yet their middle-aged children may be experiencing another transition, the "midlife crisis," during which they become acutely aware of their own mortality. In sharp contrast to their "life-review" parents, "midlife crisis" children want to recapture their past, their youthful feelings of invulnerability and immortality; they do not want to discuss death. Where these two transitions occur simultaneously, aging parents and middle-aged children will be incompatible companions, at least for a while. Naturally, such life-course transitions vary greatly among individuals (Nachman 1979).

Distance also influences the ability to help during transitions. At almost every juncture, distant children perceive their parents' lives as intimately bound up with their own. Relations between children and their parents are dominated by intimacy and positive concern, feelings of obligation, and the desire to help. Many distant children provide material and psychological supports (Blau 1973; Rosenmayr and Kockeis 1963), including money, gifts, plane tickets, material goods, and, most importantly, services organizing and supervising health care and housing, domestic tasks, and the filling out of forms for government agencies. Distant children also act as intermediaries to find out needed information. With difficulty they communicate with social workers, ministers, doctors, dentists, housing authorities, impersonal government agencies, other nearby friends and neighbors, and extended family about their parents' welfare. Distant children also provide emotional supports such as active listening, sympathetic response, advice, consolation, reinforcement, and nurturance.

Bonds between distant generations remain strong over many years (Litwak and Silverstein 1987). The desire to assist parents during health and social-status transitions is clearly present in everyone. Displaced, well-adapted, and alienated children all come forward to help their parents during a health crisis or social-status transition; none abandon their distant parents. Yet the voices of emotional attachment influence a distant child's perceptions and evaluations of his or her ability to help. For example, declining health triggers ambivalence and conflict in alienated children. The source of stress in the relationship is not the life-cycle transition itself, but the accompanying need for care and support from children who cannot do it.

It is useful to look at declining health as a continuum (Atchley 1977) with complete social, physical, and mental well-being at one extreme and death at the other. The health continuum may be divided into three key stages, with health transitions occurring as individuals move from one stage to another. The first stage is the appearance of a health problem, seeking of treatment, some restrictions on activities, self-managed illness, and signs of increasing dependency. The second stage is partial disability, when a person is unable to engage in a major activity and requires some assistance from another person. The third and most problematical stage begins when elderly parents experience health transitions leading to total disability, the need for long-term face-to-face care, and death. Such stages are arbitrary, of course. They merely provide reference points along the health continuum that can be used to describe the general course of decline and the response of distant children who want to help parents during these old-age health transitions. Typically, health transitions bring out strong emotions, either positive feelings of satisfaction and caring for a loved one, or negative emotions, anger, and conflict with roots in the past.

THE APPEARANCE OF A PROBLEMATICAL HEALTH CONDITION

Discovery of a health condition depends on the presentation and severity of symptoms, and the way individuals respond to body and mood changes. A health condition may be noticed first by an individual, a family member, or a physician. Most often a condition is first brought to light by those closest to an individual. When family members recognize changes early, chances for avoiding serious health consequences are better, as a daughter in her early thirties recalls:

> We've had a pretty easy time of it; virtually no sickness. Even my father's heart condition turned out to be the best for everyone because he had an arrhythmia that my mom really noticed. She would like lay her head on his chest and she could hear it. She said, "What's going on with your heart? It goes bee-beep, bee-beep, then there's no sound at all?" So he went in under duress; he wasn't feeling bad at all. They whipped him in, they injected dye to determine how much blockage he had. It came out something like 98 percent blockage here and 97 percent blockage there. The doctor said, "Holy cow, you better get yourself cleaned out." So they did a triple bypass within two weeks. It was successful. And everybody realized that had he not had this done, he would have keeled over with a heart attack at any time. I couldn't have been happier about the whole thing.

Parental decline into ill health often begins with an acute-illness episode. Sometimes, however, a condition causes a very gradual decline in health, and the appearance of illness is masked to those in frequent contact with the individual. Such changes, however, may be noticeable to the infrequent visitor who sees the cumulative effects and becomes aware consciously that something is wrong in a parent's appearance or behavior. In one case, everyone living near an older man knew his driving was very bad, so no one who saw him daily would drive with him. A visiting daughter went shopping with him and upon returning, her nerves shattered, she developed a strong determination to put an end to it.

In another case, everyone at home had noticed that an elderly father's cough was becoming worse but he would not listen to their suggestions that he see a doctor. A visiting daughter, however, insisted that he see a doctor before the end of her visit. In such instances a distant child may show greater perception, objectivity, and determination. The distant child may notice gradual changes in appearance more clearly than anyone living near the parent simply because he or she is not in the middle of daily events.

In addition, distant children sometimes become aware of changes in their parents' behavior that near-living relatives do not notice. Changing relationships between spouses, unusual anger, and conflict can portent health transitions. A daughter recalls a routine visit that ended with an unpleasant awareness that the relationship between her parents was changing radically, perhaps a result of ill health:

> We experienced a family crisis just prior to his death, that time I went there to visit. They were behaving oddly, snide comments, and then when they didn't think anybody was watching they were really nasty to each other. She has just a total disorientation, not remembering two seconds later what we've said to her. And she and Daddy, I think because of that, were just fighting constantly the whole time I was there two years ago Christmas. He was trying to remind her to take her insulin and she got really angry. There was a lot of hostility between them which I had never seen before.
>
> During that visit I felt sorry for my father for the first time. He was always so demanding. I just hated people who made demands all the time. But this time she had decided I'm not going to take these demands anymore. I'm going to say something back. And he was so shocked. I felt sorry for him because I realized that he didn't think he was doing anything out of the ordinary. He didn't understand why this woman was screaming at him when she'd never screamed at him before. And he wasn't doing anything different from what he'd done his whole life. She was changing. And he died shortly thereafter.
>
> Almost the same kind of thing happened to me in my previous marriage before my first husband died. I was becoming much more independent. I was starting to say I'm going back to school. And I had done strange things to my hair. He hated it and I screamed at him and said, "I don't give a shit if you like it or not. It's my hair." So I was asserting my independence and before I'd kept it inside. I had *thought* a lot but I hadn't really done anything about it. My

former husband said, "I haven't done anything different, why are you behaving this way?" I saw that was happening to my mother too.

Once a condition becomes known it may be ignored, self-treatment may be tried, or professional treatment may be sought. When it comes to treatment, not everyone is satisfied with the parent's self-assessment. If their parents reject their advice, some children become frustrated, as one daughter explains:

> The biggest thing was that she and Daddy both thought they were the picture of health even though they had all these things wrong with them. To them being sick means being in bed. They were not in bed so were not sick. When I say to her things about diet beyond not just eating sweets but diet in the sense of reducing fats and cholesterol, I say the quality of your life would be better or your health would be better. She'll say, "There's nothing wrong with my health." But that's frustrating for me, for her not to understand that there are health problems that she could change by diet and exercise. Clearly if she'd walk around the block five times every day her circulation would be better. The doctor tells her to. And if the circulation is better the memory's going to be better. But she doesn't do that.

Waiting for a parent to seek treatment after discovering something is wrong may be very stressful. In one instance, a son criticized his father's companion, claiming she did not take care of him properly. After the son's distant sister was unsuccessful in getting their father to attend to his problem, the distant son made sure his father would go to the doctor:

> Renée does the minimum, she's not conscientious. But he's not capable of doing anything and he avoids doing anything. He had a sore on his nose for a long time. My sister told him to attend to it. He had not gone to a doctor about it. So when I saw him in Atlanta that time I said, "What is that?" "Oh, it's nothing, a little sore." I just raised hell with him. I was very unpleasant. And the next week he went to the doctor and it was cancerous. He had to have a rather long and complicated piece of plastic surgery as a result of this thing which could have been taken care of easily.

Frequently, chronic health conditions are discovered during routine visits to the doctor and no hospitalization is required. Health conditions are also discovered during acute emergency hospitalizations. When a distant child is told in advance of a routine hospitalization, there is usually no reason to visit. Nevertheless, children maintain closer communications and try to help, as one daughter recalls: "The only kind of assistance would be my emotional support to my mother when she is sick and goes to the hospital. I call her every day and write to her."

On the other hand, an emergency hospitalization usually means a crisis visit out of fear that the parent may die. In deciding how to help, distant children often consider the degree of local social supports for their parent. If a spouse or nearby sibling is available, most children do not travel to visit and help unless their parent is gravely ill. But if the parent is widowed without near-living children to care for them, the distant child will come to help during an acute illness episode. In some cases a child may come even if the spouse is living.

Children provide many kinds of services during crisis visits. Both children and parents regard the visit itself as a vital aspect of moral and emotional support to the sick parent and, if both parents are alive, to the parent who is not sick. One son indicates that visits from distant family members provide moral support even when they are not needed for functional support:

> We were all together for several days on Thanksgiving, and I had no sooner got back here when my mother got really sick. My father was sort of panicky when he called me about my mother's surgery. I went there right away. I just got on a plane and left in a couple of hours.
>
> She was out of intensive care already. But then she started bleeding again and was back in. So, while he was quite scared, he was also very uncertain, because the doctors had been very reassuring. So, it was a kind of mixed-up thing, but he definitely wanted me to come and was glad when I did. He didn't ask me to come actually, but was very happy when I said I would come. It was mainly a matter of my being there. I could help drive him around. But mainly what I did for him while I was there was to be with him since he was alone.

Some children provide useful medical advice. A daughter who is a nurse helped her mother-in-law by changing physicians and getting her transferred to a better hospital for surgery. A son claims:

> I could explain what the medications were and what type of injury it was—neural injuries—and I told my dad about some of the long-range symptoms; the personality changes, the sleep disorders, and those sorts of things that happen after a stroke. Actually, the physician told him the same thing.

One of the most difficult problems in a hospital emergency is not having a precise diagnosis. Given the high expectations people often hold of modern medicine, waiting without knowing the outcome can be very frustrating. The same issues of withholding health information apply here as in the telephone discussions considered in chapter 5. Some parents prefer to share their uncertainty and fear, as a son explains:

> She had what turned out to be a bleeding ulcer. It was way up at the top of her stomach but kind of hidden by other organs. And so it bled quite a bit even after she got to the hospital. Then it stopped but they couldn't find anything.
> She had been in intensive care, but was out again and was feeling good. But then in the next couple of days, it kept happening and they couldn't find it. Finally, one of the physicians was actually there when it happened and was able to locate it. Then she was in surgery and it was very serious. They were afraid, having lost that much blood, that she wouldn't pull through. But it was a surprisingly easy operation. They were very pleased. I think that they were afraid that it probably was cancer from the way they talked, and when they found that it was this ulcer, they were pleased and she came through it fine. So, I went back there.

Early in a health crisis distant children are generally not involved. The spouse, near-living children, and their spouses carry the responsibility for emergency health care. In such circumstance, powerful emotions and conflicts may surface between family members. Several children remember important conflicts erupting between them and their parents or between their parents and other family members during a health crisis, as one son recalls:

I had a conflict with my father, and it didn't come up over the phone, but when I was there. When my mother was sick in the hospital, he really got angry at me because I had gone to the hospital early one morning and didn't come back to pick him up in time, that is, by his schedule. He felt that I was ignoring him and that his authority was being usurped. He can be really angry.

This son also remembers conflict between his father and his sister-in-law when his mother was hospitalized. It is significant that these conflicts focus on questions of parental independence, so fundamental to the process of health decline:

My parents are used to being independent, able to do everything for themselves. So it's not easy for my father to let other people really have power. When my mother was so sick and lost blood that morning, apparently he called my brother and my sister. But Louey and Karen, my sister-in-law, were there right away, when the decision was being made about what to do. Apparently he hadn't called the ambulance and the bleeding had stopped. She wasn't hemorrhaging or anything, so he didn't just call anyone. It ended up that Karen called an ambulance, and he was angry because she had taken that out of his hands. That's typical. He can get into situations where he feels really threatened and insecure.

Frequently, siblings share the tasks of staying with their parent at home and in the hospital or helping parents recuperate at home after a hospital stay, as a son recalls:

She's pretty independent. She had an angioplasty and we thought she may need a bypass operation. But here again my brother took her to Indianapolis to the hospital and came and picked her up. I stayed with her for a couple of days while he went back to work. But she likes to do things on her own.

In another instance a daughter and her sisters took turns staying with their dependent grandfather at home while their mother took care of their father in the hospital:

They called me when they learned about my dad being ill. That was a very difficult time for both of them. It was a panic in that they needed someone to come and take care of my grandfather, which I did because we were closer plus in the summer we didn't have as much responsibility as my brother and sister. My sister came and stayed with my mom while my dad was in the hospital. So everybody pitched in. And my brother also came and stayed mainly in the hospital to be with my dad.

Frequently, the early phase of an illness does not prevent a patient from carrying out major activities. Such a phase might include hearing impairment, a restriction on driving, or exertion. Self-management of the condition is the norm and preferable to any other treatment. Both self-management and independence are basic to our value system. Thousands of elderly Americans manage high blood pressure, arthritis, diabetes, and other chronic conditions with little or no assistance from their children.

Hospital emergencies may herald a more serious chronic illness and disability. The most significant outcome of a chronic condition is the health regimen, which may include medicines, a special diet, and limitations on activities. Once diagnosed, a chronic condition can have an important impact on the distant relationship since questions of assistance must be addressed for the first time.

PARTIAL DISABILITY: TEMPORARY

The second phase of health decline is partial disability, a serious restriction of a major activity. This means a parent is unable to carry out some necessary activities, such as work or housework, shopping, or transportation. Many elderly parents recuperating from surgery are partially disabled but only temporarily so. Some parents, however, are permanently disabled and require assistance in some activities and a specific health regimen. When parents are unable to engage in the major activities one undertakes in life, they approach total disability.

Once an emergency passes, children and their families begin to focus attention on their parents' disabilities and specific needs for recovery. A daughter notes that her mother has slowed down considerably since she was hospitalized:

The most important change is in my mother's ability to run us all ragged. She was a dynamo and now she's limited. We can't hop in the subway and go. We have to drive, we have to park. If it's a museum we have to get a wheelchair. You walk in with your cane and ask for a wheelchair at the door. She can't stand still or do the slow museum shuffle; she really feels pain. I used to say she has as much energy as the rest of the family together. Also they went to an elder hostel in Japan and were planning to go to one in India but changed after the accident because the walking would be too much.

Parents' illnesses can create misunderstandings that strain distant relationships. A son fears that because of her failing memory his mother will leave the stove on. A daughter explains that a series of minor strokes has affected her mother's memory; she becomes frustrated when her mother forgets she called or visited. The daughter's own guilt feelings emerge in her explanation of the problem:

The biggest difficulty is that my mother is suffering from lapses of memory. The doctor is convinced it's due to hardening of the arteries and very mild strokes. When I call and Mother doesn't sound very good I'll call back in a few days and see if she's better. A lot of times she doesn't remember whether I've called or not. This gets really sad because she'll call thinking she hasn't heard from me but she has, a week ago, and doesn't remember.

I am not as good as one of my sisters who calls once a week; it's routinized so Mother remembers. But because I tend to call whenever, she doesn't remember. If she's healthy her memory is great and we have no conflict. But I get frustrated if she doesn't remember when I called last or visited.

Another daughter expresses concern over her mother's heart condition: "If she gets a cold she gets much sicker, and it takes her a longer time to get rid of colds that most people would kick off in a week. It could get very bad very fast." And another recalls tremendous stress resulting from her mother's decision to recover at home rather than in a nursing home:

When my mother returned from the hospital having had knee surgery, she decided to come home directly rather than go into a nursing home. It was not a good idea. My father went crazy trying to help her. I suggested they have a hospital bed in the living room until she's able to move because she was trapped upstairs in the bedroom. "No that wouldn't do." He said I just didn't understand.

In most cases, the healthier spouse and near-living children care for the recovering parent. Sometimes extended family members come to help. Distant children maintain close contact with their parents and siblings and monitor their parent's progress as well as the condition of the parent care giver, as one son notes:

> I speak with my parents more frequently than with my brother. My brothers and I increasingly talk about my parents. I say, "When you're there please observe how my father is. See whether Mother found out about the volunteer who will give her some respite. Find out if she is really getting away for a while, that sort of thing."

During the recovery, care-giving parents frequently seek emotional support and reassurance from distant children. Their need emerges from the stress of caring for a spouse at home. A well-adapted son expresses admiration when his father is willing to share his feelings under difficult circumstances:

> My father understood that she was being hard on him because she wasn't fully recovered. But this went beyond the usual, and he was really quite upset. She was in that postoperative condition, feeling very negative and critical, which is not like her. She was very disturbed by the anesthetic.
>
> He was surprisingly very forbearing, and felt distressed by the way she attacked him. I don't know what she said, but it hurt him very badly. But I was proud of him because he's easily hurt, not all that secure, and very vulnerable to her criticisms. But he worked it out for himself that she really wasn't herself, that she wasn't so much recovered emotionally as she seemed to be physically, and he accepted that.
>
> A lot of what's really touched me is how open he was about how he was feeling. He was having some feelings he didn't have total access to, and it was easier to feel anger about that than to feel the other things that were going on. But also in a more complicated

190

way, he realized how she was and wanted to talk about it with me, and was happy to have me to talk to.

Several children express concern about their parents' moods following hospitalization and surgery. One daughter is particularly worried about her mother's depression caused by the recent deaths of several siblings and her unceasing pain from arthritis. She also notes the impact of her mother's depression on her father, who is dependent on her:

> My mother used to get satisfaction out of overworking. Now I think she's given up. And I think it's her health—the arthritis has been pretty much constant. My father is very emotionally dependent on her and very frightened. He believes if you don't feel well you get it fixed and move on. But at another level he understands absolutely because his mother also suffered from arthritis and she quit; she just sat, so her joints locked. And my grandfather had to nurse her. I think my father fears that the pattern will be repeated. The irony is that it's unlikely. If my mother just had a little more sympathy from him she would be fighting harder now.
>
> She's also suffered from a series of deaths of her siblings, around the same time. Her attention to her sisters when they were alive and her grief at their deaths is very threatening to him. Since she was the youngest of those children she was there to help everybody, even when she wasn't healthy. In the last couple of years my father has refused to drive her to her sister's house, so she's had to slow down.

Distant children often feel intense ambivalence, inadequacy, and guilt that they cannot be there themselves to care for their recovering parent. One daughter relates a dream filled with the symbolism of guilt and ambivalence:

> After Mom left the hospital we argued more because of my trying to persuade my father to get somebody to help in the house, do the cleaning, the garden, and he won't. It's still at that touchy level. I think we're afraid to fight.
>
> I had very strange dreams. We were in my parents' basement. But I clearly was part of it in a way that I'm not when I go home to visit them. I was doing some laundry for them, and the washing machine went berserk. It was filled with water so that the clean laun-

dry was coming out of the top of the machine on its own. The water was coming with it and sloshing over onto some dry laundry that was right next to it. It began flooding the floor.

Now I did manage to flood my own basement last week so there are some connections. But it was definitely my parents' laundry. And it was not a totally altruistic loving gesture of mine. Something had gone on between me and my father before the dream started, so there was some sort of tension. I think it was about what sorts of things I try to do to help them when I'm visiting there. My overwhelming feeling was that it just wasn't going to be enough—that I live far away and don't exactly know what I could do or how much.

PARTIAL DISABILITY: PERMANENT

Poor health is not necessarily associated with old age. As a group, however, older people suffer disproportionately from permanent disability and chronic conditions that restrict their activities. At a certain moment chronic illness can become a major limitation on participation in the distant relationship. Certain chronic conditions like Parkinson's disease, stroke, or deafness may leave a parent unable to communicate on the telephone, travel to visit distant children, or interact normally during visits. Most parents with permanent disabilities are dependent on others for daily routine activities. Illness emergencies sometimes herald a parent's transition from good health to permanent ill health. The nature of relationships change as both generations adapt to a new life-style shaped by chronic illness and disability.

In his report of his father's stroke, a son describes his father's transition to permanent disability and his role as a distant child:

My father had his stroke four years ago. I was due to get back from Scotland a few days later so they didn't bother to call me because it didn't seem to be life-threatening. When I got back to Detroit I called home to tell them about my trip and that's when they told me. They said to take a day to do my laundry, get myself together, then come to Buffalo.

They were over the initial life-threatening fears. But he was essentially unable to move or talk. The last time I'd seen him he was like you or me or anybody else. He was lying down and had a little wiggle in his fingers. My brother was feeding him and there was a lot of anxiety about the future, if he was ever going to be any better.

I saw rapid and significant recovery while I was there, especially during the first month. Then basically less. They were exceptionally happy about the recovery early because it looked real promising. Now they're frustrated that it was not a complete recovery. I know it sounds weird but my father is actually healthier now than he's ever been in his life. He rides the exercise bike I got for him. He walks. He doesn't smoke or drink anymore.

Many parents recover completely from hospitalization or surgery and continue to age gracefully without disability. Yet at some point children accept their parents' frailties, physical impairments, limitations on activities, and increasing dependencies before death. Frailty also often heralds impending disability. Once it becomes clear that a distant parent is frail or partly dependent on another person, many children help indirectly since they cannot be present to help directly. Children maintain close contacts through frequent calls to the healthier parent or near siblings who give care. Typically, daughters rather than sons take on the primary responsibility caring for a disabled parent, even when they live farther away. A son describes the frail condition of his distant parents and his ongoing communications with his sister and brother:

My parents are both eighty-eight and living together in a small house on a lake. Neither of them is in the greatest health. In the last couple of years, they've gone downhill. My mother has a bad back and difficulty walking. She wears a kind of a corset because the bones in her spine are disintegrating. My father has heart problems. She needs some help in getting around even though it's just a couple miles to the store, her friends, or to my brother's house. I think at this point, when one of them dies, the other will not be able to live alone.

My brother lives near them but he's been pretty unwell. He's sixty years old and he's had a thyroid problem, although it wasn't diagnosed right away. So, he was quite an active guy and helped them a lot, especially keeping the place up, sawing wood. But he hasn't been able to help them very much lately. He was not able to drive my father around because he was very sick, lethargic, and in a negative state of mind.

My sister, who lives about 150 miles away, is the one who's most involved with them. We talk more about my parents. Since she's been retired from teaching school she travels with them a good deal and gets them down to her house. She's more social than my brother is so she and I talk more about the plans for my parents. Because she really likes to travel and give parties, she's become the social center, organizing family reunions and stuff like that. My parents are engaged in all that, so my sister is kind of a moving force in their lives and my brother isn't.

Several children try to help their parents hire people to assist them at home. Frail parents often reject their suggestions as intrusive or as a threat to their independence. A son in his late fifties reports:

Actually right around the time when my mother was recovering they needed some help. I would say things like, "Karen (my sister-in-law) can put you in touch with a woman who could come in and clean for you." So, I give them advice like that, but it's kind of frustrating to me because they're disinclined to do those things. First, my father especially doesn't like my sister-in-law very much. I think she's terrific but he finds her bossy; he wants women to be submissive and she certainly isn't. Also, my mother would rather do it for herself and put off getting help from anybody. The young men who've helped them have moved. So I don't think that they want help, but even if they did they're not inclined to ask for it and they don't exactly know how to do it.

Many frail parents become disabled only in late old age. Commonly their own children, in early old age themselves, care for them at home. One well-adapted daughter describes her own distant parents' commitment and dedication to her extremely frail grandfather who lives with them. Sometimes she feels sorry for them, sometimes she is critical that they don't find more help to alleviate their burden. She certainly accepts their dedication to her grandfather and, in turn, dedicates herself to their needs at some future time. She also tries to alleviate their stress and feels frustrated by their inability to get out of the house and visit her more:

My parents have very little accessibility in their life-style because my mom's father lives with them. It's difficult, but they feel they have no choice. He is ninety-three. He can't be alone and he keeps them at home. He needs everything in services though he's not bed-ridden. But he doesn't walk that well and spends most of his time in a chair. They have a woman who comes in for half a day but my mom pretty much does everything for him. My dad feels really close to him and thinks of him as Dad.

They don't come here though. They're really locked in. They don't complain a lot about it but they wish they had more freedom. They've chosen their situation. They've looked into nursing homes for my grandfather, but they really don't want to subject him to that. They would never put us through this. On the other hand, as one who's seen how well it can be done, I would never want to put them in a home either. I wouldn't hesitate to take them into my home. My mom took care of her parents. And my grandmother took care of her parents. You know it goes way back, children taking care of aged parents at home, outside of institutions.

Now I could give my parents more relief than they could give me. But a year ago they could have given me a lot more because of little Jeremy. You can ask and expect more from your family than you can of friends. If they were closer it would be easy for my mom and dad to have me come spend the weekend and they could go away. Or we could all go to the movies. It would be great.

Many children realize that caring for a very old parent is stressful. A son sadly recalls his mother's last years, drained and overwhelmed caring for her own mother. When both parents are alive the most common arrangement is for the healthier spouse to care for the permanently disabled spouse. Again, the distant child's contribution is limited and indirect. Most children attempt to help the care-giving parent by listening and sympathizing with their problems, performing services and tasks during visits, and trying to find outside help. A distant son typically feels his help is inadequate:

My father has made as much improvement from his stroke as he's going to make. He can walk and talk, but with difficulty. He is dependent for just about everything. He doesn't cook. I think he still could but when he first had his stroke my mother pampered him.

So now he just relies on her for everything: shopping, cooking, laundry, housecleaning, transportation. She writes the checks and he sits and watches TV. Well, I got him an exercise bike for Christmas and he rides that every day.

If my mother is ill, my father can't drive her to the doctor so she has to call my aunt or my brother. Or, if something happens to my father, she gets very upset. So she has to call somebody to help her out. But she's basically pretty independent.

My mother feels under a lot of pressure. My father needs some stimulus to convince him that he can do things if he just tries. He lets her do things for him. But she thinks if she gets upset with him, he'll have another stroke. And when he gets upset with her she doesn't fight back. She used to yell all the time. That's a change in their relationship.

I'd like to get them out of the house more. But it's a lost cause because of my father. He just isn't all that interested. I think they have problems but I have no real response. I could be doing other things. I'm not sure what they are. I've talked with my brother about getting them a counselor. She's gone alone though, not with my father. I feel inadequate there.

Some children are not as sympathetic when care-giving parents complain. One son elaborates the stress his mother felt and her impatience during his father's long decline from Parkinson's disease. Since his mother lacked certain skills in making important decisions, he assisted her. Foremost in his mind was trying to avoid institutionalizing his father:

Before he died my mother was in relatively good health. But there was a lot of stress coping with my father's rapidly deteriorating health. I was very concerned that he would become disabled and in a nursing home because it would be too hard for her to stay home alone and she wasn't ready to go into a nursing home. Even though she's a very capable person, she wasn't quite up to making all the decisions for a person who was very ill. I intervened quite a lot by invitation. My sister lives there. And we all get along rather well. It's a very open communication system. There's a lot of assistance given both by the parent to the child and vice versa.

Basically, my mother is a kind, giving, and supporting individual. But she doesn't handle people being sick real well. She would imagine that my father was deliberately making things more difficult. And that wasn't my perception at all. I really think she exaggerated, given the stress of the situation over many years. Anyone who experiences so much stress for so long might become impatient about those things. Maybe it's a feeling of hopelessness.

Another son whose father is deteriorating from Parkinson's explains how he and his brothers began exploring ways to convince his father to accept more help in order to alleviate his mother's burden:

My mom is very self-sufficient. I talked with my brothers about how desperate her situation is getting. It's partly the result of those conversations that we decided to visit and do what we did.

My father has had Parkinson's for fifteen years. The symptoms can be controlled. But it's still degenerative. He can only walk a few steps unassisted. He needs help dressing and bathing. He regressed from a cane to a three-legged cane, to a walker, and finally, just in the last year, to an electric wheelchair. So it's been gradual but most rapid in the last five years. Until then he was quite independent.

In helping him get his shoes on I'll find myself becoming impatient. It takes forever. We'll be sitting there and I'll say, "I can do that for you." And he'll say, "No, I can do it." It's one of the things he can do. So I sense in myself something I'd have to deal with if I were there more frequently. I'd just have to deal with my urge to do things just for the sake of speed and efficiency.

Now he's become very dependent on my mother. She has no recreation and no respite from him. She's up to the task. But I don't know what it's going to do to her. In a retirement community like that there are relatively few men and they tend to be in worse shape. Occasionally she will go play bridge somewhere in the apartment building and leave my father alone. She'll come by to check on him every half hour. Shopping is also a strain. She will leave him in the car while she shops, which she's not happy about. He'll be OK alone, I suppose. But it's risky. If he tried to get up and fell down he wouldn't be able to get back up.

We were there a month ago and I talked to my father about my mother's need to have some relief. He was uncomfortable with anyone else taking care of him. My mother is getting burned out. We could tell from her letters that she was getting almost completely tied down. We went to intervene somehow, to persuade her to explore the possibilities for getting relief, and to talk to my dad about it. Well, at least he recognized that she needed to have some respite for the sake of her health. He even said something, that his objection to having a volunteer was that this was a step he didn't want to recognize, toward greater dependency.

In the retirement complex where they live there is a nursing home connected under the same administration. When the time comes it will be hard for them to make the decision. But my mother will be able to stay in their apartment if her health remains good. And he could have nursing care right there in a building across the way.

TOTAL DISABILITY

The final stage of the continuum of declining health usually begins with institutionalization or moving to live with one's children because of the need for care. This transition takes place when parents become very frail or develop a serious medical condition. Sometimes children and their parents try to adjust their life-styles in anticipation of disability and dependency. Near-living siblings often take the primary responsibility in caring for a permanently disabled parent, especially if the parent is widowed. A common response of distant only children to a parent's permanent disability is to suggest that the parent move in with them. None of the children in my study had moved their distant parents into their own homes, however. One only daughter was not satisfied with her mother's medical care following a heart attack, so her parents moved to an apartment in Lansing to be closer.

Especially during the final stage of declining health, the need for a parent's assistance places great stress on the distant relationship. In 1983 the *New York Times* (Collins 1985) ran a series of articles revealing a growing public awareness about the difficulties of organizing long-distance health care for elderly parents. According to Rose Dobroff, director of the Brookdale Center on Aging at Hunter College, only recently has a national social welfare network developed in the private sector to help children assess and respond to health and housing needs of distant elderly parents. But such services are very expensive, not widely available, and not yet reimbursable through most insurance programs.

Newsweek magazine (1985) also examined the beginning of a nationwide network to help long-distance care givers. One example is the Aging Network Services of Bethesda, Maryland, founded four years ago by social workers Barbara Kane and Grace Lebow. They noticed problems created by distance in their social work cases. As Kane says, "Doctors were sending us middle-aged patients with stress-related complaints like backaches and headaches. They had already had some therapy and they felt the only thing that would help was if we could do something to help their parents in Chicago, or somewhere like that." Because of this experience they developed a long-distance management system. A daughter, for example, will tell them she is worried about her recently widowed mother who is not dealing well with the death of her husband but refuses to move from her own distant locality. The network of 150 social workers around the country will find the local neighborhood and community supports. The local social worker becomes the contact person for the worried daughter.

A number of studies also focus on the impact of care giving on the adult child care givers themselves (Cantor 1979; Horowitz 1975, 1985). Although practically no one abandons distant parents, children reveal a wide variety of perceptions regarding their distant care-giving responsibilities. Displaced and well-adapted children typically accept their responsibilities as a loving expression of family concern. Predictably, alienated children cannot cope with the time, money, and effort.

The responsibility for distant care giving places great stress on both generations. Children report instances of severe stress, broken marriages, financial crises, and jobs lost due to the burdens of distance care giving. Disagreements with spouses or siblings may involve not just the expense and time of traveling to visit the parent, but also long-dormant emotional issues of child-parent conflicts triggered by the stressful situation.

Most parents who enter nursing homes usually do so after a variety of alternatives have been tried, including living with children. When institutionalization does occur, it seems to signal an imbalance between the needs of the individual and the community to meet those needs (Ward 1978). The decision to institutionalize a parent is extremely stressful for everyone. Both relief and guilt are common feelings immediately following institutionalization (Smith and Bengston 1979). Distant children agonize as much or more than children who live nearby. And, if an aged spouse is living independently, he or she carries the major burden of maintaining family bonds with the institutionalized spouse. If the institutionalized parent is widowed, the responsibility usually falls to a near-living child. Virtually no long-term care institutions take the initiative to contact distant children unless the child initiates and maintains the contact. Moreover, professionals in long-term care institutions still regard distant children de facto as irresponsible and unreliable. One alienated daughter, a distant only child in her fifties, narrates the story of her mother's mental deterioration from Alzheimer's disease and her eventual institutionalization:

> My mother is in a nursing home in California an hour away from my father. She's been there for two years; she has Alzheimer's disease. It is further complicated because both my parents are Christian Scientists. One doesn't get anything diagnosed, although that's slightly complicated, as you can imagine. Until recently they would never go to doctors or take any medicine.
>
> My mother had this condition for seven or maybe ten years. When she got progressively worse, I finally encouraged my father to find a place for her because his life was becoming completely unmanageable. She did not recognize him or me. He tried to place her in a Christian Science nursing home there which would be in accordance with their beliefs. But she was so advanced with Alzheimer's that none of them could handle her.
>
> The only place that handles Alzheimer's Christian Scientists is in New Jersey. He didn't want to relocate there and he didn't want to part with her, living so far away. So he and I looked at the other homes and found this one. A doctor there sees her once a month and they have been administering insulin. Other than that, virtually no medication. But even that's contrary to religion, so in that area my father sent her off to be cared for and doesn't inquire.
>
> When I went abroad in 1978 she was just horrified. They then decided to go to California from Washington. So they packed up the house that year and moved. And I got these letters from my

mother saying how could I be in Poland the year they decided to move. Here she was all by herself and why wasn't I there to help her. I knew she was crazy because they could have waited a year.

My mother showed the first signs when we went to China about eight years ago. They came up from L.A. to San Francisco to see me. My mother's behavior then was definitely Alzheimer's. I knew there was something wrong. I don't think I had a name for it then. But I had a feeling. She was spending so much of the time going through suitcases and not being able to find things. She was getting frustrated and crying about it. Even before that, though, she told me she was having trouble remembering my children's names. She had to wake my father up and things like that.

And I think because they were Christian Scientists and I knew that nothing was going to be dealt with medically I blocked out being concerned about what was happening. I simply had as good a relationship as I could. And I convinced myself since they were old and going to die anyway, that I shouldn't worry about it.

My mother's deterioration was slow. A lot of the behaviors have been there for many years, because the best I can determine my mother has been mentally and emotionally ill all the time I've known her, from my childhood. But it didn't dawn on me that she was really ill for a long time; it was just Mom. Her love was so unhealthy. I didn't get loved. She wasn't mature enough to be able to love. She needed me. She was desperate. I was playing some kind of a role to fulfill her needs. It wasn't nurturing because that sounds too much like I understood it. It was more of being a victim by playing a role to survive. I always had a sense something was strange. But since all adolescents complain about their parents I just thought . . . well, that I had gotten locked into adolescence. It's so painful to talk about it, but what I know now is that she really was mixed up for a long time.

Christian Science is not just positive thinking about the condition you're in. There is a denial of being mortal and of having any problems because you are perfect as God created you. So you have that energy and that's all you talk about. You always have to conceal how you feel physically. One doesn't raise this to consciousness. That was why in high school I began to think this stuff was really pretty bad. Not only that I couldn't say what I needed. But I remember them teaching me that if you have the pleasures of your body, then you have to suffer the pain in your body. So you had to deny all of your body. I thought, "My God that's terrible." I'd go out on a Saturday night date and Sunday I'd think I'm never going to get things together. I mean it didn't match my reality.

I left home originally to go to college. I negotiated to go to New York, as far as they would let me go. I knew I needed to get out and be on my own because it was far too controlling at home. My mother literally followed me to the bathroom.

After we were married Tom would vacillate between thinking my mother was crazy and evil. If my mother were still with it mentally, we would still have the same conflict. I left the religion and my mother told me that I might as well be a prostitute, that I was a failure, that she had been a failure as a mother. The main thing was to raise me as a Christian Scientist. I can't win. I don't think my mother ever found solace though. No.

I know the effects on me were incredible. I don't know where to start, but when our first child was born seems right. My husband and I had delayed having children. We just didn't feel we were ready. But when we decided and the first one was born I knew I had parenting issues I had to deal with. I thought I had to be perfect and I had no idea what a perfect parent was. I knew I didn't want to be like my mother. So I got some counseling. That was supportive and helpful once a week for a year, then every other week for a year.

Toward the end it was difficult communicating with her. I would call and if my father were out she would say, "I'm so glad you called. I don't know where your father is. I'm so upset." And I could tell she'd been crying and was in distress, and disoriented. We didn't have any substantive discussions but she knew who I was and I was so glad I called.

Now I visit several times a year. But my mother hasn't recognized me for four years. Two years before she went in the hospital, I had figured out that she didn't really know who I was. She had a lot of cover-up behavior so that one could think she knew. But she could be talking to a stranger. Suddenly she would be looking at a picture of me and say, "Who's that?" And if I told her it was her daughter she would go on about it. But if I told her it was me, she would say, "Really, that can't be." One time in front of her I called my father "Daddy," and she turned to me and said, "Is he your father?" and I said, "Yes, he is." So she said, "How can that be?" So she was totally lost. Actually she got nicer the sicker she got. She would begin to let me help her and she was distractible like a child so that she wouldn't bore in on something. That's why I was able to help her.

My father involved me completely in solving the problem of what to do with my mother. I told him, "When I come to California we need to go out and look at places." When I got there he had these places for us to go see. When we found the right one my father said, "Fine, we'll place her in there." He was ready. It was important to him that I was there. That was a crisis and there isn't any other family. I'm an only child.

They were in a condominium out there and my father was doing the shopping and the laundry and everything. My mother didn't know anything that was going on. But he didn't want to part with her. I said, "Why don't you move to an apartment, one of those places there where you can get your meals and someone will clean the house for you so you won't have all those things to do." He agreed to that. So I went out and spent a week packing them up.

He had packed up for maybe two weeks before that. She had all these sets of china. Then I went out and still had an incredible amount of packing. And we did it all by ourselves. I thought, "But where are their friends?" He called on no one. No one came over to help. Just the two of us did this, with my mother in this bizarre state the whole time. She was interfering although it was so childlike by that point that I could distract her.

I think emotionally he was so relieved to have her gone because he had let it go too far. For a year every time I talked to him he said he was getting better every day. He had never complained before. He never would say how bad he felt physically anyway. But after she left he just kept saying how much better he felt. So I helped my father move to the apartment and he gets all his meals there. It's really worked out nicely.

It is difficult to live far away now that she's in an institution. Institutionalizing my mother made it hard to fill out the forms there. I keep the amount of time I go there to a minimum. Now when I go I spend the whole day there. And I know I'm doing that for me; there are things I get out of it. I sit and write. I talk to her. I see her. Recognition is a game that one plays. I imagine that she knows who I am during some of that time. But that's because I wanted to. . . . That isn't so painful. The hurt is [crying] . . . that it couldn't be a better relationship. It's not so bad if parents are far away if they have Alzheimer's. If they had all their facilities that would really be distressing to me because I would want to do more. Now there isn't really much I can do.

There was a period when I wanted to tell them I was having some really difficult times at work. But when I attempted to do it they couldn't hear my problems. They gave me back such unreal responses it wasn't worth it. They'd say, "Everything will be all right." I realized I can only mention successes, no problems.

I can't imagine what her problems are now because my father and I don't talk about the medical problems. I guess I avoid them. Now I ask him questions that I could never have asked before. How did my mother look? Is she eating? What did the doctor say? I can get my father to give me information but I have to phrase everything in the right way. I can't say, "How is she?" But as long as I don't involve him directly. . . . For example, from his Christian Science perspective, he and I both know the doctor doesn't know anything. But I can ask what the doctor says as long as I don't involve my father. They won't ever volunteer personal information. And they need to be asked in a very special way.

Certain fundamental issues about people's conditions must remain unexpressed. It is difficult for Christian Scientists to live away from their parents, especially having the thought and wanting to know those things. They aren't things you're supposed to want to know. For example, I didn't find out about their friends dying either. It was curious because people their age would die and they wouldn't tell me. And I considered them my childhood friends too. They go into so much denial themselves about anybody dying because life is eternal. They would block it. And to say it out loud to me was to have to deal with it on another level. They wouldn't have told me if I were close by, either.

Now I speak several times a week on the phone with my father. Very little of our communication is about my mother. First of all, he doesn't even really know what's happening or ask questions. He doesn't pursue it. I don't think he wants to know. In Christian Science the physical condition is not important anyway. And she recognizes him. He goes to visit her. He spends the time with her. He tells me he's been to see her but I can't get much information from him because he doesn't comment. So we talk about what he's doing.

When my mother was around, even when she was her sickest, I still didn't know my father as well as I did once she went away. She dominated so much that at least now, even though he's not a great listener, I get to listen to him. In the past she totally controlled the conversation. And all through these years I mostly spoke with her.

I speak to my father on his terms, about his subjects mainly. I don't expect a normal conversation. I patronize him, absolutely. I must say. We don't really tell each other how we feel. He won't talk about physical needs. But I was really raised to feel I was to be independent and on my own.

Sometimes my self-esteem is affected by such calls, depending on my needs at the time. Now he kind of backs off. Most of the time his message is that I'm pretty amazing, that I am a rock, that I am tough. He complements me. But he's really amazed with my emotional strength. It makes me feel good now. But I went through such a long period of needing their approval. I extended it and had it all mixed up so that I had a lot of meaningless approval from my mother. A lot of overflow of things that I didn't value that she pretended to stress. Now I'm rather detached from the approval. It's just not an issue now. It took me till middle age.

COPING WITH TERMINAL ILLNESS AND DYING

When a distant parent's health begins to decline dramatically, many children initiate a crisis pattern of contact, visiting and calling far more often than previously. The distant child's need to visit frequently during a terminal illness is greater than at any other time. Crisis visiting patterns allow sorely needed direct face-to-face interactions, health arrangements, and care.

Sons and daughter see and care for their dying distant parent, comfort and provide emotional support and comfort for the surviving parent, and reaffirm bonds of affection before their parent dies. Regardless of their emotional attachment, distant children take time out from their lives to be with a terminally ill parent because they realize their chances to see their parent in the future are limited.

Several children recall their parent dying as a period of intense, long-term stress. Combined with the normal grief and anxiety, modern medicine has prolonged the dying process sometimes more than a year. During this time children travel and visit many times, as one daughter recalls:

"My father developed emphysema, then lung cancer followed. During the time he was ill I visited him very often. I went alone and stayed about four days at a time. It was important to me that I'd been there the week before he died."

Frequent visiting from far away carries an immense emotional cost. The child's nuclear family often suffers a great deal. A daughter's narrative of her mother's terminal illness illustrates how frequent crisis visits disrupt the normal routines of the distant child, cause financial hardship, and upset virtually every aspect of family life:

> I had a new job and was sick with the chicken pox when she called in July to say she had ovarian cancer. She lied at first; she said it was uterine, which is less serious, because she was worried about me. I wasn't going to come in at first. I didn't have any sick leave. The girls were three and four. But I did go because my dad called and was furious. She went in for surgery and I found out it was ovarian as I walked around with my dad. I looked up ovarian cancer. The survival rate at her stage—distended stomach—was one in five. The surgeon said he took out only 80 percent of the cancer.
>
> After six months of chemo she was nauseous all the time. She didn't eat and she threw up. Then she had a turnaround and dealt better with the chemo. She had moments when she felt she's going to beat it, moments I thought she was going to beat it, moments when I believed her. You know that woman who helped her mom commit suicide? It was a very controversial book. I bought it but I couldn't bring myself to read it.
>
> By January she went on vacation for three days. In April my husband Ken had his heart attack. They came Mother's Day to help out. She was feeling great. No sooner did the doctor declare Ken OK than she got sick again. The day after she returned home she had a bowel obstruction from cancer. She was operated again, in and out of the hospital. She took a lot of pain killers.
>
> The summer before she died I flew in every other weekend. I feel guilty spending so much. I thought she was dying so many times. She'd be rushed in the hospital, "Bring my bathrobe, my nightgown. . . ." My brother would call at 6 A.M., we answered thinking he would say she was dead. I was angry with my brother because all this was just after Ken's heart attack. But he'd call up and say he just couldn't do anymore. I could come home and get away a bit but my brother was there all the time. The pressure to visit my mom and have Dad over was tremendous. And he lives an hour away from the hospital. But when I'm here I can't do spontaneous things like take Dad for coffee and hug him.

Sometimes I'd go by myself, sometimes together. On those regular visits we all drove and she'd be at home. We'd stay at my in-laws', not my parents' house. The girls got on Mom's nerves. Mostly I would just visit with her and my father. My father would cry and go upstairs. She'd come down and we'd eat dinner. Then Dad would cry again. My oldest girl Rachel was angry with me. She felt very little sympathy. Lisa, the younger one, accepted it all very well. She had a delayed reaction.

My mother said she loved me. She had no regrets about our relationship. She couldn't talk about dying with my dad or my brother. Dad brought clothes from the cleaners and she said, "I'll never wear that cause I'll never live to see the winter." Mothers and daughters share things as women that fathers and sons don't share—fertility problems, menstrual pains, planning menus for a party. Also I'm getting older. Mother even said, "We don't share the way we used to. Living out of town you've become more self-reliant." It's true. Many times I call a friend rather than family. If I stayed in town I wouldn't go through the same process of independence. I would have been more dependent if I stayed there. Certain friends become substitutes for family.

They put her on an I.V. until she died. Now my dad is remarried. I'm happy for my father. I used to tell my mother things and she would tell him. I'm still close to him but I got closer during Mom's illness. I told him, "Someday it will be over and you will have some moments of happiness again." I gave him moral and emotional support during the worst of it. My husband gave me support.

In the final weeks, children help make important health decisions for their distant parents. A common decision involves nursing homes, since the caregiving parent often cannot manage such extreme changes in health any longer:

I would call and there were lots of conversations about where he was going to go. We were not sure whether we would be able to bring him home or put him into a nursing home. And, of course, we went through a lot of searching to try to find alternatives to the nursing home.

Spouses and other family members often make valiant efforts to keep their loved ones at home. At a certain point, however, many concede to the institution, as a son explains:

207

My mother had a bad stroke in 1980 but she was beginning to recover. And my father decided a mad thing, that he would take care of her at home. He wouldn't have nursing care. Then she had a second stroke that left her unconscious, really semi-comatose for four years. When my mother was in a nursing home, I would spend a moderate amount of time just sitting there holding her hand and saying nothing.

The only time my father has ever needed support is when my mother was sick. I'm afraid I wasn't in a position to do very much. I would call him often. I visited a couple of times too. Then, when my mother died, I was supportive. She was virtually unconscious. We had concern periodically when someone would come to visit her. We were afraid someone would say something about my father's girlfriend, Renée.

In the process of dying, distant parents may be admitted to the hospital, released, then readmitted several times over a period of months. One son recalls that his father returned home from the hospital, then had a massive stroke that left him brain dead; the family had to deal with questions of withdrawal of life supports. When families make decisions in a crisis, old patterns of cooperation and conflict surface. Well-adapted and displaced children sadly recall such crises. Yet they report that the family clung together and displayed sensitivity toward one another. Openness of communications prevailed and they made decisions naturally, as a son reports:

> There was a decision early on after the stroke: whether or not to take my father off a respirator. Can he breathe without it? We don't know. It was the question of how much life support to provide . . . force feeding for twenty days? My telephone communications with my mother and sister were very open and candid in all ways. My mother and I from the outset had a similar understanding of the situation. My sister was initially more reluctant; she had some glimmer of hope that something dramatic might happen. But after she started going to the hospital and seeing what was happening, she came around to our viewpoint. So there was never any argument about it and no one was trying to conceal information from other members of the family. By the time the decisions actually had

to be made, we were all in agreement. So I helped my mother in that way.

In contrast, alienated children relive unresolved relationships and an inability to generate genuine communications during a crisis. Ambivalence and emotional repression are recurrent themes. An alienated son remembers:

There was about a month where it was very clear to everyone in the family that his situation was hopeless. But the doctors wouldn't quite say that. They gave him many things in the hospital including chemotherapy. So when he went in, my expectation was that this could be dealt with, that there was a procedure for it. But he never came back. I was with my father when he died. I went down there for the weekend to see him. I didn't get down a lot because, well . . . that was a very tough year for me. . . .

When my father was dying, that's when the emotional swallowing took place. I think nobody was willing to say to my mother that her husband was terminally ill, that the treatment will not help him, that the only thing we can do now is make him as comfortable as possible and prepare ourselves for his death. By the time I got down there he wasn't even coherent. In some ways it really did matter. I couldn't really say good-bye or I loved him. Instead we said he's getting this treatment. But at the same time his treatment is not working and his doctor is stupid.

Why don't we just say we don't want any more of this treatment and take him home? There was a typical inability of the family to talk about touchy issues. In this case we needed immediate action. Somebody needed to say, "Hey everybody, attention, our father, Herbert Howell, is about to die. Let's get ready for that. Let's not think something is going to happen or that we don't really know what's happening."

I think we bungled our way to a solution. I must have said something to my mother that it looks like he's beyond help. I remember asking her if she asked what the chances were that the procedure will work. But we were busy suspending all of our rational judgments. People are really geniuses about handling things by not saying certain things. Maybe we all knew what was going on, that it was over. But that the easiest way to play it out psychologically was through a feeling of sort of we don't know. Or, the doctor told us to do this so we'll do it—to play along and get through this horrible time.

209

If we had all gotten together and acknowledged the fact that he is dying, that would have put an emotional pressure on everyone that might have been too hard for them to deal with. So it was a kind of unconscious family strategy. But that was very typical for us. My family could do better if we'd talk more. Things get done by default because people aren't willing to make decisions.

Alienated children often report less direct involvement in the decision-making process and are more critical of the medical care their parents receive, whereas well-adapted and displaced children express faith in their families and doctors, even when they know their parent is dying. A displaced son describes a similar death scene in a radically different light:

The doctor is actually hiding from the Medicare authorities to prevent them from moving my father from the hospital. Under the new regulations they want to get you out of the hospital and into the nursing home because they're saying it's not diagnostic treatment anymore. We know what's wrong with this person and that's the end of it. Their opinion would be that he's going to die anyway and they're bureaucrats. But our doctor ordered a whole new round of diagnostic tests to stall the whole process because it's not in the patient's best interest to move him to the nursing home. Even though everyone knows he's going to die, the medical facilities in the nursing home are not going to be as good under any circumstances.

The voices of emotional attachment are not only expressions of attitudes and feelings, but also of behavior. Regardless of their voice, children desire to help their distant parents when they need assistance. Yet well-adapted and displaced children feel more capable and confident in their ability to help than alienated children, who feel frustrated and powerless as a result of unresolved and painful conflicts from the past.

CHAPTER 8

Social-Status Transitions of Parents and Children

In this chapter we will consider the assistance children and distant parents provide during social-status transitions. As with health transitions, the voices of emotional attachment do not influence the desire to help as much as a child's perception of his or her capacity to help. The most important social transitions of parents are death, widowhood, relocation, remarriage, and retirement. We will also consider the help distant parents provide during their children's social and health transitions.

DEATH AND GRIEF

When a parent has a terminal illness, some distant children begin grieving even before the parent dies. Their grief is no less real but begins sooner because distance obstructs regular face-to-face contacts. The death of one distant parent often results in widowhood of a surviving parent. So the distant child must deal with two major life-cycle transitions at the same time: grieving for the dead parent and maintaining the distant relationship with the widowed parent.

Most distant parents who have lived away from their children for many years relocate to live with or near them or another child when they are dying or become seriously ill. Yet confronting death is always difficult. It generates powerful emotions and intense conflicts often surface. A son reports that his father and alienated brother are beginning to talk to each other again, ten years after their conflict at the time of his mother's death:

> My brother and my father's views are really quite opposite. And when my mother was dying down there that was a very difficult time. My parents moved back from Puerto Rico to get her medical help in Phoenix. So they were in fact living with them when she died. In fact, my father had bought my brother and his wife a house. It had a kind of mother-in-law wing where they lived. Well, it was just a very hard time. The real reason my brother didn't come to my mother's funeral was because of conflict with my father. I spoke with my brother on the phone and asked if he were coming and he said he couldn't and he sent a headstone for her grave.

In anticipation of the end, some distant parents want to talk about death with their children. Well-adapted children are sometimes put off but tolerant of their parents' concerns. A well-adapted son in his fifties describes his ambivalent response to his father's thoughts about death:

> In October I was out walking with him and he said, "Your mother doesn't mention this but I know I've gotten much weaker. I don't think I'll last till my next birthday." I said, "But there are things that you still enjoy, aren't there?" "Not really," he said. So I think he does recognize his decline and he is depressed; he's given up. I'm very conflicted about my father now because I feel like Dylan Thomas: "Do not go gentle . . . Rage, Rage against the dying of the light." I hate to see him give up. On the other hand, if I imagine myself to be in his position where life in physical terms can't get better, it can only get worse, I don't think I would have a strong urge to struggle. I don't know why I should insist that he do so. I grasp at things. In a way I want him to fight for life because I would

hate to see him go. In another way I can see that since no one lives forever, there's a time when you're just too tired, and ready. And it's not bad to be ready.

In contrast, alienated children find it very painful to listen because past conflicts intervene. An alienated daughter received a letter about death from her mother that reawakened intense feelings of emotional and geographical distance:

My mother writes letters about her preoccupation with all these people dying, and telling us all the funeral arrangements they made for themselves. I got a letter outlining all their choices for funerals: what music, what Psalms, who's to talk, the whole thing. That's because my brother-in-law's mother died and my sister made the comment when they went to clear out the house that it would have been helpful had they known about some of these things. So my mother was going to make it easy for us. She went through the house and wrote down the things that she thought were of interest and said who was going to get what and sent copies of this to everyone.

I was extraordinarily hurt and I did not contact her for a month because there were some things from the grandparents, and all three of my sisters were named for those things. But I was not named for anything. We have contemporary tastes and she thought, "Well, Linda isn't going to want that because it's not going to fit into her house." That would be her way of thinking rather than thinking that I would value it as a family item. It hurt me that she knew me so little.

I kept thinking should I write, should I call, should I never speak to her again? I was very upset. I finally waited long enough for them to return from a trip. She wrote again: "Oh, I went through what I had written before I went on the trip. I wrote it in a hurry and I realized that I forgot to ask you if you wanted to have this cream and sugar set that belonged to your grandparents?" So it was her sloppy carelessness rather than a deliberate thing.

I would have said something. But I didn't want to disturb the holidays. I just want to let it all out and tell her how I feel. But the other part of me says she's not going to react the way I want her to react. She's just going to be hurt. And she isn't going to change. So what's the point? I have these conflicting ways of handling it. Usually, if I wait long enough I stew and I sweat it out. It was a week before I even told my husband I got this letter. I couldn't sort out my own feelings about that. I felt very much like I was not a part of the family. Maybe because I live away I've developed different ideas and attitudes. I see and do things differently and I have different interests. I have more education too. And I've been exposed to different ideas. But I always knew I was different. I never really got along well with my mother even while I was growing up.

Living far from parents may promote guilt due to the children's own health problems and their inability to be there when their distant parents need them. Adult children often suffer from intense guilt if they are not present when their parent dies. Guilt is the emotional reaction to a personal sense of having violated a rule combined with a need to punish oneself. Problems arise when distant relationships are based on guilt or when a child feels guilt, as a well-adapted daughter recalls:

We got a call on Friday that he'd gotten a heart attack. I had a conference to go to that week in New Orleans. I had just visited them there the month before and Mom and Dad were fighting. I felt so stressed and I was just beginning to get over that bad cold, getting asthma, and not feeling up to par for that whole term. I really didn't want to go back then if it wasn't absolutely necessary. I talked at length with my sister, who lives right there, about whether I should cancel the conference or go. We were planning to go to Florida except after a few hours the doctor said he'd stabilized. Well, he'd had a lot of those mild heart attacks and had always pulled right through them. We decided she'd check with the doctor and he said I shouldn't come, that my daddy was doing just fine.

So I talked to him on the day before I left to go to the conference. That morning I left for the conference and he died while I was en route. Even my sisters who live three and five hours away didn't go. So we were all feeling the same kind of upset. That was really a terrible thing for all of us.

Children frequently call attention to the difficulties they face grieving for family members far away and alone. One theme involves the recognition that grieving is collective as well as individual, a family matter as well as a personal one. Moreover, distant children feel a special kind of loss or abandonment when their grief is postponed beyond the grief of their families because of distance, or when their grief is completely individual without the proximity and support of family and friends. A daughter in her late thirties experienced these feelings when her parents did not tell her about her aunt's death until she arrived for a visit:

> My mother's eldest sister was a fascinating lady who was dying for the last twelve winters. A little medicine and she was fine again. She was just getting old. But after she moved into her eighties it was clear she was in decline. I had said earlier in my letters if it looks as if Aunt Mary's really going to die let me know. I can come earlier if I need to because I want to see her.
>
> When I came home that summer my father met me. I asked how my aunt was and he said, "Well, we buried her last week." I was furious, absolutely furious because I could have come home earlier. They just didn't get around to telling me she had died. They waited until I got there.
>
> There was a certain logic. There was nothing I could do about it. But that's a very alienating experience. I feel very left out. I find that when there are deaths in England, if I don't hear until after several weeks I feel very isolated because I have to go through my grieving alone. Obviously everyone goes it alone. But I believe it would feel different if I felt we were doing it on both sides of the Atlantic at the same time. You don't even have to be there but know at the same time and be able to think, "Well they're hurting there and I'm hurting here." There's a kind of bonding. It's less lonely. The way I've felt in the past is, well, "I'd better hurry up with this because, well, they've dealt with it and it's all over there and I'm three weeks behind.

A displaced son explains his feelings of guilt at not being with his mother and sister when his father was dying:

> There was a lot of stress because I couldn't decide whether I should physically come down there. Because to me the decisions were fairly clear-cut. We agreed as a family that we did not want to prolong a hopeless situation. But I had some feelings of guilt and anxiety about being physically removed from the situation because I couldn't provide any emotional support to the other members of the family.

They of course were not attempting to lay a guilt trip on me about it. It was self-imposed. I thought my physical presence would have made a difference. I guess I was thinking, well, they're having to go through all this trauma of being there and dealing with this, staying at the hospital where this person is just waiting to die. Actually, even that was traumatic because the quality of life . . . well, there was no quality of life. Here is a person who is brain-dead so you're seeing all this physical deterioration. The less rational part of you says, "This is terrible, we've got to do something about this." And you're talking about dehydration and all those things that happen after you take away life supports. You provide minimum amounts of sustenance through an I.V. So that's why I felt a greater anxiety and it was more difficult. They were reporting to me what was happening over the phone. I was feeling really bad about it for a full twenty days. I suspect in some ways it was more . . . well, maybe this is an exaggeration . . . but I think my family feels like it was more difficult on me than it was on them. They understood why I felt guilt and anxiety, because I was so far away and unable to provide any support. Well, then he just died in that condition. Everyone felt immediate relief about it.

Grieving a parent's death may take many years. But it can be particularly painful when a distant child cannot air his or her feelings of loss. A well-adapted daughter believes her family has developed an unspoken taboo about discussing her deceased father. She wants to discuss her unresolved emotions, yet finds it difficult to break the conspiracy of silence:

A lot of the visit is just getting through the day, being with the kids, making meals. It's a lot of time and energy spent, and the true conversation level is fairly limited. So much hasn't been talked about: feelings, my interests, and my needs. My mother always talks about herself. So I feel a missing connection, that she really hasn't understood what I'm about even though she cares. At her house in particular, she gets very caught up wanting to cook us a fabulous meal.

I'd probably still talk about my father's death. It's like a big space we all walk around, and nobody's ever ventured in to talk about it and resolve it. I don't talk about it, my brother doesn't, my mother doesn't, everyone walks around it. We all know it's there. We lived through it. I think it's harmful in a way. Sometimes the most important things are the things people don't talk about.

It's a very bad feeling, unresolved. I don't know if loss would be the best term. It's got a lot of mystery, things I don't know about. Nobody wants to talk about it because it's too scary. Well, I do, but I don't. I avoid it also. I contribute to maintain this whole syndrome. I dismiss references that are made, I don't take them any farther than the superficial element.

I just talked to my brother, just working through what that time was like. And you know, I can't remember my brother during that time period at all. I don't even have a picture of him. For years, I'm not talking about a day. I don't remember the gap. I'm moving toward asking him. The most frustrating thing during visits has to do with that lack of connection.

Well-adapted children commonly arrange local memorial services for their parents after their distant funerals. I was invited to a memorial service in the home of a well-adapted son whose father had died of cancer. The ceremony was brief and featured religious and secular readings about life and death. He invited friends who knew his father from visits over the years and those who did not. He said the service in his home enabled his friends to help his family through the transition. The ritual eulogized his father and emphasized the love his family feels for his father. His father's life was reviewed and he was praised for helping his children, being kind to his grandchildren, and providing material and emotional support to his son and family.

Immediately after a distant parent's death, many children try to adapt their schedules to spend extra time with their widowed parent, as one well-adapted son explains:

We knew he had congestive heart failure for two years but we didn't know it was so serious. It worked out well because he died in June and classes are out here, so I flew immediately. When my other brothers left to go back to their families, I stayed with my mother for two weeks after that. Then I came back here because I had just left everything. Then I returned again for a few more weeks.

At the same time, children remember their efforts to comfort the surviving distant parent, as a well-adapted son recalls:

He doesn't want help, that's clear. When my mother died I was living in Austria. In fact, he wrote me a letter which took a couple of weeks to get there. I was writing home every day at that time. I'd been remembering pleasant things about my childhood and writing autobiographically about them. And the nice thing was that after my mother died my father got one of those letters each day. And it meant a lot to him.

When I got off the plane he said he was glad I was here because they were going to have a memorial service to my mother. He said, "You're the writer in the family; I'm glad you're here. You can write the memorial service and give it." And that was very, very difficult. I did that really without complaint. We had the memorial service in North Carolina, where she was buried and where they both grew up. Many of their relatives still live in that area. Really, Jane and I and the kids did it. That meant a great deal to him. So I helped him through my mother's death.

ASSISTING THE WIDOWED AND SINGLE PARENT

Children have very little responsibility as long as distant parents are married and living together. The household of an independent married couple is by far the most satisfying for the elderly because spouses provide each other with emotional and instrumental supports. Of course, some children assist distant parents by performing tasks that neither parent does well. A number of children are involved in their parents' financial planning, though here again children report variations in the way families identify and solve problems. One displaced son recalls his problems when he tried to involve his parents in a real estate business:

I was always ambitious. I was always the driving force to get my family moving with regard to business. I had some struggles at that point with my father because he was not a great risk taker. They were not major arguments but they were definite value differences about achievement.

Probably the fact that there was a family business might have enhanced the frequency of communications. But if the feelings weren't there to begin with, being in business together would have been worse. I have managed the family assets for years. That's something a lot of parents would never turn over to their children. I suppose it's helped my self-esteem. There was a lot of responsibility placed at my disposal.

Another displaced son explains:

> Mom's been an artist all her life. Unfortunately she has been reduced to painting ceramics on glazed porcelain since the blood vessels in her retina dried up and she sees less and less. We live in a place where you just can't get anywhere unless you drive. Mom always wants to go somewhere. When I'm home there's always a half dozen things she asks me to do, which means going over here and picking up some paint, and there for some china, and going to pick up shades for lamps she's just painted and so on.

The real burden of a child's responsibility often begins with the death or divorce of a distant parent. Sixteen children had widowed mothers, three had widowed fathers. Only three had divorced parents. An alienated son fears his mother will become emotionally dependent following her recent divorce:

> I was fairly anxious about my mother's divorce. For one thing, I had just gone through a painful divorce. For another thing, suddenly the possibility was there that my mother might be on her own. And if she doesn't have a husband, she's certainly not going to remarry at her age. What's she going to do? I don't mean financially. She's not well off but she has means. Where will she live? I have this fear that my mother might be coming to depend on me. I would feel stressed if she could no longer manage. Mother would not consider moving to Lansing with my wife here, so there's a saving grace there. I would say that she is less manipulative because I'm not alone.

After the death of a spouse the surviving parent reveals in one way or another the nature and extent of his or her dependencies, both emotional and instrumental. In general, the adjustment to widowhood is more difficult for older than for younger parents. Most sons tend to address their widowed parents' instrumental needs while daughters talk more about their parents' emotional dependencies. Yet such distinctions are not universal. Sons are also responsive to their distant parents' emotional needs and daughters routinely assist in very practical ways. A well-adapted son comments:

> She confides in me about her childhood. I consult with her on a computer. She calls me up when she has a problem with her program. She also sometimes calls up distressed about getting along with people in her church. She'll call and try to talk through things. Now I know that she's generally made up her mind. And usually my role is listening, it's to confirm for her that she is indeed doing what she wants to do. I will not disagree. She does the church budget. The minister considers her way very tight money. So she wants to defend her position. My role is to listen to her talk.

Another son notices confusion in his mother's behavior:

> Recently, her ability to analyze situations is beginning to slow down. I think she gets confused more easily. She has to think things through more carefully. I noticed when I was there this weekend once or twice I became a little impatient with her. I had to slow down more when I was around her. She went to the airport with me to pick up my son. She's not used to being in the airport and sometimes it's hard for her to see where we should go. I had to tell her two or three times.

Well-adapted and displaced sons stress their help with instrumental tasks:

> It was critical to help when my father died since they had lived together for fifty-three years and they were very close. She was much more needy and dependent. I just stayed at her house as opposed to staying at the cottage. There were a lot of very specific tasks she wanted to perform as quickly as possible: insurance policies, pensions for the company Dad worked for. It was difficult because it was concentrated and we were more emotional. I went through documents, papers with her and helped make the decisions. I transported her to various agencies of government and offices of the company.

Daughters also help solve practical problems:

> One big problem is how to provide routine help when Dad may
> need it. I'm just thinking of someone who can't drive. Going to the
> doctor and picking up groceries and going to clean the house. That
> becomes a problem. We're beginning to feel that we'd like to help
> out more.

Another daughter explains that her brother helps her mother
more with financial matters such as advice about taxes and bank
accounts, then proceeds to relate how she rather than her brother
helps financially when her mother goes on trips. Children often feel
helpless when distant parents require things they cannot provide.
One son complains that his brother who lives nearer (but not close)
does not help enough: "I feel I've been called upon to take on too
much responsibility. I wish my brother would do more. On the
other hand, I'm the one who's prepared through my background to
advise her in financial matters. And she follows my advice."

Typical emotional problems of widowhood are those of loss,
grieving, and loneliness. Such problems may be expressed in the
fear of social interaction, loss of confidence, depression, and anxiety
about the future (Lopata 1981). Recently widowed parents often
feel socially and emotionally isolated. Of course, distant parents express their dependency needs in a variety of ways. Some experience
difficulty forming new social networks and emotional bonds. For
others, widowhood is a time for experimenting with new relationships and trying new activities and life-styles. Several children help
their distant parents consider such options. One daughter sends her
mother books to support her return to evening college:

> My mother had a job teaching English for several years, then she
> retired. I take her and her ideas seriously and I send her books to
> read. I think that really matters to her because she has a lot of
> trouble finding books where she lives. I'll send her anywhere from
> six to twenty books at a time. And because I've sent them she'll
> read them.

A son claims his mother consults him when she travels: "Now she
travels a great deal, especially to California, so she asks me about

how long she should go. She doesn't like to fly but I've convinced her that her beloved bus is becoming inappropriate at her age." Another daughter encourages her mother to socialize:

It's her best friend from college's son who's getting married in North Carolina and she said she couldn't decide whether she should go or not. So I said, "You should go and have a good time." She said, "I don't know." She was concerned about going out socially by herself. I reminded her that her friend came alone to my wedding. I encouraged her.

Several well-adapted children praise their widowed mothers' growing independence in both social skills and emotions. A son expresses satisfaction that his mother controls her finances even when it means rejecting his advice. Another son notes that his mother is more sociable and feels entitled to her own opinions since his father died. A daughter is happy to report her mother's self-sufficiencies:

Since my father's death, my mother has found a new independence; she's turning into a self-sufficient person. She did try to learn to drive while my father was sick with cancer. She had a minor accident in a shopping center. It was a disaster. People often try to do new things and change during a crisis. But what she's done now is mastered the city bus system to go all over. Her neighbors are amazed because everyone drives. She lives within walking distance of a shopping mall and she walks every day to the center to exercise. People offer to drive her and she doesn't want rides. She occasionally does things with the senior citizens' houses and she's starting to make friends on her own too. So in many ways she's adjusting to a new phase in her life. Now she sees my brother's family once a week instead of every day.

Satisfaction with distant contacts often remains low for some time, especially from the child's perspective. Since so much attention is focused on the surviving parent's problems, the adult child's grieving about his or her parent's death may be lost in the shuffle. Certain routine concerns are often put on hold because of the priority given to the grieving parent. A son laments that for a long time after his father died his mother did not inquire about the grandchildren because of her sorrow. Most children provide far more emotional support to widowed parents than to married parents. A well-adapted daughter, who had been a widow herself, explains that her widowed mother confides in her rather than in her sisters because of her experience:

> My mother and I talk about my father or my late husband, who died in an automobile accident. It seems to me that my mother remembers the past better than she remembers the present. And she also likes to talk about things that are painful. I don't know if it's therapeutic for her. Since my sister hasn't lost anyone but my father, she probably doesn't do that quite as readily with her. She uses me more as the person who understands what she's going through because of my having gone through similar things.

When widowed parents complain, it represents a symbolic expression of underlying insecurities and conflicts that surface during times of grief and loneliness. A well-adapted daughter was amazed when her mother began to discuss marital intimacies she had never spoken about before:

> We didn't talk about sex when I was growing up. When I was a teenager, at the appropriate time, she never mentioned a word to me about sex. So I just had very limited information before I married the first time. There was never any discussion for years and years that I lived away till after my daddy died. Then when I was there last summer she suddenly broke into this conversation about their sex life and my sex life and just informed me of all sorts of things and about Daddy that I never dreamed of. It was shocking and embarrassing to say the least, after a mother and daughter never having any conversation about things like that. My mother acted as if she never had any sex life all those years.
>
> I'm a feminist. I always said my father was too chauvinistic toward her and I felt bitter growing up with an overbearing father. I think that has freed my mother up a great deal to talk about things like that with me, about women being more self-possessed. So I think she was breaking out and deciding that, well, she didn't have a very good sex life because she liked sex, and well, my father was very quick to have it over with, and she was never very satisfied.

I tried to help her: "Well Daddy probably didn't know any better." Or that if they had been able to talk about those things the way husbands and wives should be able to talk, the way I'm able to talk about them with my husband. . . . Telling her that probably did help her in some sense. And also telling her that I've had many conversations with women my age who've said they've experienced exactly the same thing probably helped her. She never had anyone validate those feelings for her.

Many widowed parents develop a greater need for distant communications immediately following their loss. Thus much of the child's relationship with a distant grieving parent focuses on issues of loss and loneliness and the reconstruction of a satisfying lifestyle. Since the distant relationship itself is often plagued by feelings of loss and separation, this task is very difficult for many distant children to address, particularly when their own memories of the past are unresolved or filled with conflict.

During the year after the death of a parent/spouse, all forms of communications increase as both generations cope with grieving and assess the extent of the surviving parent's needs for assistance. Both generations feel and express a sense of profound loss at not being together to share their grief. A widowed parent may call more often than before. Children too may call more often to console their distant parent. On the other hand, children with recently widowed mothers report slightly less desire to call. They often feel stress over their inability to provide face-to-face services previously performed by the spouse. While his father was dying, one son called every other day. Immediately after his father's death he called his mother twice a week. His mother also called twice a week. But their conversations now are shorter; they focus on her feelings of depression and loneliness, whereas before they focused on his father's deteriorating condition. He claims he calls less frequently now because he wants to encourage her to make new friends to fulfill her needs for companionship.

Visits also decrease markedly a year or so after the parent dies. While his father was dying a son flew to New Jersey from Michigan about ten times in one year. But he did not visit his mother during the year after his father's death:

My emotions fluctuated greatly after those visits. Sometimes angry, sad, and sometimes happy and peaceful. It was all colored by my father's illness. Shortly before my father's death it became very difficult for Mother to cope. Her depression affected everyone in the family. Now, as she moves through her period of mourning, she is beginning to feel part of her extended family again. I believe I will be able to enjoy visits once again though clearly not in the same way as when my father was alive and healthy. We're going to see her more often now that she is coping better with her own life, traveling and doing things with friends.

When visiting occurs it usually focuses on the child's home and family since few elderly widows feel comfortable entertaining their children's families. In part, this may reflect a let-down from the sometimes frantic crisis-visiting patterns immediately prior to a distant parent's death. But the decrease in visits also signifies a change in communication patterns, which is symbolic of a social-status transition.

Some distant widowed parents fantasize about visiting their children. This is probably a common experience and enables them to express their loneliness. Graham Rowles (1978:183) perceives such fantasizing as a healthy process of identification with the child and believes distant parents' lives are enriched through vicarious participation in the environments of others:

> Marie was often involved in the worlds of her children. Sometimes she "traveled" to Florida. On other occasions she "visited" a Gary home. . . . And Evelyn participated in an Arizona environment: "I watch the map on the TV and they've got cool; and it's going down to about, like in the forties, forty-five. He's in the center of Arizona."

Widowed parents must learn to perform the duties of the deceased spouse or find someone else to do them. Many of these duties can be learned, but when they are too difficult to learn, a widowed parent may turn to a distant child for assistance. Distant communications often change to accommodate these needs. An only son in his early thirties persuaded his mother to remain in her large house after his father died. At the same time he had to take on more responsibilities maintaining the house since she couldn't do it alone:

> I knew things needed to be done around the house that I would enjoy doing, so I made that an excuse to go. We help with house maintenance. I go every summer to repair what needs to be done. We also established a house fund if she needs to have a window repaired or something so that she has some money available and doesn't need to go into savings. I write her a check on a monthly basis.

Finally, the distant child's marital status influences assistance. Married children with their own children must divide their commitments among more people, that is, their spouse, their children, and their spouse's parents, than unmarried children whose commitments to their own parents remain relatively undivided. Married children without children must balance the needs of their spouse and their in-laws with those of their own distant parents. Frequently, married couples must assess the relative needs of both sets of distant parents. In some cases, one spouse lives far from parents while the other lives close. Providing help is very difficult and places great stress on a marriage when both sets of distant parents require assistance at the same time.

REMARRIAGE

Remarriage is an important transition for elderly parents. Actually, more elderly men remarry than women because the high ratio of women to men permit them a greater pool of women from which to select a mate. Remarriages in old age are generally successful; couples claim to be happy and divorce and separation rates are low. On one level both sons and daughters encourage their widowed or divorced distant parents to remarry. Children often express relief when a distant father remarries. They are pleased that he has found companionship and someone to look after him. On a significant emotional level, however, old age remarriages frequently cause problems, especially for adult children. Remarriage involves changes in financial and inheritance arrangements that were made when both parents were alive. Moreover, relationships change, especially prior patterns of emotional support.

Many children are unhappy because stepparents represent a source of tension in their relationships with their biological parent. Some children complain that their father's new wife or companion has taken him away from his family and friends. One son makes a point of asking his father about his entire extended family when he calls and privately blames his father's companion when his father is out of touch. Similarly, a daughter criticizes her distant father's wife for encouraging him to move, leaving behind extended family that the daughter used to contact through her father. Another daughter says she feels uncomfortable talking to her distant mother about her deceased father when her stepfather is around.

Another common fear is that relationships stepgrandparents form with young grandchildren will threaten the memory of the deceased biological grandparent. A well-adapted daughter explains her conflict in these terms:

> She wanted to be like a grandmother to my children. And I said, "Well OK, the kids really seem to like her." But then she wants me to call her "Mother." So I told my father, "No way I'm going to call her Mother." I have a mother and she's dead." I have this conflict about what this relationship is going to be like. The kids didn't really get to know my mom. I feel they were gypped.

Sometimes the degree of acceptance depends on the way a father handles the relationships. After many years an alienated son continues to reject his father's companion because his father began their relationship while his mother was still alive:

> After my mother had her second major stroke she had to be put into a nursing home. At some point he was at a party and met this woman who had been in a wedding with him of a very good high school friend. And I disapproved. This was a standard reaction of a son, who was very close to his mother.
> I just thought it was terrible that he was living with her. I never said anything to him. Both my sister and my wife thought this was probably a good thing because he was very distraught, and frankly

he had been drinking too much and that all stopped when he met her. So really in many ways this had been a good thing for him. But I really do not approve. My objection was that my mother was still alive. But I will say it's a good thing for my father. I realize that he's taking terrible advantage of this woman. She would like nothing more than to get married. It's one of these classic old-fashioned man-woman relationships. He refuses to get married.

His sister also has a problem explaining her father's companion to her small children:

> My sister can't stand her either and that's a great source of satis-faction. It's harder for her because she is hopelessly romantic and believes in the family. I do too. But my sister is slushy and my father doesn't respond to this at all. There is also the fact that she has children. My sister has this conflict about the relationship because their grandfather isn't really married.

The problem of the stepgrandparent is often symbolic of a more fundamental issue: children feel regret or even anger that another woman has displaced their mother. The son who criticizes his father's companion acknowledges that his own anger comes from a deeper emotional source:

> I am really very moralistic about this. I said my public objection was on moral grounds. But of course I didn't believe any of those things. If this had been someone other than my father I would have thought it the most normal thing in the world. My real objection was a personal one. That this was a person who was in the way, who was replacing my mother.

Remarriage of a widowed mother is less common but similar in many ways except that emotions toward the new stepfather are usu-ally not as intense. Children see remarriage as a desirable way for their mother to combat the loneliness of widowhood and reenter the important world of socializing couples (Blau 1973). Ultimately, both sons and daughters recognize the benefits of their distant fa-ther or mother having a spouse. But most children continue to be reminded of their deceased parent's absence in their face-to-face contacts with a stepparent. Even after many years children reveal problematical relationships to stepparents. An unmarried, well-adapted daughter in her early forties whose distant mother remarried when she was in college explains:

> I get along OK with my stepfather. But he's probably the primary source of tension at home because he has a different attitude. In some ways I'm fortunate in that I had been shaped by the life with my mother and father and didn't live with him. He has problems with independent, intelligent, talk-back women. It didn't get to that point with my real father since I was only twenty-one when he died and he was proud of his smart daughters. But Steven is different. He didn't have any input, so when we disagree with him about how family members are treated it's harder for him. He'll simply say this is how it ought to be and he doesn't feel comfortable engaging in a lot of discussion. I generally try to avoid confrontations since I'm only home a few days out of the year. He can't be educated at this point. Most of my sisters like talking things out. But these different styles create tensions. Family disruptions are often related to my stepfather.

VOLUNTARY RELOCATION

Relocation represents an important social transition for many parents. Voluntary migrations often evolve over a number of years, beginning with vacations in an attractive location along with a pleasant social life with friends from the same city. After retirement some elderly parents from northern climates spend their winters in Florida, California, or Arizona as "snowbirds," then eventually move completely. Voluntary migrations are common in early old age. They differ from later relocations, which increasingly become adaptations in response to widowhood and declining health.

Because these moves are voluntary, desirable, and elderly migrants are generally healthy and active, they require little or no assistance from distant children beyond emotional support and encouragement. Most children do not assist in the actual move if distant parents are healthy. Nevertheless, children invite their parents to stay in their homes at some helpful moment during the move. Children also take an active interest in their parents' social networks and the kinds of communities they are seeking. Typically, a daughter describes her distant parents' relocation in these terms:

> They just moved last month to Long Meadow, Massachusetts. They had a certain area in southern Massachusetts picked out because of the price of the homes, and because they were very involved in the cultural life of New York City but knew as retired people they couldn't afford to stay there and live the kind of life-style they had. So this seemed like a good compromise. It's a culturally rich area; concerts and movies, and restaurants. Long Meadow also has a community center, which helped make their decision. And they have some friends there.

Some children feel regret or loss when their distant parents move, particularly if they still have a psychological attachment to their childhood homes, communities, or extended families. One daughter whose parents moved from New York City to Florida expressed regret at not being able to go "home" to New York. Miami didn't offer the same cultural environment either. Also, when the parents lived in the old location it was easier for children to visit and maintain contact with extended family. Without parents there, maintaining contacts becomes more difficult. More importantly, a near-living child may be left behind when parents move. Most children continue telephoning and visiting their distant siblings. In some cases, however, parental relocations disrupt prior patterns of contact.

Nevertheless, most children support such moves and continue visiting and calling their parents as if they had not moved at all. In some cases the initial adjustment is difficult for the parents. But most speak positively about it to their children and adapt well to the new location. Concern about relocated elderly parents may reflect past migrations of the family. Response to moving differs among families who changed residence before, perhaps during an individual's childhood, and families where parents have lived in the same residence for many years. Children whose parents have never moved express greater concern that their parents will miss relatives and friends, local organizations, activities, and favorite places left behind. On the other hand, children whose parents have moved before express greater confidence that the move will invigorate them by providing new activities and social opportunities.

Some parents ask for advice and assistance when they move. Others reject the advice and solutions of their children. A principle of generational independence emerges as children and distant parents exercise the freedom to accept or reject help. Many parents talk about moving long before they need to move. For example, shortly after her husband died, a widowed mother wanted to talk about giving up her home and moving into an apartment. In fact, she did not want to make this move but the nearness to her husband's death and the emptiness in the house encouraged her to think and speak in those terms.

Distant parents resist making decisions quickly because they feel overwhelmed by the pressure to change. When children hear their parents talking about making important transitions they often make the mistake of understanding only the surface motives and not the underlying ones. Children who try to make unilateral decisions must be prepared for rejection. A son in his fifties remembers:

> About five years ago my brother and I decided that they should consider moving to another house. They were getting old and the house was too big and maybe they'd want to move into a condominium. They didn't bring it up as a problem; we did. But they didn't really want to discuss it. They had decided they were going to stay where they were, and so I guess in their minds it was not a problem. So it didn't need to be solved.

The outcome is better when children offer assistance rather than make decisions. An only child was very concerned about her mother and father living alone in a New York City apartment. Her mother had recently suffered from a rather severe heart attack and she resolved to have them move to an apartment near her. But in discussing the matter with her parents she never demanded or acted as if she had made this decision alone. Her parents responded positively. They had no friends or organizational ties and also wanted to move closer to their only daughter and grandchildren.

The daughter made most of the arrangements, with her parents' approval. She rented an apartment near a supermarket and contacted a local geriatric physician whom she trusted. She was eagerly awaiting her parents' arrival in March, but on the telephone her mother suddenly said she couldn't come until May. Faced with this unexpected two-month delay, it took all her self-control to contain her disappointment. After hanging up she initially felt her parents would never come. Then she realized her mother and father needed to make the final decision themselves, in their own way, in their own time. By avoiding conflict with their schedule, she opened channels for a much improved relationship after her parents arrived.

A well-adapted daughter in her early thirties makes a very positive statement of the principle of generational independence: "I discuss important issues over the phone with them, like buying a new house. They've used us as people to talk with in helping them think about these issues. But they make their own decisions."

Children help more in the moving process when their distant parents are widowed or divorced. They assist in the physical move itself, provide emotional support, and may help their parents financially by outright gifts or making financial arrangements. Major marital rifts such as divorce and separation add stress to the distant relationship. Several children spoke of the need to maintain separate relationships, communications, and assistance with divorced and separated mothers and fathers who may be living far apart. An only son recalls his difficulties helping his divorced mother move:

> Mother and Father are divorced for a long time. My mother moved to North Carolina six years ago. My father had a small cottage and a six-bedroom house in North Carolina, which I inherited when he died. My original intent was that my mother move down to that cottage but it was not what my mother wanted. She started talking about how she didn't like the cottage. So I said, "If you don't like the cottage why don't you move into the big house?" I didn't think she'd take me up on it because that's where her ex-husband had lived. But it didn't bother her in the least.
>
> As an only child I have a lot of responsibility. You can't pass it on. Well, I organized the move and I brought my truck. I assisted her financially, because I could have rented it to somebody else. So I guess I'm subsidizing her. The move was difficult for her. She was sixty-five and very reluctant to part with any of the possessions that she had accumulated, as ridiculous as that might be. At that point I

was still thinking of moving her things into the cottage. And all the things she wanted to take obviously did not fit. I tried to convince her to leave some of it behind, or to get rid of it. But she fought vigorously against that. I remember one statement she made: "At my age these things are what you are and to leave them is very difficult." I recognized that those things that she surrounded herself with were an important element in her security. At age twenty, one would have an opportunity to get new ones. But when you're sixty you don't vision the financial resources. So everything came, from mops to pans, to things that I just would have tossed out. It was also hard for her to leave her friends. But my mother is very adaptive in that way.

Some widowed parents move in with an extended family member. One daughter provided emotional support and advice when her widowed mother and her aunt tried to live together:

One of my mother's two sisters came to live with her about two years ago. She really made a lot of mistakes and suffered. I encouraged her to talk about her expectations with her sister before they did it. But her sister is a very closed person who never talked. They had not agreed on space management beforehand. So when it didn't go as my mother had dreamed, problems arose. They fought over who should pay to mow the lawn. Things had broken down so badly by then. I tried to get her to initiate conversation with her sister and I gave her some words to use, like "Charlotte, we need to talk," or "I'm not happy and I don't see how you could be either."

Well-adapted and displaced children frequently invite their distant parents to move into their homes or a nearby apartment. One year after his father's death, a married, displaced son without children is preparing his house and his wife for his widowed mother:

After my father died, it became obvious that it was too much of a house for my mother to take care of alone, so we made this decision to have a six-month split between my sister and me. My wife, Beth, can see a difference between having a very positive relationship seeing them probably twice a year for many years and living together. And we used to go there far more than they came here. There have been lots of weekly calls. So I'm less concerned about the relationship with my mother. Naturally, even though they get along very well, getting along with someone for a short visit is different. Well, there's never been any problems. But you don't know until she's here.

Probably it will work all right because we're trying to create an environment that will have a self-contained living and cooking area within the house. If she wants to she can be alone and likewise we can isolate ourselves. We haven't yet finished the remodeling the way we're going to have it. We're arranging it so she will have a bedroom and bath plus a little family room of her own. We intend to set up the maximum amount of choice for everyone.

She'll probably come here for the spring and summer and stay in Texas for the winter with my sister. This obviously wouldn't work for a lot of families because of the personalities of individuals. My mother has always been a person who has been not intrusive with her relatives but very connected and interested in their lives. She's the kind of person who will join in chores in the household and provide all kinds of assistance. And she provides emotional support. She's more family-oriented than friend-oriented. My mother has always been involved in my sister's social life. I don't feel as comfortable about it as my sister. It's not that I object to her becoming involved with my friends. But I would not want to feel the obligation every time I had a dinner party to have my mother in on it. I think she's flexible enough to understand that, but that's something we haven't experienced yet. The other thing that makes it a little more complex is that she doesn't know anyone. That's something we'll have to do. I may attempt to find a network through the church just to be helpful to her. I've actually brought my mother together with the parents of some friends of mine.

In sharp contrast, alienated children usually do not encourage distant parents to live near them, though they may help arrange and implement the move, as a daughter recalls:

She had been living alone for about twelve years. Then she got frightened because the house was broken into and robbed. So she decided to sell the house and go to a retirement community. She relied on me and my husband to help her. We went through her finances and talked about if she could afford it. It turned out she really could pay for it.

Before that she was thinking of living here. We didn't say no but

234

we didn't encourage her either. I did show her Meadowhills Estate. She was kind of hinting that, well, soon the children will be gone and there will be all those empty rooms in your house. Well, I'd say, "That's true, Mother." I didn't encourage and I never did say, "Mother, we'd like to have you," because it never got to that point. She must have been aware that I wasn't encouraging her. And she didn't ask directly either. I didn't encourage her hints so it ended there. We went down there physically and helped her move.

Some parents move many times without finding the home they seek. A well-adapted son in his mid-fifties recalls:

My mother-in-law's husband died and she found herself having a difficult time living in that town. So she came to live with us for a year. Then she lived with her other daughter in California, then went back to that town again and then came back here. The death of her husband put her in a state; she was never able to get her life on track again.

RETIREMENT

A distant parent's retirement usually has no direct impact on the child. Yet many children remember their parents' retirement as a difficult transition. For a few distant parents the increasing freedom of retirement permits more visits and the development of stronger bonds with children and grandchildren. Other parents wish to find satisfying work or activity in retirement. If carving out a new routine proves difficult, the distant relationship may be strained.

As a major life transition, retirement often heralds a reevaluation of one's identity and perceptions of others. Several distant mothers are beginning to retire. Yet none of the children report difficulties. On the other hand, retiring distant fathers commonly develop medical, emotional, and financial problems and children try to help them. One recurrent theme is a father who retires early because he is not happy with his work. One son claims his father died of a heart attack shortly before retirement. He became depressed anticipating the future and did not take steps to diagnose his heart problems. Another son tells of his father's poor health immediately following retirement:

It's sad. He retired in April at sixty-two, as early as he could. He had all kinds of plans, gardening and this and that. Then he had a stroke in September so all the things he'd hoped to spend the rest of his life doing as far as he's concerned, he can't do anymore.

Some distant parents recognize their need for emotional support when they retire. But they communicate personal needs differently, depending on their relationships. With the advantage of hindsight a son remembers his father's increasing contacts as a sign of trouble: "After my father retired in his early sixties, he had more time. His visits and calls became more frequent. Then he became suicidal. He didn't know how he would go on so he started back to work in the business with my brother."

An alienated daughter believes her father's complaints stem from his need for emotional support in retirement:

My phone communication with my father is changing. He feels that the roles should reverse a little more; that all this time he's been supportive of me, my getting established and doing my dissertation, my career. And now, since it's kind of a transitional time for him, he feels the support should go in the other direction. But he doesn't think it's worth coming here. So when we talk on the phone he's very abrupt. He complains that I don't call enough, I haven't been supportive enough, I haven't come to visit enough.

Several children recall their distant father's retirement as a time of financial difficulty. An unmarried daughter says:

I helped them. He retired early and he wasn't sure how it would work financially. He asked me to lend him money, which I did happily. Now they ask me frequently if I have enough money. Well, I never have enough money. But it's all relative.

In the last couple of years he has given me money in small amounts; that comes from their relaxing about money. Mother needed knee surgery. My father was urging her to have it done privately because then she could get in much more quickly. The national health system in England is fine for emergencies. But if it's not an emergency you've got to wait your turn. She was in a lot of pain but not a prime candidate for immediate care. She kept resisting it. She said, "Well, we're saving for our old age." And Father and I both said, "You've reached it." So my father more easily than my mother realizes they have been saving long enough now.

It's very distressing. I just wish they would have a lot more fun and spoil themselves. It's very painful and I feel guilty because I see they are living far more carefully than they need to. I think some of what's going on is that they want to save money to leave to me. I'm an only child.

A few children whose distant parents have financial difficulties in retirement join their siblings to help. A daughter describes her contribution as minimal:

Before my father retired they were clearly better off. Now we're about the same. We're going to help them out more monetarily, not send them money every month, but when we're with them, my father was always very generous. If all of us would go out to dinner my father would pick up the tab. And we all know it's very difficult for him to relinquish that; it has to do with his identity. But he simply can't do it anymore. So my sister and I have made a very serious effort to arrange ahead of time how things will be paid, and that we will take care of it. Things like that don't necessarily make an enormous impact but will ease the burden. Our fear was that they wouldn't want to do things like that anymore because of this need that my father had to pay for it.

PARENTAL ASSISTANCE DURING CHILDREN'S TRANSITIONS

In their interviews, children focus on their assistance during their distant parents' transitions. But many children acknowledge that distant parents are as likely to assist them during transitions as they are to receive assistance from them; thus distant parents remain an important resource for their children. Children report special visits and help from their parents for their graduate educations, careers, weddings and divorces, purchase of homes, the births and graduations of grandchildren, and when they are sick.

Many children say their distant parents helped them raise the down payment on a house. Well-adapted children are generally happy to use their parents experience and advice. In contrast, alienated children feel their parents' involvement is intrusive. One well-adapted son set clear limits to his parent's involvement when he was looking to buy a house:

> They just didn't quite understand the market up here. They were criticizing but they were actually parroting back to me the problems I said I was having. I would say I would like to spend more time doing research. Then, in another conversation, they would say, "Why aren't you spending more time on research?" And I would brush off their criticism. They know I'm looking for a house now, but they know they can't participate in that, that will just be part of the conversation. My mother and dad are totally independent from the decisions I make.

Distant children also report many parental supports to grandchildren, such as financial support for their education. A daughter in her late forties says both her parents and her in-laws came for her children's graduations. A son indicates the importance of his mother's visit when his son was born: "She stayed a week with us. She traveled by plane. She doesn't like to travel and that was the first time she had ever been on a plane. So it has to be a major event."

Well-adapted children generally report strong parental supports when they marry or divorce. A well-adapted son whose father is disabled explains that his parents' second visit in four years was to his wedding. A well-adapted daughter who married in her late thirties explains her parents' feelings:

> We've grown closer as adults in the last ten years. She has changed a lot since my father's death. She was real pleased when I finally got married. They didn't put pressure, except that as they aged and my father got ill—he had open heart surgery—he said he wanted somebody to take care of me. I don't think they meant it in a paternal way, just someone to be there. They had expressed the desire that I not live alone.

Another well-adapted daughter recalls that her parents helped her financially after her divorce. Several children comment on their distant parents' feelings toward their ex-husbands and wives. One daughter remembers that her mother disliked her ex-husband in-tensely because of the way he treated her. A well-adapted son claims his divorce after twenty years was difficult for his parents because they liked his ex-wife:

> They've been enormously supportive of me through my separa-tion and divorce. It must have been very hard on them because they liked my wife. But they never criticized me or her and were very generous. They listened, they expressed sympathy and sorrow. They never acted like it was somebody's fault. I really respected them for that. It could have been problematical at that time in my life.

One theme that is often carried over from a child's adolescence is parental disapproval of real and potential mates, reported mainly by unmarried and alienated children. An unmarried daughter of thirty-eight complains that her widowed mother did not want her sleeping in the same room with her friend. Another unmarried daughter reports a long-unresolved conflict:

> I think the one conflict that has survived is their idea of appro-priate male friends. I clearly never found their appropriate ones. When I was living with them they were very strict. They just didn't want me to go out at all. As soon as I left for the university I was encouraged to bring people home. But it didn't seem to work out practically. I'm not sure why. I had one friend who was in the navy so he was fine because my father had been in the navy. The others were more questionable. I think in fairness it was in part because my parents wanted to be sure I just didn't fall into a pattern that so many girls fall into: they just marry quickly and get stuck in the town. They wanted to be sure I left home, got a university education and had choices.
>
> When they visited they met a friend of mine with the university and decided they didn't like him. It was terrible. He tried to be friendly to my mother, and she misunderstood most of what he said, then reported it to my father. I was very unhappy. They essentially said they didn't want to be in the house when he was there. So when my friend came over he and I had to sit in the garden. I thought, "This is insanity. This is my house."

Alienated sons also suffer from parental rejection of their spouses, as a son reports:

239

The conflict that survived most fully from my adolescence might be described as the conflict surrounding the significant female-other in my life. Or, to put it in another way, my mother seems not to get along with my female companions. That goes beyond my two wives, to my earlier girlfriends as well.

Unexpectedly, several alienated children report parental support when they divorce. But they typically emphasize underlying conflicts. Regardless of their parents' public support, they seem to know that their parents fundamentally disapprove. An alienated daughter recalls:

> My divorce was not problematical for them because they are Catholic. The fact is I had this odd telephone conversation with them on one of these annual birthday calls. When I got off the telephone I realized that, in effect, my father was giving me his permission to divorce my husband, which really wasn't what I asked for. But it was supportive. It's a big thing. And they haven't made judgments to me about what I've done. They've kept it to themselves. They probably disagree. I know this because I know they freely and openly voiced their disapproval of one of my younger sisters when she divorced her husband. In the overt things, they've kept out of my life. My daughter loves them dearly. I suppose that's one reason I make a point of going there.

Distant parents and siblings make special visits during a health crisis. A daughter describes her father's visit when she had surgery:

> We were trying to have a child. And the pregnancy wasn't proceeding normally. So I went and had some tests, and a sonogram, and my blood count said I should be two months pregnant, but they didn't find anything in my uterus. I was in the hospital with a tubal pregnancy.
> My father came and my sister came; they took shifts. We got a chance to talk more on different levels, but that kind of talk is really very rare. My father said it was his best vacation here. I mean he wasn't happy at my state. My mother had to stay there because they were in the process of signing contracts for the house at that point.
> After my operation, my parents were very concerned about whether or not I'd be able to have a child. They did a lot of reading

and found out a lot of information. They wanted to know how impaired my fertility would be. They wanted to be grandparents. So they were sad about my miscarriage, losing a child. I think they were more concerned about my health.

When distant children become ill it is usually acute and temporary. Parental visits are short-term, special events. In one exceptional case, however, a daughter recalls that her distant mother and father actually relocated in order to help her brother's family through a long-term health crisis:

Five years ago my mother and father moved from Chicago to Lexington to be near my brother. I was very skeptical because they had to uproot themselves. My father was already retired and my mother retired to make this move. They went at my brother's request because my sister-in-law was seriously depressed and had been hospitalized. They were in a cycle. Every time my sister-in-law was not able to take care of the children, my brother was on the phone calling my parents in a panic, saying couldn't you come stay with us for a few weeks. And they would immediately just throw things in a suitcase and drive there. After doing this for a couple of years my mother just thought it made more sense to move to Lexington. But they still had to leave their family, their friends, and their community behind.

I was very worried about my parents losing a sense of their identity. At the time they decided to move we had some rather heated conversations. I tried to warn them. But they didn't understand what I was talking about. I said you're going to leave your family and friends. Cindy needs to work these things out for herself. Dad was already in poor health.

My mother was very troubled about the situation with my sister-in-law not being able to care for the children. And the move, selling the house, and buying a condo near my brother was a very difficult experience for her. She lost a lot of weight and had difficulty sleeping. It was very uncharacteristic for her to have to operate at a high pitch. She's very low-keyed.

When they moved they were immediately busy with my brother's family. My father threw himself into driving the kids to school. He drove from his condo to my brother's house, then he would drive the kids to two different private schools in two different directions,

241

then pick them up in the afternoon. In the summer, when the kids weren't in school they spent every day at my brother's house. I didn't realize this before, but my nephew picked up all these gestures and mannerisms from my father. After my father died there was Jamie walking around, gesturing and acting just like him.

Actually, I think it turned out to be a very good thing for my parents. My father had sort of withered into a retired person without much purpose in life. Suddenly he had a purpose: to chauffeur his grandchildren. Then he became ill with cancer and was hospitalized. He died about two years ago.

My mother was very pleased to just move in and take over my sister-in-law's house. My mother is the classic mother-in-law. Her daughter-in-law could never take care of the house or care for the children very well. So it's been hard on my sister-in-law, who's a weak person.

I have mixed feelings about it because I know it was good for my parents. But it was not good for my sister-in-law to have my mother interfere so much. It gave my parents a sense of importance and identity, throwing themselves into their immediate family. My sister-in-law tended to be passive. She just let my mother take over the cooking and cleaning and care of the children in her absence. Then my mother continued to do it even when she was back in the home.

Since my father's death my mother isn't spending all that time at my brother's house anymore. That gives my sister-in-law a chance to take charge again and she is doing better. She's been out of the hospital and they finally found the right balance of drugs.

Social-status transitions of distant parents include death, widowhood, relocation, remarriage, and retirement. All adult children express a desire to help their distant parents during these transitions. Yet the voices of emotional attachment influence their capacity to help.

As distant parents anticipate death and wish to talk about it, well-adapted children are more tolerant whereas alienated children find it too painful as past conflicts intervene. Regardless of emotional attachment, most children experience intense guilt if they are not present when a distant parent dies. Moreover, children frequently call attention to their own suffering if they are not with their families when a distant parent is dying and when they are grieving for family members far away and alone. Yet only well-adapted children believe they provide effective emotional supports for grieving widowed parents, and commonly report arranging memorial services in their own towns for their parents after their distant funerals.

Most children provide less assistance to distant parents living as a couple, though some displaced children report helping distant parents in important work-related or financial matters. After a parent's death the widowed parent often reveals the nature and extent of his or her emotional and practical dependencies. Here again, well-adapted and displaced children report being able to provide emotional supports and help with instrumental tasks. They also encourage and praise their widowed parent's growing independence in social skills and emotional self-sufficiencies and show tolerance for recently widowed parents' increased needs for emotional intimacy and more frequent communications.

On one level children encourage their distant parents to remarry; they express happiness when their parent has found companionship. Many children are also unhappy, however, because stepparents can create tensions between children and their biological parents. Acknowledging that such problems are universal, well-adapted and displaced children tend to accommodate better and with less intensity and regret than alienated children.

Voluntary relocations are common in early old age while parents remain active and healthy. Beyond emotional support most parents require little assistance. Some children express regret when their parents relocate if they still have psychological attachments to their childhood homes, extended families, or cities. Most children support such moves and adapt previous patterns of routine visiting and calling to the new geography. Children provide more help when their relocating parent is widowed or divorced. Well-adapted and displaced children frequently invite distant widowed parents to move into their homes or a nearby apartment. In sharp contrast, alienated children usually do not encourage a distant parent to live near them, though they may help arrange and implement the move.

Soon after retiring, fathers often develop medical, financial, or emotional problems. Several well-adapted children relate incidents of providing financial assistance to recently retired distant parents. An alienated daughter suggests her father's recent complaints that

CHAPTER 9

Distant Living as a Growing Social Problem

In this book I have explored distant adult–child elderly parent relationships and tried to explain why this ambivalent connection is rapidly emerging as a widespread yet neglected social problem in contemporary America. Although long-term family separations are characteristic of our times, until now systematic information concerning the special problems of distant relationships and the efforts of individuals and families to deal with them has been unavailable to the public.

The distant, isolated, nuclear family represents the clearest behavioral expression of our cultural norm that encourages generational differences and independence. In distant relationships both adult children and elderly parents are free to develop attitudes and life-styles independently from each other, and make life choices with as much or as little involvement of the other generation as they desire. But if isolated nuclear families are so satisfying, why are so many people unprepared emotionally for the stresses distance creates? Why is there so much unresolved conflict in distant relationships? And why do adult children feel ambivalent about their relationships with distant parents? Frequently, neither child nor distant parent is satisfied with so much independence. For along with nuclear-family freedom, distance brings a subtle yet gnawing demise of certain key elements of family protection, support, and security.

Many adult children are unprepared to deal with all the emotional requirements of this new life-style despite cultural, economic, and social approval of geographic mobility and distant living. In describing their relationships with distant parents, children often fluctuate from positive to negative feelings, with intense emotions, revealing not only that their relationships are in flux but also that they feel ambivalent. Surely distant children are not alone. Near-living adult children also experience ambivalent feelings as a result of generational differences, individuation, social separations, life-style differences, attitudes and orientations toward family, occupational and financial differences, the education gap, and differences in ideology, politics, and religion.

But distant children experience a particularly intense kind of ambivalence, which they express in three distinct voices of emotional attachment. Displaced children are not satisfied with distant living. The displaced voice expresses a wish to reunite with parents. Well-adapted children accept distance in their relationships as a normal result of occupational and educational mobility. The well-adapted voice maintains close contacts and communications and feels affection without desiring to change the situation. Yet even well-adapted children express ambivalence, often desiring closer relationships and better mutual understanding, particularly during major life-cycle transitions. Alienated children are glad to be living away from their parents because their relationships are unsatisfying and filled with unresolved conflicts from the past.

These distinctive voices of emotional attachment reveal the ambivalent connection to distant parents. They are dramatically expressed in four problem areas that place special stress on distant child-parent relationships. The first problem involves the persistence of past conflicts in present relationships. Of course, not every distant parent-child relationship suffers from memories of the past. But the evidence suggests that a significant proportion of children continue to experience leftover emotions from unresolved family conflicts, often from the time they left home originally as young adults but also from unresolved, deeply rooted family problems of an earlier time.

Ambivalence emerges when children desire to discuss past and present relationships with parents: their childhoods, repressed emotions, the death of a parent or sibling, a divorce, or a family trauma with significant losses that was not satisfactorily resolved. But they do not raise the subject because the risk is too great that their parents will not understand or will criticize or interpret past events too differently for any genuine reconciliation. And if past relationships cannot be reconciled, neither can present relationships with husbands, wives, companions, and even one's own children. The losses are only aggravated by distance and the risk for further conflict is too great.

A second difficulty concerns the most obvious limitation of distant living: that routine communications and contacts are less frequent or less meaningful. Distortions and conflicts easily arise in routine telephone calls and visits because of the nature of language and distant contacts. On the telephone, miscommunications and misunderstandings arise that require patience and tolerance from both generations. The alternative is continued misunderstanding and an inability to transmit affection and other positive emotions that sustain familial bonds. Children may want to share information about themselves or learn about their parents' health, but they do not want to burden their parents or be burdened with problems when they cannot contribute to the solutions. The same may be said for routine visits. Since routine visits require planning and daily face-to-face interactions, often in close quarters, misunderstandings and life-style differences in activity level and habits arise as potential disruptions in distant relationships.

Finally, health-status and social-status transitions in old age often lead to increasing dependency on adult children and feelings of ambivalence or anxiety in distant parents who wish to remain independent. The child also experiences ambivalence and intense emotions as a result of role conflict; on the one hand he or she feels responsible for providing face-to-face care and services when needed, while on the other hand, because distance creates obstacles and complications in providing assistance, the child feels guilt, stress, and frustration. It is significant that today many children and distant parents experience more stressful and painful relationships as a result of parents' late-life illness and the children's inability to provide direct assistance.

Distant parents and children must make a particularly strenuous effort to communicate recent transitions, changes in personality, and new life goals and statuses, so that the other generation can accept them and adjust. But such tasks are extraordinarily difficult because the impact of distance on relationships has not yet been acknowledged. In spite of widespread feelings of ambivalence and role conflict, distant living is not a generally recognized social problem in contemporary American family life. The placid acceptance of distant living with virtually no public awareness of the problems that accompany it is strange indeed, especially when we consider that distance and prolonged separations can literally tear the generations apart, sometimes requiring them to live separately for the remainder of their lives.

In addition to this book's contribution to social science, I hope it will have the effect of making lay people aware of the limitations and potentialities of their distant familial relationships. The experiences and interpretations revealed here should capture the attention of many children and distant parents and alert them to the fact that this unacknowledged social problem has direct and immediate consequences for their lives. Becoming aware of the unique problems of distant relationships is the first step toward individual and social mobilization to improve relationships that can be changed, to learn how to cope with relationships and circumstances that cannot be changed, and to learn how to distinguish between the two.

IMPROVING THE DISTANT RELATIONSHIP

Early in the book I discussed four mistaken assumptions about the effects of distance on the parent-child relationship. I wrote that the assumption that distant relationships cannot be improved is clearly the most harmful one because it leads to despair. With the revelations of this study, however, we can now consider both the barriers to improving distant relationships and the real improvements children have made in their distant relationships and communications.

The first barrier to improving distant relationships is the inability to view communication as a skill that can be improved. Most children take their communications for granted as simply part of who they are. Unless there is an explicit misunderstanding, they assume what they intended to communicate was received in its intended form: they assume accuracy.

Most children and distant parents have not learned to use distant telephone technology effectively or even to express themselves clearly in face-to-face interactions. It is not surprising, then, that only a few maintain satisfying communications on the telephone or during visits. Many express awareness of special difficulties involved in telephone communications, such as the absence of body language or tone of voice, as one daughter says:

> We used to have anger and miscommunication on the telephone. I've just learned to be more patient. In the first few years of my remarriage there were times when I would try to emphasize things on the phone to get a clearer understanding. Perhaps the tone of my voice would create a mixed message itself, which would then start an argument. I remember getting off the phone wishing I hadn't said or made a big deal out of something.

Many difficult family situations require complex decisions. Since most children and parents are not accustomed to negotiating the details of such decisions over long distances, there is a high probability that communications will break down. In an exceptional case, a daughter recalls that through a difficult process of negotiation she was able to convince her parents not to appoint her the trustee of their will:

> We did a good deal of talking about their latest redraft of their will. They decided not to leave my sister the money outright but to set up a trust for her because my father is convinced she's irresponsible and would run through any money they gave her in no time. They wanted to make me trustee and every time they'd say it on the phone I would just say, "Please don't do this to me," until finally they agreed not to.

Fortunately, many telephone communication and face-to-face interaction skills can be learned. Edinberg (1987) has identified several such skills that can increase social effectiveness. Such skills can also improve distant relationships. These include the skills of talking about ourselves, active listening, and asking appropriate questions. One of the most difficult yet important skills in telephone communication is distinguishing facts from opinions and feelings. Talk about oneself describes facts and events, the outer happenings in one's life. Opinions present one's inner thoughts and beliefs, a personal point of view rather than an objective frame of reference. Feelings express one's emotional reactions to experience. In face-to-face interactions people often show feelings through gesture, facial expression, or body language. In telephone conversations, however, the difference between fact and feeling must be made explicit.

Children may avoid feeling-level disclosure for a number of reasons. First, personal expressions of feelings make us more vulnerable to other's negative evaluations. It hurts more to be rejected after revealing our private experiences. The risk may be too great for children who are insecure. But the price of having relationships without regular, feeling-level disclosure is a narrowed and restricted emotional existence, a deadening of our selves. For example, when a recently widowed distant mother comes on the telephone with sad and lonely feelings, it may be very difficult for the adult child to help her. Or when parents and children feel differently about religion it is difficult yet possible to avoid conflict by developing communications that distinguish feelings from facts. A son reports that his mother alerts him when she is going to talk about this sensitive topic so he is prepared:

> We don't argue or express anger because we respect each other and we've agreed to live and let live. We're careful not to have any miscommunications. For instance, for a long time my mother was hoping that I would get myself and my family back in the church I was raised in. I think that now she's pretty much given that up because she doesn't talk about it. There was a moment where she would say, "I wish you would, I think you ought to go to church." Now she says, "Now I'm not going to talk about this topic," so we never fight. What we talk about instead is her church, which is a breakaway from another church. My grandparents were founders of that church and it means a lot to her; her feelings are very strong.

Our strong cultural value on logic and efficiency may also discourage feeling-level disclosure. In our culture the priority of instrumental values over intimacy is more closely associated with men than with women. Women generally disclose at a more personal level. Mothers and sons, and fathers and daughters, must confront this difficulty in distant communications. It is easier for a listener to get involved and empathize with us when we include the details of our reactions using vivid emotion words to paint word-pictures of our experiences. People skilled at talking about themselves will also provide some cues about the sort of reaction they expect— admiration or agreement and positive reinforcement, advice or a new way of looking at the problem, or maybe just a sympathetic ear.

Active listening is another important skill that can be cultivated. The feeling of making contact and being understood has an important healing effect. Yet people often comprehend only a small portion of what they hear. The potential for improved listening is therefore substantial. Edinberg's suggestions for enhancing active listening include: (1) make prompts such as eye contact, nodding (and verbal prompts on the telephone such as "Mmm, hmm" or "Tell me more"); (2) give feedback, ask for clarification, or paraphrase; (3) be empathetic, try to put yourself in the other's place; and (4) avoid being judgmental.

The final skill is in asking questions. Questions set the mood and tone of the conversation because of their strong impact. Personal questions ask the speaker to reveal very private parts of themselves. And since the adult child–elderly parent relationship is intimate, it will include personal questions that are emotionally charged. When people can anticipate these matters and decide in advance how much they want to reveal, chances are better that the communication will be satisfying rather than threatening.

Family telephone communication patterns vary greatly. In some families the norm is to ask directly for personal information while in others people feel they should volunteer the information. Volunteering information raises the intimacy level and carries with it the implicit understanding that if one wants to talk about something he or she will, so questions become unnecessary. On the other hand, the norm of asking implies that if one wants to know something he or she will ask. When both child and distant parent use the norm of volunteering, the conversation moves smoothly, with partners taking turns recounting their experiences.

Children and distant parents who possess these interaction and telephone communication skills maintain more satisfying contacts. Even difficult long-distance problems can be addressed, such as arranging health care by telephone, monitoring parents' health status through direct calls to the parents, friends, and professionals, and confronting common miscommunications.

Yet since the emotional bonds between children and distant parents are so intense, it would be naive to assume that improvement in distant relationships will somehow emerge mechanically, with the acquisition of skills alone. Communications can improve only when children know their own areas of sensitivity and when their own strong and perhaps irrational needs distort what they hear. The real differences between displaced, well-adapted, and alienated voices do not lie in communication skills but in differing emotional attachments and needs from the relationship. On a rational level acquiring such skills may be clear enough. But implementing them in telephone conversations and visits with distant parents is extremely difficult and painful.

A second barrier to improvement emerges when children refuse to believe distant parents can change, or when they fear that change will make things worse. Such fears are often based on stereotypes of aged parents; thinking they are irrational, senile, rigid, unwilling to listen, domineering, or ill because they are old. Several children made comments that reinforce stereotypes of the aged. A daughter, for example, says: "My mother is in fair health. She's sixty years old, so she couldn't be in excellent health. I say fair just because of her age. She hasn't been hospitalized recently and she has no chronic medical conditions." And a son says:

> Barbara's father is old enough now so that sometimes he isn't aware a whole lot of what's going on. Sometimes people will be talking to him and he'll ask a question which is somehow a repetition of what they've just said to him. He'll tell the same stories over and over. He has a repertoire and doesn't go beyond it. When he's really engaged I don't see a great difference from what his mind was

years ago, but when he's tense or when there's too much going on he sometimes gets kind of a far-away look in his eyes. I don't think he has Alzheimer's; he's just very old.

Though widely held, such stereotypes of the elderly—the belief they cannot change their perceptions or ways of interacting—are quite wrong and can yield harmful and counterproductive results. Current research indicates that successful aging calls for many behavioral adaptations in perceptions by the social world. A more accurate image of people who age successfully is that of the pioneer (Silverman 1987) or the survivor, a person who shows great capacity for altering even the most enduring values and relationships (Clark and Anderson 1967).

In fact, many children, especially well-adapted and displaced but also alienated ones, report finding ways to improve their relationships. Several recall incidents of distant parents learning to adapt to changes in their lives. A son notes that his working-class parents have become more tolerant of different people as a result of his influence. A well-adapted daughter recognizes that she can listen to her parents' advice but still do things her own way. She notes the importance of developing patience and avoiding conflict:

> I've learned over the years, because I'm this far away and I can listen to whatever advice. But I can still do things the way I think they need to be done. I'm forty years old and can make the decisions I need to make that have to do with my life and my children. I really value their input but I don't necessarily have to take that as the only possibility. Sometimes I decide not to say things that will muddy the waters; there's no point. It used to seem to be important to be stubborn and make my stubbornness known. If it were an important enough issue I got angry. But now with age and health being an issue, I don't want to have a cow over the phone four hundred miles away where she hangs up crying or I hang up crying. So I've gotten more patient. I'm able not to say everything I think all the time.

The same daughter also explains that her mother has learned that she can contribute to her daughter's important decisions without intruding:

I do discuss important decisions with her. But she's learned now that it's a discussion, not a situation. Once when my husband and I lived in Georgia and we were going to open a store in New Orleans, my mother said, "Now, you have no business going to New Orleans. You can make just as much money in Georgia as you can in Louisiana . . . you'll be so much further away . . . ," and I got so angry at that kind of butting in that I really flew off the handle and said a lot of things I probably shouldn't have said. But after that she decided that she had really stepped out of line and that it was really not her place to say what we should and should not do financially. That didn't happen again when I named off the places I was thinking of when I was looking for jobs after graduate school. One of the places had been a suburb of Los Angeles. After I made the decision to come here she told me later she was glad we didn't go to California. But she didn't tell me that beforehand, so I think the other incident had really made her aware of her overstepping as far as a move is concerned.

A well-adapted son in his early fifties avoids conflict with his father about the telephone by ignoring his complaints:

He still doesn't like the telephone. But I'm working on improving its use with him. We went up to the cabin for a few days to see him, and the first thing he said to me was, "You know last night the phone rang at 4:30 in the morning and it was a person who had the wrong number." The conversation was closed. What he thinks about telephones hasn't changed. But I just let it ride rather than engage in a discussion with him.

Even alienated children recall their own life-cycle changes that led to greater emotional independence from their parents. An alienated son suggests that his relationship with his mother improved as a result of life-cycle convergence:

The patterns of contact changed; we are closer now. We have more reasons to be in touch with each other. Neither of us have spouses. When my father was alive I felt they were taking care of themselves and it wasn't so necessary. I took my father's attitude. If your health is OK and there are no emergencies, what can I do? I know everything I need to know.

Another alienated son explains that his relationship has improved as a result of insights he gained through therapy:

> I need to keep in touch, not to have more visits. I would change the pace; less running around, more actual exchanges of feelings and ideas. My relations with my mother have gradually improved. Since I was psychoanalyzed I was able to tell her just what it is I've been feeling. And she accepted responsibility for that and didn't deny that as children she basically ignored us. She was listening. It transpired over the course of the therapy. When Louis finally got me to see what happened, I was full of rage. The minute that I saw what had happened, my life fell into place. After that it wasn't complicated. I was able to take stock, get my shit together, and eventually remarry successfully.

A daughter's remarriage initially made her parents very unhappy:

> I've made them adjust to a lot of things, not the least of which is marrying a man twelve years younger than me the second time around. It threw both of them for a huge loop. I was thirty and he was eighteen. That was very hard for them at first. Also, we got married and told later. And of course that was a shock too from someone who always seemed like the perfect daughter, who had not been perfect all along, and had been trying for a long time to say, "Look this is not perfect here." Well, suddenly, I pulled the rug out from under them.
>
> She was angry the time that I called up and said that I got married. But that probably helped my parents grow and change and broaden their way of thinking about things more than anything else that's happened in our family. When they figured out a way to accept that, then my family seemed a lot different. Actually, they managed with it much better after I told them that the Baptist minister who married us said that we had a more perfect marriage than most people who were the same age or females who had spouses twelve years older than them. Of course, when the minister put his seal of approval on it, then it became all right for my mother and Daddy.

An alienated daughter explains that she needs less approval from her parents now that her children have grown: "Things used to bother me more. I wanted approval. You're trying to tell them something that's good about your children and you don't get that approval. It's frustrating when the children are little. Now that they're grown I'm not so needy." Another alienated daughter has improved her distant relationships by finding ways to spend time with her father:

> There are always those moments when visits are difficult. But I'm learning. I'm mellowing a bit. And I'll say things like, "Dad, why don't you and I go down and get some bagels," or something that very pointedly doesn't include her so that I can have some time with my dad. Communicating with my father is more satisfying for me because it's only been recently that I have figured out ways to do this. And I'm enjoying that time with him. He doesn't initiate it if my mother is talking. But it's very disturbing to me to be with them when she corrects my dad or interrupts him or speaks for him or doesn't let him have a thought of his own. If we ask him about a trip they've been on, for example, she may say, "Oh Charles, it wasn't like that." He's hard of hearing but we all suspect he's hard of hearing at some times more than others.

The help children can provide for a distant parent is limited. Yet their desire to help and remain close persists. To improve relationships children must come to terms with the physical limitations of distance and prolonged separation along with the resulting role conflicts, frustrations, guilt, anger, and, ultimately, feelings of loss. For in the end, we must acknowledge that some relationships cannot change. The other side of initiative is passivity, feelings of powerlessness, and guilt. When alienated daughters despair they often focus on their own inability to improve their distant relationships, as one daughter typically explains: "It's kind of an unfortunate thing. I can never really relate to them as adult equals. Not so much necessarily in the way that they treat me, but the way I treat them. I'll only be an adult when they're dead." However, some minor improvement can emerge even from the realization that the relationship is never going to change; for having made that judgment, one can turn one's attention and energy away from trying to change the relationship to learning to cope with it, as another alienated daughter observes:

"Some day you're going to be sorry that you treated me that way, some day when it's too late." She's talking about when she's dead and gone. It goes back and forth between anger and guilt. But now it's more just that she wants something and I want something. But I don't know how to bridge that gap. My mother wants to be closer. And she wants to have this mother-daughter type of relationship. And I want it. But she makes it impossible to have that. So I feel bad. But I don't see any way that it's ever going to change. And it's only been in the last couple of years that I realize it isn't going to change. I was always holding out hope when there never was any chance. It's really more of an acceptance.

An alienated son expresses a similar sentiment:

You realize once you've been in therapy that the real change comes from within. You can't bring it about in someone else. My mother does not wish to change. Most people don't change. So that my mother divorcing is an external change, but it hasn't changed the dynamics of their relationship.

The most significant improvements children note always include a measure of self-help along with recognition of their increasing emotional independence from distant parents. Moreover, whenever children acknowledge their distant parents' ability to adapt successfully or change, they also refer to some insight of their own, some area in which they have attained greater consciousness and control over their own lives and an ability to communicate that insight. Consequently, the most significant improvements come in the area we control most, our own perceptions of our responsibility toward distant parents who need our help. I believe this is the area where adult children can experience the greatest growth and success in relationships with aging distant parents. But in order to change, each child must first understand the nature of his or her own personal dilemma, particularly issues of the interpersonal self and self-esteem.

Virginia Satir (1972), a family therapist, has described four types of communication manifested by those with low self-esteem: placating, blaming, being superreasonable, and being irrelevant. Satir claims that 95 percent of us regularly use low self-esteem communication styles, but we may not be aware of doing so. From an early age parents may unwittingly direct us toward these styles by not supporting our sense of self-esteem, by modeling low self-esteem, or by giving us attention only when we display low self-esteem. After a while these styles become habitual, so we simply do not attend to what we are saying. Also, what we intend to say is often different from what actually comes out of our mouths. We are in better contact with our intended than with our actual communication.

According to Satir, the tremendous need for security among people with low self-esteem encourages social behaviors designed to keep interactions at a minimal level of contact. People with low self-esteem look without seeing, listen without hearing, speak without meaning, move without awareness, and touch without feeling. They are alive but not really living. For distant children with low self-esteem, telephone communications and visits represent two additional frustrating social contexts for personal failure.

On the other hand, high self-esteem encourages the development of congruent communications. We are freer to explore our world and let others know who we are. Since there is no need to confuse ourselves, it is also easier to be clear in what we say to others. Also, we can be congruent so that what we are thinking, feeling, saying, and doing all go together, reinforcing the same message. Congruence implies acting from the heart, so that what we feel is right coincides with what we think we should be doing. When cognitive and emotional systems are aligned, we can speak and act directly with one purpose, leading to clear and effective communication.

Self-esteem clearly has its roots in life experiences, particularly interactions with our parents. But that is now history. It can't be changed. What can raise our self-esteem now is to open ourselves up gradually to new possibilities. Satir lists five freedoms: (1) to see and hear what is, instead of what should be; (2) to say what you feel and think instead of what you think you should be feeling and thinking; (3) to feel what you feel instead of what you think you ought to feel; (4) to ask for what you want, instead of for permission; (5) to take risks instead of always choosing security.

According to Satir, self-esteem is not the result of focusing on our successes and our finest moments only. It is more a matter of accepting and respecting all that we are, including our failures. The natural outcome of this attitude is a communication style that is open, spontaneous, expressive, and congruent. Much of the meaning communicated from one person to another derives not from what we say, but from what we do. Adult children and distant parents who integrate these skills into their relationships will find greater satisfaction and understanding between them. Although high self-esteem, mutual understanding, and effective communication skills do not always lead to agreement, they almost always improve communications and satisfactions between adult children and distant parents.

IMAGES OF THE FUTURE

In fact, the problems and solutions presented here apply to all kinds of distant relationships. I believe adult children who identify with any of the three voices of emotional attachment can improve their distant relationships through a combination of developing communication skills and self-help. Clearly, alienated and displaced children have the most to gain since they express the greatest sense of dissatisfaction and urgency in their relationships with distant parents. But well-adapted children also express ambivalence and conflict in distant relationships, particularly during major life-cycle transitions.

I can envision a future in which the problems of distant living are not only seen as personal and individual, but as social. Society will play an important role reintegrating adult children and distant parents back into the family in at least two arenas: the technological arena, which will diminish the negative impact of geographic separations by facilitating face-to-face communications through advanced technology; and the emotional arena, in which a mobilized family and social system will work together consciously to learn more about the dynamics of distant relationships and alleviate their negative emotional effects.

To help advance these goals, Kent Creswell and I (Climo and Creswell 1987) conducted a teleconferencing experiment with three pairs of adult children in Lansing and their relatively healthy distant elderly parents in Chicago. Adult children and distant elderly parents visited spontaneously with each other on two occasions for fifteen minutes each, via satellite using combined audio and visual communications; both children and parents could see and hear each other at the same time. We videotaped each of the teleconferences on a split screen with the parent on one side and the child on the other.

Five themes emerged from their conversations: (1) planning future visits; (2) health status; (3) activities of other family members; (4) recent activities of the child and the parent; and (5) reactions to television communications. Of course, there may be some differences between normal private telephone conversations and experimental teleconferencing. Since the experiment was conducted in open studios, none of the conversations focused on intimate family problems. Although mild generational conflicts surfaced briefly, neither parents nor children discussed any fundamental conflicts, nor did they express conflict in their interactions. Nevertheless, I believe these five themes generally reflect the way these people normally use the telephone to reaffirm their family bonds. The visual component of teleconferencing was an added attraction and a novel experience for all the participants.

The long-run goal of this experiment was to explore the possible use of such teleconferencing communications when a distant parent is convalescing in a hospital or nursing home or living in a long-term care facility, isolated from other family members. In the present experiment, however, all of the parents and children were living independently.

The final theme in the teleconference conversations involved the parents' and children's responses to the visual dimension of the teleconference. One exchange between a son and his widowed mother was typical:

> *Son:* How do you like talking on T.V.? Do you think it's better than talking on the telephone? If it were as simple as calling on the phone, would you like to be able to talk this way routinely?
> *Mother:* Yes, if I had a button I could press when I didn't want to be seen because there are times when I answer the telephone and I run from the bathroom to the phone in my bedroom, and I probably don't have a stitch of clothing on or maybe I've got my hair all pinned up or something.

Both parents and children in the experiment had to travel several miles to their respective studio sites for the teleconference. It was not convenient for them, but someday it might be. Also, in the first conference all parents sat next to each other in the Chicago studio and heard each other's conversations. This detracted from a sense of privacy and encouraged them to provide explanations for each other and the technical crews. In spite of these and other technical problems, such as satellite transmission difficulties, both parents and children clearly enjoyed the experience. With some qualifications they felt they would use this technology regularly when it becomes available at reasonable cost. The technology is already available to place such devices all over the country and allow frequent communications with a visual component.

Finally, society must become aware of the distinct emotional problems distant children and their parents face. A growing awareness of common problems may result in the development of self-help groups, people who informally but consciously address mutual concerns arising from distant living. Such groups will alert social and health-service professionals as well as other practitioners and researchers to the growing need of reintegrating daughters and sons and distant mothers and fathers into each other's lives. I can imagine daughters and sons with distant independent-living parents maintaining more satisfying and fulfilling relationships than they do today. And I can imagine a day when hospitals, nursing homes, and long-term care facilities regularly contact adult children concerning routine and special supports for their institutionalized distant parents. But to realize this vision of the future requires conviction, courage, and commitment along with the capabilities that further basic and applied research will bring.

It is my hope that adult children and their distant elderly parents can gain from this study important insights about the natural limitations of distant communications and relationships. The alternative is to continue to hold the individual responsible for every failure in relationships. In this era of "life-style" behavior, a basic American cultural value promotes the idea that problems can be overcome if we, the public, only lived right. We do not know how to relax, so we exacerbate our hypertension; we eat greasy foods, which contribute to obesity and high cholesterol levels; we smoke too much, which leads to lung cancer; and we rely on alcohol and drugs, which addict us. Again and again we indict the individual as solely responsible for health and happiness. Irving Kenneth Zola (1979) argues that as long as such problems are defined as individual problems we will seek individual solutions:

> It seems easier to point a finger at the individual behavior and prac-
> tices that correlate with specific diseases rather than to ask what it
> is about American society economically, socially, or politically which
> makes us unrelaxed, eat unnutritiously, smoke, drink, use drugs pro-
> digiously, and what political and economic interests might be served
> by our doing so.

Turning inward with self-blame was common among the women and men I studied. It is a by-product of this dominant notion of the individualistic self in American society, which fixes responsibility for any failure to achieve the American dream in individual inadequacy. As a result, people often suffer with personal problems for a long time before they are identified as social realities. The fact that many distant adult children share such dilemmas whereas before they were thought to be only private family problems means that many more people need to learn how to cope successfully and resolve them. Only after we can identify distant living in a broader social and economic context can we begin to understand and resolve the resulting feelings of ambivalence that dominate our distant relationships.

Most of the progress in gerontology in recent years has come from the recognition that a certain group of people was suffering from some unrecognized or unacknowledged circumstance: the homebound and frail elderly, the desperate need for adult day care in many communities, and the very positive impact experienced after home services were buttressed for many elderly to avoid institutionalization. All these innovations improved the quality of life for millions of Americans—not only for the elderly, but also for their adult children who assume primary responsibility in caring for them (Brody 1988). Not long ago these were identified only as individual, personal, or private family problems.

The distant adult child–elderly parent relationship must be understood in the same light—as a growing social problem as well as an individual problem within the larger context of our highly technological civilization. We can begin to find solutions to help us cope and develop better, more satisfying relationships only when we can clearly identify and acknowledge the complications, difficulties, and obstacles distance places in the path of the adult child–elderly parent relationship. Solutions can emerge only when the causes and effects of the problem are understood. I see this book as a first step toward the development of that understanding.

Adams, P. N. 1968. *Kinship In an Urban Setting*. Chicago: Marham Press.

Aldous, Joan. 1967. "Intergenerational Visiting Patterns: Variations in Boundary Maintenance as an Explanation." *Family Process* 6, 2:235–251.

———. 1987. "New Views on the Family Life of the Elderly and the Near Elderly." *Journal of Marriage and the Family* 49:227–234.

American Association of Retired Persons. 1986. *Miles Away and Still Caring: A Guide for Long-Distance Caregivers*. AARP, A Publication of the Social Outreach and Support Section.

Atchley, Robert C. 1977. *The Social Forces in Later Life: An Introduction to Social Gerontology*. Belmont, Calif.: Wadsworth Publishing Company, Inc.

Balkwell, Carolyn. 1980. "Transition to Widowhood: A Review of the Literature." *Family Relations* (January): 117.

Bengston, Vern L., and J. A. Kuypers. 1971. "Generational Differences and Developmental Stake." *Aging and Human Development* 2:248–260.

Bierce, Ambrose. 1958. *The Devil's Dictionary; A Selection of the Bitter Definitions of Ambrose Bierce*. Mount Vernon, N.Y.: Peter Pauper Press.

Biggar, J. C., C. F. Longino, and C. B. Flynn. 1980. "Elderly Interstate Migration." *Research on Aging* 2:217–232.

Blau, Zena Smith. 1973. *Old Age in a Changing Society*. New York: New Viewpoints, a Division of Franklin Watts, Inc.

Bowlby, John. 1983. "Affectional Bonds: Their Nature and Origin." In *Loneliness: The Experience of Emotional and Social Isolation*. Robert S. Weiss, ed. Cambridge, Mass.: MIT Press.

Brennan, T. 1980. "Mapping the Diversity among Runaways." *Journal of Family Issues* 1(2): 189–209.

Brody, Elaine. 1977. *Long-Term Care for Older People*. New York: Human Sciences Press.

————. 1978. "The Aging of the Family." *The Annals* 438:13–27.

————. 1981. "Women in the Middle and Family Help to Older People." *Gerontologist* 21:471–480.

————. 1988. "Parent Care as a Normative Life Stress." *Family Relations: A Reader.* Norval D. Glenn and Marion Tolbert Coleman, eds. Chicago: The Dorsey Press.

Bultena, G. 1969. "Rural-Urban Differences in the Familial Interaction of the Aged." *Rural Sociology* 34 (March): 5–15.

Bultena, G. L., and V. Wood. 1969. "The American Retirement Community: Bane or Blessing?" *Journal of Gerontology* 24(2): 209–217.

Butler, Robert. 1975. *Why Survive? Being Old in America.* New York: Harper and Row.

Cantor, Marjorie. 1979. "Neighbors and Friends: An Overlooked Resource in the Informal Support System." *Research on Aging* 1:434–463.

Chernin, Kim. 1983. *In My Mother's House: A Daughter's Story.* New York: Harper Colophon Books.

Cicirelli, V. G. 1981. *Helping Elderly Parents: The Role of Adult Children.* Boston: Auburn House.

Clark, Margaret. 1967. "The Anthropology of Aging, a New Area for Studies of Culture and Personality." *The Gerontologist* 7:55–64.

Clark, Margaret, and Barbara Anderson. 1967. *Culture and Aging.* Springfield, Ill.: Charles C. Thomas.

Climo, Jacob J. 1988. "Visits of Distant-Living Adult Children and Elderly Parents." *Journal of Aging Studies* 2(1): 57–69.

————. 1992. "The Role of Anthropology in Gerontology: Theory." *Journal of Aging Studies* 6(1) (Spring).

Climo, Jacob, and Kent Creswell. 1987. *Long-Distant Teleconferences between Adult Children in Lansing and Elderly Parents in Chicago.* Videotape (22 minutes). Michigan State University, East Lansing, Michigan.

Cohler, Bertram J., and Morton A. Lieberman. 1979. "Personality Change across the Second Hand of Life: Findings from a Study of Irish, Italian, and Polish-American Men and Women." In *Ethnicity and Aging,* vol. 5. Donald E. Gelfand and Alfred Kutznik, eds. Springer Series on Adulthood and Aging. New York: Springer.

Collins, Glenn. 1983. "Long-Distance Care of Elderly Relatives Is a Growing Problem." *The New York Times,* December 29, sec. A1.

Cummings, E., and W. Henry. 1961. *Growing Old: The Process of Disengagement.* New York: Basic Books.

Croog, S. H., A. Lipson, and S. Levine. 1972. "Help Patterns in Severe Illness: The Role of Kin Network, Non-Family Resources, and Institutions." *Journal of Marriage and the Family* 34 (February): 32–41.

DeVos, George 1965. Social Values and Personal Attitudes in Primary Human Relations in Niike. *Occasional Papers, Center for Japanese Studies*, 53–91. Ann Arbor, Mich.: University of Michigan.

Dewit, David J., and B. Gail Frankel. 1988. "Geographic Distance and Intergenerational Contact: A Critical Assessment." *Journal of Aging Studies* 2(1): 25–43.

Dobroff, Rose, and Eugene Litwak. 1977. *Maintenance of Family Ties of Long-Term Care Patients: Theory and Guide To Practice*. Washington, D.C.: U.S. Government Printing Office.

Dono, J. E., L. M. Falbe, B. L. Kail, E. Litwak, R. H. Sherman, and D. Siegal. 1979. "Primary Groups in Old Age: Structure and Function." *Research on Aging* 1:403–433.

Douvan, E., and J. Adelson. 1966. *The Adolescent Experience*. New York: Wiley.

Dunkle, Ruth E., Marie R. Haug, and Marvin Rosenberg, eds. 1984. *Communications Technology and the Elderly: Issues and Forecasts*. New York: Springer.

Edinberg, Mark A. 1987. *Talking with Your Aging Parents*. Boston: Hambhala.

Elkind, David. 1984. *All Grown Up and No Place to Go: Teenagers in Crisis*. New York: Addison-Wesley.

Federal Council on Aging. 1982. *The Need for Long-Term Care*. Washington D.C.: U.S. Department of Health and Human Services.

Francis, Doris. 1984. *Will You Still Need Me, Will You Still Feed Me When I'm 84?* Bloomington: Indiana University Press.

Frank, Gelya. 1980. "Life Histories in Gerontology: The Subjective Side To Aging." In *New Methods for Old Age Research*. Christine Fry and Jennie Keith, eds. Chicago: Center for Urban Policy, Loyola University.

Frank, Gelya, and Rosamond M. Vanderburgh. 1985. "Cross-Cultural Use of Life History Methods in Gerontology." In *New Methods for Old-Age Research: Strategies for Studying Diversity*. Christine L. Fry and Jennie Keith, eds. New York: Bergin and Garvey Publishers.

Gallup Report, The. 1989. "The American Family." Report no. 286 (July).

Garrison, D. Randy, and Myra Baynton. 1987. "Beyond Independence in Distant Education." *American Journal of Distance Education* 1(3): 3–16.

Gelfand, Donald E. 1982. *Aging: The Ethnic Factor*. Boston: Little, Brown and Co.

Glascock, Anthony. 1990. "By Any Other Name, It's Still Killing: A Comparison of the Treatment of the Elderly in America and Other Societies." In *The Cultural Context of Aging: Worldwide Perspectives*. Jay Sokolovsky, ed. New York: Bergin and Garvey Publishers.

Glascock, Anthony, and S. Feinman. 1982. "Social Asset or Social Burden: Treatment of the Aged in Non-Industrial Societies." In *Dimensions: Aging, Culture, and Health*. Christine Fry, ed. New York: J. F. Bergin Publishers.

Glick, P. C. 1975. "Living Arrangements of Children and Young Adults." Paper presented at Population Association of America, April, Seattle.

Gmelch, George, and Walter P. Zenner. 1980. *Urban Life: Readings in Urban Anthropology*. New York: St. Martin's Press.

Gober, Patricia, and Leo E. Zonn. 1983. "Kin and Elderly Amenity Migration." *The Gerontologist* 23(3): 288–294.

Gold, Herbert. 1983. *Family*. New York: Pinnacle Books.

Granovetter, Mark. 1973. "The Strength of Weak Ties." *American Journal of Sociology* 78: 1360–1380.

Gray, R. M., and T. C. Smith. 1960. "Effect of Employment on Sex Differences in Attitudes towards the Parental Family." *Marriage and Family Living* 22(1): 36–38.

Gullotta, T. P. 1978a. "Leaving Home: Family Relationships of the Runaway." Paper presented at the University of Arizona Symposium on Families and Adolescents.

———. 1978b. "Runaway: Reality or Myth?" *Adolescence* 13(52): 543–550.

Hagestad, G. O. 1979. "Problems and Promises in the Social Psychology of Intergenerational Relations." In *Stability and Change in the Family*. R. Fogel, E. Hatfield, S. Kiesler, and T. March, eds. Annapolis, Md.: National Research Council.

Hammel, E. A., and Charles Yarborough. 1973. "Social Mobility and the Durability of Family Ties." *Journal of Anthropological Research* 29: 145–163.

Hays, Judith A. 1984. "Aging and Family Resources: Availability and Proximity of Kin." *The Gerontologist* 24(2): 149–153.

Hess, Beth, and J. M. Waring. 1978. "Parent and Child in Later Life: Rethinking the Relationship." In *Child Influences on Marital and Family Interaction*. R. Lerner and G. Spanier, eds. New York: St. Martin's Press.

Homer. 1950. *The Complete Works of Homer*. New York: The Modern Library.

Horowitz, Amy. 1975. "Family Caregiving to the Frail Elderly." *Annual Review of Gerontology and Geriatrics*. M. Powell Lawton and George Maddox, eds. New York: Springer.

———. 1985. "Sons and Daughters as Caregivers to Older Parents: Differences in Role Performance and Consequences." *The Gerontologist* 25:612–617.

Johnson, E. S., and B. J. Bursk. 1977. "Relationships between Elderly and Their Adult Children." *The Gerontologist* 17:90–96.

Jorgensen, S. R., H. D. Thornburg, and J. K. Williams. 1980. "The Experience of Running Away: Perceptions of Adolescents Seeking Help in a Shelter Care Facility." *High School Journal* 64(3):87–96.

Kaufman, Sharon. 1986. *The Ageless Self: Sources of Meaning in Later Life.* Madison: University of Wisconsin Press.

Kennedy, Robert E., Jr. 1986. *Life Choices: Applying Sociology.* New York: Holt, Rinehart and Winston.

Krause, C. 1978. *Grandmothers, Mothers, and Daughters.* New York: Institute on Pluralism and Group Identity.

Lee, A. S. 1974."Return Migration in the United States." *International Migration Review* 8:282–300.

Lee, Gary R., and E. Ellithorpe. 1982. "Intergenerational Exchange and Subjective Well-Being among the Elderly." *Journal of Marriage and the Family* 44:217–224.

Leichter, Hope J., and William E. Mitchell. 1967. *Kinship and Casework.* New York: Russell Sage Foundation.

LeVine, Robert A. 1982. *Culture, Behavior, and Personality: An Introduction to the Comparative Study of Psychosocial Adaptation.* New York: Aldine.

Levinson, Daniel J. 1978. *The Seasons of a Man's Life.* New York: Ballantine

Litwak, Eugene. 1960. "Geographic Mobility and Extended Family Cohesion." *American Sociological Review* 25:385–394.

———. 1965. "Extended Kin Relations in an Industrial Society." In *Social Structure and the Family: Generational Relations.* Ethel Shanas and Gordon Streib, eds. Englewood Cliffs, N.J.: Prentice-Hall.

———. 1982. *The Modified Extended Family, Social Networks, and Research Continuities in Aging.* New York: Center for Social Sciences, Columbia University.

———. 1985. *Helping the Elderly: The Complementary Roles of Informal Networks and Formal Systems,* New York: The Guilford Press.

Litwak, Eugene, Steve Kulis, and Wendy Worth. 1982. *Technology, Proximity, Gender, and Ethnicity as Factors Affecting Kins' Service to the Aged, and an Elaboration of the Modified Extended Family Model of Kin Structure.* Center for Social Sciences, Columbia University, Preprint Series No. 86.

Litwak, Eugene, and M. Silverstein. 1987. "Changes in Caregiving over Distance with Disability." Paper presented at the Gerontology Society of America Meetings, November 20, Washington, D.C.

Litwak, Eugene, and Charles F. Longino. 1987. "Migration Patterns among the Elderly: A Developmental Perspective." *The Gerontologist* 27:266–272.

Longino, Charles F., Jr. 1979. "Going Home: Aged Return Migration in the United States, 1965–1970." *Journal of Gerontology* 34:736–745.

Longino, C. F., R. F. Wiseman, J. C. Biggar, and C. B. Flynn. 1984. "Aged Metropolitan–Non-Metropolitan Migration Streams over Three Census Decades." *Journal of Gerontology* 39:6:721–729.

Lopata, Helena Z. 1981. "Loneliness: Forms and Components." In *Loneliness: The Experience of Emotional and Social Isolation.* Robert S. Weiss, ed. Cambridge, Mass., and London: MIT Press.

Lowenthal, M. F., and C. Haven. 1968. "Interaction and Adaptation: Intimacy as a Critical Variable." In *Middle Age and Aging.* B. Neugarten, ed. Chicago: University of Chicago Press.

Marshall, Victor M., and Carolyn J. Rosenthal. 1985. "The Relevance of Geographical Proximity in Intergenerational Relations." Paper presented at the Annual Meeting of the Gerontological Society of America, November, New Orleans.

Mercier, Joyce McDonough, Lori Paulson, and Earl W. Morris. 1989. "Proximity as A Mediating Influence on the Perceived Aging Parent-Adult Child Relationship." *The Gerontologist* 29(6):785–791.

Moos, Rudolf H., and Bernice S. Moos. 1983. "Family Process: A Typology of Family Environments." In *Families: What Makes Them Work.* Beverly Hills, Calif.: Sage Publications.

Moss, Miriam, Sidney A. Moss, and Elizabeth L. Moles. 1985. "The Quality of Relationships between Elderly Parents and Their Out-of-Town Children." *The Gerontologist* 25:134–139.

Munro, G., and G. R. Adams. 1978. "Portrait of the American Runaway: A Critical Review." Paper presented at the University of Arizona Symposium on Families and Adolescents, Tucson.

Myerhoff, Barbara. 1978. *Number Our Days: A Triumph of Continuity and Change among Jewish Old People in an Urban Ghetto.* New York: Simon and Schuster.

Myerhoff, Barbara, and Andrei Simic, eds. 1978. *Life's Career Aging: Cultural Variations on Growing Old.* Beverly Hills, Calif.: Sage Publications.

Nachman, Gerald. 1979. "The Menopause That Refreshes." In *Socialization and the Life Cycle.* Peter I. Rose, ed. New York: Springer.

Newman, Sandra J. 1976. "Housing Adjustments of the Disabled Elderly." *The Gerontologist* 16:312–316.

Newsweek. 1985. "Who's Taking Care of Our Parents?" May 6.

Nydeggar, Corinne N., and Linda S. Mittness. 1988. "Etiquette and Ritual in Family Conversation." *American Behavioral Scientist* 31(6): 702–720.

Orton, J. D., and S. K. Soll. 1980. "Runaway Children and Their Families: A Treatment Typology." *Journal of Family Issues* 1(2): 249–261.

Parkes, C. Murray. 1981. "Separation Anxiety: An Aspect of the Search for a Lost Object." In *Loneliness: The Experience of Emotional and Social Isolation.* Robert S. Weiss, ed. Cambridge, Mass., and London: MIT Press.

Parsons, Talcott. 1943. "The Kinship System of the Contemporary U.S." *American Anthropologist* 45: 22–38.

Rallings, E. M. 1969. "Problems of Communication in Family Living." *Family Coordinator* 18: 289–291.

Ruesch, J., and G. Bateson. 1968. *Communication: The Social Matrix of Psychiatry.* New York: W. W. Norton.

Rosenmayr, Leopold, and Eva Kockeis. 1963. "Propositions for a Sociological Theory of Aging and the Family." *International Social Science Journal* 15: 410–426.

Rosow, Irving. 1967. *Social Integration of the Aged.* New York: Free Press.

———. 1970. "Old People: Their Friends and Neighbors." *American Behavioral Scientist* 14: 59–69.

Rowles, Graham D. 1978. *Prisoners of Space? Exploring the Geographical Experience of Older People.* Boulder, Colo.: Westview Press.

Rubinstein, Robert L., and Pauline T. Johnsen. 1982. "Toward a Comparative Perspective on Filial Response to Aging Populations." In *Aging and the Aged in the Third World: Part I.* J. Sokolovsky, ed. Publication No. 22, Department of Anthropology, College of William and Mary, Williamsburg, Virginia.

Satir, Virginia. 1972. *People Making.* Palo Alto, Calif.: Science and Behavior Books, Inc.

Schooler, K. K. 1979. *National Senior Citizen Survey, 1968.* Inter-University Consortium for Political and Social Research, Ann Arbor, Michigan.

Schorr, A. 1980. *Thy Father and Thy Mother: A Second Look at Filial Responsibility and Social Policy.* Social Security Administration Publication 13–11953. Washington, D.C.: U.S. Department of Health and Human Services.

Seelback, W. C. 1978. "Correlates of Aged Parents' Filial Responsibility, Expectations and Realizations." *Family Coordinator* 27: 341–350.

Shakespeare, William. 1975. "43rd Sonnet." *The Complete Works of William Shakespeare.* New York: Avenel Books.

Shanas, Ethel. 1979. "Social Myth as Hypothesis: The Case of Family Relations of Old People." *The Gerontologist* 19:1, 3–9.

Shanas, E., and M. B. Sussman. 1981. "The Family in Later Life: Social Structure and Social Policy." In *Aging: Stability and Change in the Family.* R. W. Fogel, E. Hatfield, S. B. Kiesler, and E. Shanas, eds. New York: Academic Press.

Silverman, Myrna. 1978. "Class, Kinship, and Ethnicity: Patterns of Jewish Upward Mobility in Pittsburgh, Pennsylvania." *Urban Anthropology* 1:25–43.

Silverman, Philip, ed. 1987. *The Elderly as Modern Pioneers.* Bloomington and Indianapolis: Indiana University Press.

Simmel, George. 1980. *Essays on Interpretation in Social Science.* Totowa, N.J.: Rowman and Littlefield.

Smith, Kristen Falde, and Vern L. Bengston. 1979. "Positive Consequences of Institutionalization: Solidarity between Elderly Parents and Their Middle-Aged Children." *The Gerontologist* 19(5):438–447.

Sokolovsky, J., and Carl I. Cohen. 1981. "Measuring Social Interaction of the Urban Elderly: A Methodological Synthesis." *International Journal of Aging and Human Development* 13:233–245.

Spense, D., and T. Launer. 1972. "Career Set: A Resource through Transition and Crises." Unpublished. Department of Psychology, University of Rhode Island.

Sussman, Marvin B. 1965. "Relationships of Elderly Parents with Their Adult Children in the U.S." In *Social Structure and the Family.* E. Shanas and G. Streib, eds. Englewood Cliffs, N.J.: Prentice-Hall.

Thornburg, Hershel D. 1982. *Development in Adolescence.* 2d ed. Monterey, Calif.: Brooks/Cole.

Tobin, Sheldon, and R. Kulys. 1979. "The Family and Services." In *Annual Review of Gerontology and Geriatrics.* C. Eisdorfer, ed. New York: Springer.

Treas, J., and V.L. Bengston. 1982. "The Demography of Middle and Late-Life Transitions." *Annals of Political and Social Science* 464:11–21.

Troll, Lillian. 1972. "Is Parent-Child Conflict What We Mean by the Generation Gap?" *Family Coordinator* 21:347–349.

———. 1979. *Families In Later Life.* Belmont, Calif.: Wadsworth Publishing Company.

———. 1982. *Continuations: Adult Development and Aging.* Monterey, Calif.: Brooks/Cole.

Troll, Lillian E., and Jean Smith. 1976. "Attachment through the Life Span: Some Questions About Dyadic Bonds among Adults." *Human Development* 19:156–170.

Wake, Sandra B., and Michael J. Sporakowski. 1972. "An Intergenerational Comparison of Attitudes toward Supporting Aged Parents." *Journal of Marriage and the Family* 34:42–48.

Ward, Russell A. 1978. "Limitations of the Family as a Supportive Institution in the Lives of the Aged." *The Family Coordinator* (October):365–373.

Weiss, Robert S. 1983. *Loneliness: The Experience of Emotional and Social Isolation.* Cambridge, Mass., and London: MIT Press.

Wilkening, E. A., S. Guerrero, and S. Ginsberg. 1972. "Distance and Intergenerational Ties of Farm Families." *Sociological Quarterly* 13 (Summer):383–396.

Wolk, S., and Brandon, J. 1977. "Runaway Adolescents' Perceptions of Parents and Self." *Adolescence* 12(46):175–188.

Wood, Vivian, and Joan F. Robertson. 1978. "Friendship and Kinship Interaction: Differential Effects on the Morale of the Elderly." *Journal of Marriage and the Family* (May):367–375.

Zenner, Walter P. 1981. "Reactions of the Contemporary American Jewish Family to Individualistic Migration: The Problem of Cultural Reproduction." Prepared for the Conference on the Evolving Jewish Family, Queens College, June 22–24.

Zola, Irving Kenneth. 1979. "Oh Where, Oh Where Has Ethnicity Gone?" In *Ethnicity and Aging*, vol. 5. Springer Series on Adulthood and Aging. Donald E. Gelfand and Alfred Kutznik, eds.